Religion in Human Culture

The Jewish Tradition

WORLD RELIGIONS CURRICULUM DEVELOPMENT CENTER
MINNEAPOLIS, MINNESOTA

Project Co-Directors: Lee Smith and Wes Bodin
Project Assistants: Joan Voigt and Pat Noyes

Argus Communications
Niles, Illinois 60648

Photo Credits

Cover Photos

John J. Cumming   middle left
Mark Link, S.J.   bottom, middle right
Courtesy of the Maurice Spertus Museum
   of Judaica, Chicago; photo by
   Weems Hutto   top, center

Page Photos

2 John J. Cumming
5 Mark Link, S.J.
8 *Noah and His Sons*, Moshe Tamir,
   private collection,
   courtesy of the Maurice Spertus
   Museum of Judaica, Chicago;
   photo by Weems Hutto
13 The British Museum, London
17 Erich Hartmann/MAGNUM
   PHOTOS, INC.

21 John J. Cumming
24 Courtesy of the Maurice Spertus
   Museum of Judaica, Chicago;
   photo by Weems Hutto
29 *Moses*, Abraham Rattner, courtesy of
   the Maurice Spertus Museum
   of Judaica, Chicago; photo by
   Weems Hutto
30 Courtesy of the Consulate General of
   Israel, New York
33 Micha Bar-Am/MAGNUM PHOTOS, INC.
36 Charles Harbutt/MAGNUM
   PHOTOS, INC.
40 John J. Cumming
45 Al Greenberg/ALPHA PHOTO
   ASSOCIATES, INC.
46 Mark Link, S.J.
49 The Bettmann Archive
53 Lee Smith
56 Henri Bureau/SYGMA

61 Philip Jones Griffiths/MAGNUM
   PHOTOS, INC.
64 Historical Pictures Service, Chicago
69 Leonard Freed/MAGNUM
   PHOTOS, INC.
73 Lee Smith
76/77/81 John J. Cumming
84 Courtesy of the Maurice Spertus
   Museum of Judaica, Chicago;
   photo by Weems Hutto
89 GLOBE PHOTOS
92 Lee Smith
96 David Margolin/GLOBE PHOTOS
98 Courtesy of the Maurice Spertus
   Museum of Judaica, Chicago;
   photo by Weems Hutto
101 John J. Cumming
105 Tamar Grand
109 Raymond Darolle/SYGMA
112 Lee Smith

116 Courtesy of the Maurice Spertus
   Museum of Judaica, Chicago;
   photo by Weems Hutto
120/129 John J. Cumming
133 W. Karel/SYGMA
136/140 John J. Cumming
144 Lee Smith
155/156 Yivo Institute for Jewish Research
165 Museum of Dachau, West Germany
168/169 From *I Never Saw Another Butterfly:
   Children's Drawings and Poems from
   Terezin Concentration Camp
   1942–1944* (New York: McGraw-Hill
   Book Co., 1964), pp. 44, 52
170 Adam Kaczkowski
173 Micha Bar-Am/MAGNUM
   PHOTOS, INC.
174 W. Karel/SYGMA
184 Cornell Capa/MAGNUM PHOTOS, INC.

Acknowledgments

Designed by Gene Tarpey

Excerpt from *The Book of Jewish Knowledge* by Nathan Ausubel. © 1964 by Nathan Ausubel. Used by permission of Crown Publishers, Inc.

Excerpts from *The Complete Bible*, trans. by J. M. Powis Smith and Edgar J. Goodspeed. Copyright © 1923, 1927, 1948 by The University of Chicago. Reprinted by permission of The University of Chicago Press.

Excerpts from *The Book of Psalms.* Copyright © 1972 by The Jewish Publication Society of America. Reprinted by permission.

Excerpts from *To Be A Jew: A Guide to Jewish Observances in Contemporary Life*, by Rabbi Hayim Halevy Donin, © 1972 by Hayim Halevy Donin, Basic Books, Inc. Publishers, New York.

"Is There a Jewish View of Life?" by Albert Einstein. First published in *Opinion: A Journal of Jewish Life and Letters*, Sept. 26, 1932. Reprinted by permission of National Jewish Post, Inc., New York.

Excerpts from Isidore Epstein: *Judaism* (1959), pp. 19–20, 319–20, 322. Copyright © the Estate of Isidore Epstein, 1959. Reprinted by permission of Penguin Books, Ltd.

Excerpt from *The Service of the Heart* by Evelyn Garfiel. © 1958 by Evelyn Garfiel. Reprinted by permission of A. S. Barnes & Co., Inc., Cranbury, N.J.

Excerpt from *A Jewish Reader* edited by Nahum N. Glatzer. Copyright © 1946, 1961 by Schocken Books. Copyright renewed © 1974 by Schocken Books Inc. Reprinted by permission of Schocken Books Inc.

Excerpts from *Likrat Shabbat*, comp. and trans. by Rabbi Sidney Greenberg. Copyright © 1975, 1973, by The Prayer Book Press of Media Judaica, Inc., 1363 Fairfield Avenue, Bridgeport, Ct. 06605. Reprinted by permission of the publisher.

Excerpt from *A Rabbi's Manual*, edited by Rabbi Jules Harlow, © 1965 by The Rabbinical Assembly. Reprinted by permission of The Rabbinical Assembly.

Excerpt from *Judaism* by Arthur Hertzberg. Copyright © 1961 by Arthur Hertzberg. Reprinted with the permission of the publisher, George Braziller, Inc.

Excerpt from *Israel: An Echo of Eternity* by Abraham Joshua Heschel. Copyright © 1967, 1968, 1969 by Abraham Joshua Heschel. Reprinted with the permission of Farrar, Straus & Giroux, Inc.

Excerpt from *Horeb: A Philosophy of Jewish Laws and Observances* by Samson Raphel Hirsch. Published 1962 by Soncino Press, London. Reprinted by permission of Soncino Press.

Excerpt from *Babi Yar* by A. Anatoli (Kuznetsov), translated by David Floyd, English translation copyright © 1970 by Jonathan Cape Ltd. Reprinted with permission of Farrar, Straus & Giroux, Inc., and The Daily Telegraph, London.

Excerpt from *A History of the Jews in the United States* by Rabbi Lee J. Levinger, Ph.D., 1949, 1962. Reprinted by permission of the publisher, Union of American Hebrew Congregations.

"A Community of Hasidic Jews" from the *Minneapolis Star*, March 2, 1974. Copyright © Washington Post. Reprinted by permission of Los Angeles Times/Washington Post News Service.

Excerpts from *A Rabbinic Anthology*, edited by C. G. Montefiore and H. Loewe. Reprinted by permission of The Jewish Publication Society of America.

Excerpts from *The Way of Torah: An Introduction to Judaism*, 2d ed., by Jacob Neusner, pp. 41–42, 43–46. Copyright © 1974 by Dickenson Publishing Company, Inc., Encino, California. Reprinted by permission of the publisher.

Excerpt from *Writings of the Nazi Holocaust*, by Ernst Pawel. Reprinted with permission of the Anti-Defamation League of B'nai B'rith.

Excerpts from *Sabbath and Festival Prayer Book*, published by the Joint Prayer Book Commission of the Rabbinical Assembly of America and the United Synagogue of America. Reprinted with permission.

Excerpt from *The Last of the Just* by Andre Schwartz-Bart. Copyright © 1960 by Atheneum House, Inc. Reprinted by permission of Atheneum.

Excerpts from *The Jewish Catalog*, comp. and ed. by Richard Siegel, Michael Strassfeld, and Sharon Strassfeld. Copyright © 1973 by The Jewish Publication Society of America. Reprinted by permission.

Excerpts from *The Religions of Man* (hardbound edition) by Huston Smith. Copyright © 1958 by Huston Smith. By permission of Harper & Row, Publishers, Inc.

Excerpts from *Basic Judaism*, copyright, 1947, by Milton Steinberg; renewed, 1975, by David Joel Steinberg and Jonathan Steinberg. Reprinted with a simplified vocabulary by permission of Harcourt Brace Jovanovich, Inc., and Russell & Volkening, Inc.

Excerpts from *The Torah: The Five Books of Moses*, 2d ed. Copyright © 1962 by The Jewish Publication Society of America. Reprinted by permission.

Excerpt from *The Burden of Guilt: A Short History of Germany, 1914–1945* by Hannah Vogt, Introduction by Gordon Craig, translated by Herbert Strauss. Copyright © 1964 by Oxford University Press, Inc. Reprinted by permission.

Excerpt from *Weekly Prayer Book*, © 1961 by The Rabbinical Assembly. Reprinted by permission of The Rabbinical Assembly.

Excerpts from *The Encyclopedia of the Jewish Religion* edited by R. J. Z. Werblowsky and Geoffrey Wigoder. Copyright © 1965 by Massada—P.E.C. Press, Ltd. Reprinted by permission of Holt, Rinehart and Winston, Publishers, and Massada—P.E.C. Press, Ltd., Jerusalem.

Excerpt from *Night* by Elie Wiesel. Translation copyright © 1960 by MacGibbon & Kee. Originally published in French by *Les Editions de Minuit*, copyright © 1958. Reprinted with the permission of Farrar, Strauss & Giroux, Inc., and Georges Borchardt, Inc., 145 E. 52nd St., N.Y., N.Y.

Excerpts from *This Is My God* by Herman Wouk. Copyright © 1959, 1970 by the Abe Wouk Foundation, Inc. Reprinted by permission of Doubleday & Company, Inc. and The Harold Matson Company, Inc.

Every effort has been made to trace the owners of copyright material in this book. Should any material have been included inadvertently without the permission of the copyright owner, acknowledgment will be made in any future edition.

Religion in Human Culture is a Project of St. Louis Park Independent School District #283, Title III/IV (Part C), ESEA, and the Northwest Area Foundation. The opinions and other contents of this book do not necessarily reflect the position or policy of the State of Minnesota, the U.S. Government, St. Louis Park ISD #283, or the Northwest Area Foundation, and no official endorsement should be inferred.

Argus Communications
7440 Natchez Avenue
Niles, Illinois 60648

International Standard Book Number:
0-89505-011-0

Library of Congress Number:
78-52802

0 9 8 7 6 5 4 3 2

Contents

Note to the Reader

This book is a collection of readings which have been taken from a variety of sources. It is not to be considered or used as a textbook; rather, the readings are intended as a source of data or information on various practices and concepts found in the Jewish tradition. A study and analysis of this data should increase your understanding not only of Judaism but of the people who practice this tradition.

To facilitate your reading, a glossary of terms relevant to Judaism is provided at the end of this book. As you encounter words you are unfamiliar with, refer to the glossary for their definitions.

Note that the spelling of some words may vary from one reading to another or from these readings to other sources on Judaism—for example, Hanukkah-Chanukkah-Chanukah, Rosh Hashanah-Rosh Hashana, bat mitzvah-bas mitzva. Such variation in spelling is a result of transliterating Hebrew words and only the spelling is different. Some alternate spellings are noted in the glossary.

Members of the congregation follow the sequence of the worship service in their prayer books.

READING 1
What Is a Jew?
JONATHAN PARADISE

Religion is an institution where the weight of *tradition* is considerable. Anyone familiar with the musical *Fiddler on the Roof* knows that the Jews and Judaism present a good example of this rule. Yet like so many of our social patterns in contemporary America, the basic assumptions and values which have long been associated with the varieties of Judaism are in a very fluid state.

The way Jews express their Jewishness, or, for lack of a better term, their *Jewish identity,* may differ considerably from one congregation to the next or one city to the next.

Children and parents may be worlds apart, Jewishly speaking. One might assume that the younger generation, or part of a general rejection of traditional attitudes and values, is moving toward a more diluted form of Jewish culture and belief. While this is frequently the case, it is equally true that the very opposite is often true.

In order to illustrate the dynamic state of the patterns of Jewish identity, it is necessary to use family profiles which reveal these shifts of direction, emphasis, and degree of commitment.

Rachel

Rachel is always somewhat more reserved than the other students. Her hemline is always a trifle on the long side regardless of the popular style. She usually wears long-sleeved blouses and little, if any, make-up.

Rachel only eats food prepared at home or by another Orthodox family, so her social activities and dates are confined to her Orthodox friends. She has never attended a football game or school dance held on a Friday night since these conflict with Sabbath observance. However, she does not mind; she regards most of "teenage culture" as frivolous and devoid of serious values. More importantly, her belief that she lives her life in accordance with God's sacred laws gives her a sense of joy and purposeful living.

She looks forward to marrying a strictly Orthodox Jew who has studied in a Yeshiva, a school where the Talmud is studied. Although he will have rabbinic training, he probably will earn his living in another profession. It is possible that within a few years they will decide to settle in Israel as an expression of their commitment to total Jewish life.

Her husband will pray daily (both morning and evening) at home or, if he has time, at the synagogue. Rachel will usually remain at home with the children.

Rachel is a new student in Park High. Unlike most of the other Jewish students, she did not attend public grade school or junior high. She studied in an Orthodox academy where half the day was spent in Hebrew and religious subjects and the remaining half in "secular" studies.

Marvin

Marvin is a successful businessman. He came to the United States at the age of fifteen. Until then his life was full of the danger and turmoil which was the daily fare of Jews caught up in the aftermath of World War II and the rise of the communist revolution. He speaks Yiddish, Russian, Polish, German, and English—none of them very well. Although his parents were strictly Orthodox, he never attends the synagogue except on the anniversary of their death and on Yom Kippur. Marvin is a member of the Reform temple, but he takes no interest in any of the synagogue activities and has little regard for its rabbi whom he considers inadequately trained in traditional scholarly sources—surprising, inasmuch as Marvin abandoned these studies at age fifteen and never gave his children training in Hebrew or even a Bar Mitzvah ceremony. But Marvin is full of contradictions. He insists that the meat his wife prepares be kosher, yet when he eats in a restaurant he eats lobster or shrimp with great relish. When in a hurry for lunch he eats a cheeseburger.

Marvin's wife is totally uninterested in Jewish practices except on rare occasions. Yet, in many subtle ways, both parents have made it clear to their children that they want them to marry Jews. The children know that even dating a gentile friend will meet with the severest opposition.

Marsha

Despite the aloofness of Marvin and his wife, their daughter Marsha actively expresses her Jewish identity. She regularly attends Friday evening services and participates in the discussion group which follows.

She is active in a temple youth group, spending two days each week in related activities and projects. She enjoys singing and dancing to Israeli songs which she learned at the organization's summer camp. She is close to the synagogue and devoted to the rabbi. She is proud of her Judaism, seeing it as a force for progressive liberalism, civil rights, and social welfare.

Howard

Howard considers himself a secular Jew. He does not attend synagogue, keep dietary laws, or observe the holidays. However, he regards himself as intensely Jewish. His major interests are Jewish history, the Hebrew language, the state of Israel, and the fate of Jews living under totalitarian regimes.

Howard belongs to a Hebrew-speaking club. They meet for a variety of cultural activities, all conducted in Hebrew. He corresponds with a pen pal in Argentina who, he fears, will soon be forced to flee as a result of anti-Semitic violence. Recently Howard tried to organize a hunger strike to protest the fate of Jews living in Syria.

When considering possible plans for study and career training, Howard's primary consideration is whether he could pursue it in Israel. Although he is not unhappy in the United States, he plans to settle in Israel permanently. His parents are not active in Zionist organizations, though, like most Jews in Minneapolis, they contribute a large sum to the annual fund drive for Israel. His father has played an active role in several fund-raising groups and is a member of a Jewish lodge and a Jewish country club.

His parents have a great love for Israel, which they have visited in connection with their fund-raising missions, yet they themselves have no thought of emigrating.

Nancy

Nancy's family belongs to a Conservative congregation. They are moderately active in the synagogue. Her father's two brothers married non-Jewish women. One of her aunts converted to Judaism, learned Hebrew, keeps a strictly kosher home, and observes all holidays. Indeed, for several years the aunt wouldn't eat at Nancy's home because her family didn't "keep kosher." All that has changed now. Last summer, after receiving a synagogue scholarship, Nancy attended a religious, Hebrew-speaking camp. She was immersed in prayer services, Kashrut (dietary laws), Hebrew, Israeli songs and dances, and Jewish study. When she returned home, she insisted that her mother keep a kosher kitchen. Although her parents and her brother and sister have changed little in their Jewish observance, Nancy has re-enrolled in the Talmud Torah (she had quit after her Bat Mitzvah ceremony), she doesn't write or ride in a car on the Sabbath, and she tends to associate more and more with friends she met at the summer camp.

Recently the family had a large reunion on the occasion of a wedding. Relatives came from all over the United States. Yet Nancy's other uncle (who married a Catholic) did not attend. He had raised his children in his wife's faith. These children, Nancy's cousins, were active in a local church and had virtually no contact with the family. For all practical purposes, they were not part of the family.

Shlomo

Shlomo is a young Hasidic Jew. When he walks to the synagogue on the Sabbath, his outward appearance is unmistakable. He wears a brimmed hat and a gabardine coat; he has a beard; side locks are tucked behind his ears.

Despite the Eastern European style of his dress, Shlomo was born in this country. He can converse in Yiddish as easily as in English, something which sets him apart from other Orthodox Jews. His Hasidic sect stresses the joy of living according to the *mitzvot,* the divine commandments. In group celebrations this joy reaches heights of ecstasy. Through exuberant melodies called nigunim, sung (usually without words) over and over, they express the total exultation that they feel. Often the men will dance to these melodies. The energetic circle dance could easily last an hour! If the women were to dance, they would form a circle of their own since modesty requires that men and women not dance together in public.

For practical reasons our sketches of Rachel, Marvin, Marsha, Howard, Nancy, and Shlomo are brief and superficial. (To do otherwise would require a novel.) They fail to correspond fully to any actual Jewish person. The truth is that each Jew is a complex combination of each of these types in varying proportions. Notice that Marvin, whose daily life is basically devoid of Jewish content, does maintain a link with more traditional ways by keeping a kosher kitchen at home. Furthermore there may be other subtle, intangible "identity builders" in Marvin's Jewishness which have influenced the daughter, Marsha, in her active synagogue participation.

READING 2
The Search for Meaning*
HUSTON SMITH

A modern-day goatherd guards his flock.

The real impact of the ancient Jews . . . lies in the extent to which Western civilization took over their angle of vision on the deepest questions life poses.

When, mindful of the impact the Jewish perspective has had on Western culture, we go back to the land, the people, and the history that made this impact, we are in for a shock. We might expect these to be as impressive as their influence but they are not. In time span the Jews were latecomers on the stage of history. By 3000 B.C. Egypt already had her pyramids and Sumer and Akad were world empires. By 1400 Phoenicia was colonizing. And where were the Jews in the midst of these mighty eddies? They were overlooked. A tiny band of nomads milling around the upper regions of the Arabian desert, they were too inconspicuous even to be noticed.

When they finally settled down, the land they chose was equally unimpressive. One hundred and fifty miles in length from Dan to Beersheba, about fifty miles across at Jerusalem but much less at most places, Palestine is a postage stamp of a country, about one-eighth the size of Illinois. Nor does the terrain make up for what the region lacks in size. Visitors to Greece who climb Mount Olympus find it easy to imagine that the gods chose to live there. Palestine, by contrast, was a "mild and monotonous land." "Did the Prophets, in their gloom of foreboding, flash their lightning of conviction from these quiet hills, where everything is open to the sky?" asks Edmund Wilson on one of his visits. "Were the savage wars of Scripture fought here? Did its paeans first sound from

*From Huston Smith, *The Religions of Man* (New York: Harper & Row, 1958), pp. 225–26.

these pastures? . . . How very unlikely it seems that they sprouted from the history of these calm little hills, dotted with stones and flocks, under pale and transparent skies."[1] Even Jewish history when viewed from without amounts to little. It is certainly not dull history but by external standards it is very much like the histories of countless other little peoples, the people of the Balkans, say, or possibly our own Indian tribes in pre-Columbian times. Small peoples are always getting pushed around. They get shoved out of their land and try desperately to scramble back into it. Compared with the history of Assyria, Babylon, Egypt, and Syria, Jewish history is strictly minor league.

If the key to the achievement of the Jews lies neither in their antiquity nor the proportions of their land or history, where does it lie? There are a number of ways that this question, which has been one of the greatest puzzles of history, might be approached. At least a partial clue to the mystery, however, is this: What lifted the Jews from obscurity to permanent religious greatness was their passion for meaning.

[1] *The New Yorker,* December 4, 1954, pp. 204–05.

READING 3
The Concept of God:
Selections from the Holy Scripture

The following passages are representative selections of biblical literature from several different chronological and developmental stages in the formation of biblical theology.

Genesis 1:1–5, 24–28*

When God began to create the heaven and the earth—the earth being unformed and void, with darkness over the surface of the deep and a wind from God sweeping over the water—God said, "Let there be light"; and there was light. God saw that the light was good, and God separated the light from the darkness. God called the light Day, and the darkness He called Night. And there was evening and there was morning, a first day. . . .

God said, "Let the earth bring forth every kind of living creature: cattle, creeping things, and wild beasts of every kind." And it was so. God made wild beasts of every kind and cattle of every kind, and all kinds of creeping things of the earth. And God saw that this was good. And God said, "Let us make man in our image, after our likeness. They shall rule the fish of the sea, the birds of the sky, the cattle, the whole earth, and all the creeping things that creep on earth." And God created man in His image, in the image of God He created him; male and female He created them. God blessed them and God said to them, "Be fertile and increase, fill the earth and master it; and rule the fish of the sea, the birds of the sky, and all the living things that creep on earth."

*Passages from Genesis and Deuteronomy are from *The Torah: The Five Books of Moses,* 2d ed. (Philadelphia: The Jewish Publication Society of America, 1962).

Genesis 6:5–8

The Lord saw how great was man's wickedness on earth, and how every plan devised by his mind was nothing but evil all the time. And the Lord regretted that He had made man on earth, and His heart was saddened. The Lord said, "I will blot out from the earth the men whom I created—men together with beasts, creeping things, and birds of the sky; for I regret that I made them." But Noah found favor with the Lord.

Noah and His Sons.

Deuteronomy 6

And this is the Instruction—the laws and the rules—that the Lord your God has commanded [me] to impart to you, to be observed in the land which you are about to cross into and occupy, so that you, your son, and your son's son may revere the Lord your God and follow, as long as you live, all His laws and commandments which I enjoin upon you, to the end that you may long endure. Obey, O Israel, willingly and faithfully, that it may go well with you and that you may increase greatly [in] a land flowing with milk and honey, as the Lord, the God of your fathers, spoke to you.

Hear, O Israel! The Lord is our God, the Lord alone. You shall love the Lord your God with all your heart and with all your soul and with all your might. Take to heart these instructions with which I charge you this day. Impress them upon your children. Recite them when you stay at home and when you are away, when you lie down and when you get up. Bind them as a sign on your hand and let them serve as a symbol on your forehead; inscribe them on the doorposts of your house and on your gates.

When the Lord your God brings you into the land which He swore to your fathers, Abraham, Isaac, and Jacob, to give you—great and flourishing cities which you did not build, houses full of all good things which you did not fill, hewn cisterns which you did not hew, vineyards and olive groves which you did not plant—and you eat your fill, take heed that you do not forget the Lord who freed you from the land of Egypt, the house of bondage. Revere only the Lord your God and worship Him alone, and swear only by His name. Do not follow other gods, any gods of the peoples about you—for the Lord your God in your midst is an impassioned God—lest the anger of the Lord your God blaze forth against you and He wipe you off the face of the earth.

Do not try the Lord your God, as you did at Massah. Be sure to keep the commandments, exhortations, and laws, which the Lord your God has enjoined upon you. Do what is right and good in the sight of the Lord, that it may go well with you and that you may be able to occupy the good land which the Lord your God promised on oath to your fathers, and that your enemy may be driven out before you, as the Lord has spoken.

When, in time to come, your son asks you, "What mean the exhortations, laws, and rules which the Lord our God has enjoined upon you?'' you shall say to your son, ''We were slaves to Pharaoh in Egypt and the Lord freed us from Egypt with a mighty hand. The Lord wrought before our eyes marvelous and destructive signs and portents in Egypt, against Pharaoh and all his household; and us He freed from there, that He might take us and give us the land that He had promised on oath to our fathers. Then the Lord commanded us to observe all these laws, to revere the Lord our God, for our lasting good and for our survival, as is now the case. It will be therefore to our merit before the Lord our God to observe faithfully this whole Instruction, as He has commanded us.''

I Kings 8:22–29*

Then Solomon stood up before the altar of the Lord in the presence of the whole assembly of Israel and spread forth his hands toward the heavens, and said,

"O Lord, the God of Israel, there is no God like thee in the heavens above nor upon the earth beneath, who keepest loving faith with thy servants who walk before thee with all their heart, who hast kept with thy servant David, my father, that which thou didst promise him; for thou didst speak with thy lips, and with thy hand thou hast fulfilled it, as it is this day. Now therefore, O Lord, the God of Israel, keep with thy servant David, my father, that which thou didst promise him, saying, 'You shall never lack a man in my sight to sit on the throne of Israel, if only your sons take heed to their way, to walk before me as you have walked before me.' Now therefore, O God of Israel, let thy word be confirmed, I pray thee, which thou hast spoken to thy servant David, my father.

"But can God really dwell with men on the earth? Behold, the heavens and the highest heaven cannot contain thee; how much less this house which I have built! Yet turn thou to the prayer of thy servant and to his supplication, O Lord my God, to listen to the cry and to the prayer which thy servant offers before thee this day, that thine eyes may be open toward this house night and day, even toward the place of which thou hast said, 'My name shall be there,' to listen to the prayer which thy servant shall pray toward this place.''

Ezekiel 34:11–17

"For thus says the Lord God: 'Behold, here am I, and I will seek and search for my flock. As a shepherd searches for his flock on a day of whirlwind, when his sheep are scattered, so will I search for my flock, and rescue them from all the places to which they have been scattered on the day of clouds and thick darkness. I will lead them out of the nations, and gather them from the lands; and I will bring them to their own country, and tend them on the mountains of Israel, in the valleys, and in all the best

*Passages from I Kings, Ezekiel, Isaiah, and Job are from *The Complete Bible,* trans. by J. M. Powis Smith and Edgar J. Goodspeed (Chicago: University of Chicago Press, 1948).

places of the land. In good pasture will I tend them, and on the high mountains of Israel shall be their fold; there shall they lie down in a good fold, and on rich pasture shall they graze on the mountains of Israel. I myself will tend my flock, and I myself will lead them to their pasture,' is the oracle of the Lord God. 'I will seek out the lost, I will bring back the strayed, I will bind up the wounded, I will strengthen the sick; and I will watch over the fat and strong ones, tending them rightly.' And as for you, O my flock, thus says the Lord God: 'Behold, I will judge between sheep and sheep.'"

Isaiah 2:1–5

The word that Isaiah, the son of Amoz, received concerning Judah and Jerusalem.

It shall come to pass in days to come
That the mountain of the Lord's house will be
Established as the highest mountain
And elevated above the hills.
All the nations will stream to it,
And many peoples will come and say,
"Come, let us go up to the mount of the Lord,
To the house of the God of Jacob;
That he may instruct us in his ways,
And that we may walk in his paths.
For from Zion goes forth instruction
And the word of the Lord from Jerusalem."
Then shall he judge between the nations,
And arbitrate for many peoples;
And they shall beat their swords into plowshares,
And their spears into pruning hooks;
Nation shall not lift up sword against nation,
Nor shall they learn war any more.

O house of Jacob, come and let us walk in the light of the Lord!

Job 38

Then the Lord answered Job from the whirlwind, saying,
"Who is this that obscures counsel
By words without knowledge?
Gird up, now, your loins like a man,
That I may question you, and do you instruct me.

"Where were you when I laid the foundations of the earth?
Declare, if you have insight.
Who fixed its measurements, for you should know?
Or who stretched a line over it?

Upon what were its bases sunk,
Or who laid its cornerstone,
When the morning stars sang together,
And all the heavenly beings shouted for joy?

"Who enclosed the sea with doors,
When it burst forth, issuing from the womb,
When I made the cloud its covering,
And dense darkness its swaddling-band;
When I imposed upon it my decree,
And established its barrier and doors;
And said, 'Thus far shall you come and no farther,
And here shall your proud waves be stayed'?

"Have you ever in your life commanded the morning?
Or assigned its place to the dawn,
That it should lay hold of the corners of the earth,
And the wicked be shaked out of it?
It changes like clay under the seal,
And is dyed like a garment.
Their light is withdrawn from the wicked,
And the arm of the proud is broken.

"Have you gone to the sources of the sea,
Or walked in the hollows of the deep?
Have the gates of death been revealed to you,
Or can you see the gates of darkness?
Have you considered the breadth of the earth?
Tell, if you know all this.

"Which is the way where light dwells,
And which is the place of darkness,
That you may take it to its border,
And that you may perceive the paths to its home?
You know, for you were born then,
And the number of your days is great!

"Have you been to the storehouses of snow,
Or do you see the storehouses of hail,
Which I have reserved against the time of distress,
Against the day of war and battle?
Which is the way to where light is distributed?
Where does the east wind spread itself over the earth?
Who cleaved its channel for the torrent,
And a way for the thunderbolts,
To send rain on a land without people,
On the steppe where there is no man;

To satisfy the waste ground and desolate,
And to cause the blade of grass to spring up?

"Has the rain a father?
Or who brought forth the dew drops?
From whose womb did the ice come forth?
And who gave birth to the hoarfrost of the skies,
When the waters congeal like a stone,
And the surface of the deep is frozen solid?

"Can you bind the chains of the Pleiades,
Or loosen the girdle of Orion?
Can you send forth Mazzaroth in its season,
And lead forth the Bear with its satellites?
Do you know the laws of the heavens?
Or do you appoint the arrangements of the earth?
Can you lift your voice up to the clouds,
That a flood of waters may cover you?
"Can you send forth the lightnings that they may go
And say to you, 'Here we are!'
Who put wisdom in the inner parts,
Or who gave insight to the mind?
Who counts the clouds by wisdom?
And who tilts the waterskins of the heavens,
When the dust runs into a mass,
And the clods stick together?

"Do you hunt prey for the lioness,
Or satisfy the hunger of young lions,
When they crouch in dens,
Or lie in wait in the thicket?
Who provides its prey for the raven,
When its young ones cry unto God,
And wander without food?"

Psalm 23*
A psalm of David.

The Lord is my shepherd;
   I lack nothing.
He makes me lie down in green pastures;
   He leads me to water in places of repose;
   He renews my life;
   He guides me in right paths
   as befits His name.

*Passages from Psalms are from *The Book of Psalms* (Philadelphia: The Jewish Publication Society of America, 1972).

Though I walk through a valley of deepest darkness;
   I fear no harm, for You are with me;
   Your rod and Your staff—they comfort me.

You spread a table for me in full view of my enemies;
   You anoint my head with oil;
   my drink is abundant.
Only goodness and steadfast love shall pursue me
   all the days of my life,
   and I shall dwell in the house of the Lord
   for many long years.

Psalm 121
A song of Ascents.

A harpist, part of a bronze pedestal from Cyprus, twelfth century B.C.E.

I turn my eyes to the mountains;
   from where will my help come?
My help comes from the Lord,
   maker of heaven and earth.
He will not let your foot give way;
   your guardian will not slumber;
See, the Guardian of Israel
   neither slumbers nor sleeps!
The Lord is your guardian,
   the Lord is your protection
   at your right hand.
By day the sun will not strike you,
   nor the moon by night.
The Lord will guard you from all harm;
   He will guard your life.
The Lord will guard your going and coming
   now and forever.

Psalm 139
A psalm of David.

O Lord, You have examined me and know me.
When I sit down or stand up You know it;
   You discern my thoughts from afar.
You observe my walking and reclining,
   and are familiar with all my ways.
There is not a word on my tongue
   but that You, O Lord, know it well.
You hedge me before and behind;
   You lay Your hand upon me.
It is beyond my knowledge;
   it is a mystery; I cannot fathom it.

Where can I escape from Your spirit?
  Where can I flee from Your presence?
If I ascend to heaven, You are there;
  if I descend to Sheol, You are there too.
If I take wing with the dawn
  to come to rest on the western horizon,
  even there Your hand will be guiding me,
  Your right hand be holding me fast.
If I say, "Surely darkness will conceal me,
  night will provide me with cover."
Darkness is not dark for You;
  night is as light as day;
  darkness and light are the same.
It was You who created my conscience;
  You fashioned me in my mother's womb.
I praise You
  for I am awesomely, wondrously made;
  Your work is wonderful;
  I know it very well.
My frame was not concealed from You
  when I was shaped in a hidden place,
  knit together in the recesses of the earth.
Your eyes saw my unformed limbs;
  they were all recorded in Your book;
  in due time they were formed,
  to the very last one of them.
How weighty Your thoughts seem to me, O God,
  how great their number!
I count them—they exceed the grains of sand;
  I end—but am still with You.

O God, if You would only slay the wicked—
  you murderers, away from me!—
  who invoke You for intrigue,
  Your enemies who swear by You falsely.
O Lord, You know I hate those who hate You
  and loathe Your adversaries.
I feel a perfect hatred toward them;
  I count them my enemies.

Examine me, O God, and know my mind;
  probe me and know my thoughts.
See if I have vexatious ways,
  and guide me in ways everlasting.

READING 4

The Concept of God: Selections from Rabbinic Literature and Prayer Book

JONATHAN PARADISE

Much of rabbinic thought is expressed through parables rather than abstract theological statements. In reading rabbinic legends and parables it is important to distinguish the story, or parable (sometimes naive or fanciful), from the thought it expresses. The most outlandish rabbinic legend often conceals a profound concept.

The following selection deals with the nature of God. Although God appears to act in a variety of ways, His nature is nevertheless constant and unchanging.

> God said to Israel, 'Because ye have seen me in many likenesses, there are not therefore many gods. But it is ever the same God: I am the Lord thy God.' Rabbi Levi said: 'God appeared to them like a mirror, in which many faces can be reflected: a thousand people look at it; it looks at all of them. So when God spoke to the Israelites, each one thought that God spoke individually to him. So it says, "I am the Lord *thy* God"; not collectively, "I am the Lord *your* God."' 'The Word of God', said Rabbi Jose b. Hanina, 'spoke with each man according to his power. Nor need you marvel at this. For the manna tasted differently to each: to the children, to the young and to the old, according to their power. If the manna tasted differently according to men's power, how much more the word. David said, "The voice of the Lord with power" (Ps. XXIX, 4). It does not say "with His (God's) power", but "with power", that is, according to the power of each. And God says, "Not because you hear many voices are there many gods, but it is always I; I am the Lord thy God."' [pp. 6–7][1]

---

[1] This and the following selections are from C. G. Montefiore and H. Loewe, eds., *A Rabbinic Anthology* (Philadelphia: The Jewish Publication Society of America, n.d.).

Frequently, rabbinic Judaism represents a stage of development which puts it beyond, and in conflict with, a biblical notion. The following selection is a counterweight to biblical passages which portray God as wrathful or avenging.

(Rabbi Johanan expressed the view that God does not rejoice in the downfall of the wicked.) The ministering angels wanted to sing a hymn at the destruction of the Egyptians, but God said: 'My children lie drowned in the sea, and you would sing?' Rabbi Elazar said: He does not rejoice, but He causes others to rejoice. [p. 52]

What are the ingredients that make up righteousness from God's point of view? A partial answer is contained in this comment about the only man who was righteous enough to be saved from the Flood.

Rabbi Tanhuma b. Abba cited Proverbs (XI, 30), 'He that is wise, wins souls.' The Rabbis said: This refers to Noah, for in the Ark he fed and sustained the animals with much care. He gave to each animal its special food, and fed each at its proper period, some in the daytime and some at night. Thus he gave chopped straw to the camel, barley to the ass, vine tendrils to the elephant, and grass to the ostrich. So for twelve months he did not sleep by night or day, because all the time he was busy feeding the animals. [pp. 47–48]

Where is God's presence to be found? If one worships at a holy place, or sanctuary, is God somehow limited?

It is written, 'And Moses was not able to enter into the tent of meeting, because the glory of the Lord filled the sanctuary' (Exod. XL, 35). Rabbi Joshua of Sikhnin said in the name of Rabbi Levi: The matter is like a cave which lies by the sea shore; the tide rises, and the cave becomes full of water, but the sea is no whit less full. So the sanctuary and the tent of meeting were filled with the radiance of the Shechinah [the presence of God], but the world was no less filled with God's glory. [p. 15]

The rabbinic conception of God is very warm and intimate. Moreover, it frequently attributes totally human characteristics to God. A striking example is the notion that God, like a pious Jew, prays each day. Even the text of his prayer was composed.

May it be my will that my compassion may overcome mine anger, and that it may prevail over my attributes (of justice and judgment), and that I may deal with my children according to the attribute of compassion, and that I may not act towards them according to the strict line of justice. [p. 368]

Several key rabbinic values are revealed in these passages:

Rabbi Judah said in the name of Rab: The day has twelve hours. In the first three God sits and busies Himself with the Torah; in the next three He sits and judges the whole world, and whenever He sees that the whole world is guilty [i.e., deserves to be condemned], He arises from the throne of justice, and sits on the throne of mercy; in the next three He sits and feeds the whole world from the horned buffalo to the eggs of the louse; in the last three He sits and sports with the leviathan [a sea monster], as it says, 'The leviathan whom thou hast made to sport with' (Ps. CIV, 26). [p.41]

Rabbi Joshua b. Nehemiah said: Have you ever seen it happen that the rain fell on the field of A who was righteous, and not on the field of B who was wicked? Or that the sun arose and shone upon Israel who was righteous, and not upon the wicked [the nations]? God causes the sun to shine both upon Israel and upon the nations, for the Lord is good to all. [p. 43. The passage goes on to say that man is often kind to his slaves and cruel to his animals, and *vice versa,* but that God is merciful both to man and beast.]

Religious studies take a significant portion of a rabbi's time.

Through a daring reinterpretation of Exodus 34:6–7, the rabbis arrive at this profile of divine attributes:

> (1) The Lord, (2) The Lord (for Yahweh is God as the Merciful One), (3) God (usually God [Elohim] is the judge, God in his attribute of just severity, but here that usual interpretation of Elohim is ignored), (4) merciful, and (5) gracious, (6) longsuffering, and abundant in (7) loving-kindness and (8) fidelity, (9) keeping mercy to a thousand generations, forgiving (10) iniquity, (11) transgression and (12) sin, and (13) acquitting:

> Rabbi Johanan said: Thirteen kinds of mercy are written in the Scripture about God. [p. 43]

The language of the daily prayers states Jewish theology simply, directly, and briefly. The usual structure is praise, followed by petition.

Lord of Creation[2]

Praised are You, O Lord our God, King of the universe.
You fix the cycles of light and darkness;
You ordain the order of all creation.
You cause light to shine over the earth;
Your radiant mercy is upon its inhabitants.

In Your goodness the work of creation
Is continually renewed day by day.
How manifold are your works, O Lord!
With wisdom You fashioned them all!
The earth abounds with Your creations.

O King, who alone is exalted from of old,
Praised and glorified since the world began,
Eternal God, our shield and our protection,
Lord of our strength, and Rock of our defense,
With Your infinite mercy, continue to love us.

It was You, praised and all-knowing,
Who created the sun and sent forth its rays,
A beautiful creation, reflecting Your might;
The lights of the heavens radiate Your glory.

The hosts of heaven exalt the Almighty,
Forever revealing Your glory and holiness.
For the stars, so radiant with light,
For the wonder of all that You have created,
We shall glorify You, O Lord our God.

[2]From *Weekday Prayer Book* (New York: Rabbinical Assembly of America, 1961), pp. 42–43.

READING 5
Judaism Finds Meaning in History*
HUSTON SMITH

Judaism has found meaning in its concept of God. It has expressed its concept of God in the symbols and language of its culture or way of life as it has progressed through time. Human experience in time is history. Judaism has also found meaning in history or its cultural experience throughout the ages.

What is at stake when we ask if there is meaning in history? At stake is our whole attitude toward the social order and man's collective life. . . .

. . . To the Jews history was of towering significance. It was important, first, because they were convinced that the context in which life is lived affects that life in every way, setting up its problems, delineating its opportunities, conditioning its fulfillment. It is impossible to talk about Adam and Noah (the same may be said of almost every Biblical character) apart from the particular circumstances—in this case Eden and the Flood—that surrounded them and in response to which their lives took shape.

Second, if contexts are crucial for life so is group action—social action as we usually call it—for there are times when it takes group action to change contexts to the needed extent. The destiny of the individual Hebrew slave in bondage in Egypt is not depicted as depending on the extent to which he "rose above" his slavery by praising God with his spirit while his body was in chains; he had to rise with his people and break for the desert.

Third, history was important for the Jews because they saw it, always, as a field of opportunity. God was the ruler of history; nothing, therefore, happened by accident. His hand was at work in every event—in Eden, the Flood, the Tower of Babel, the years in the wilderness—shaping each sequence into a teaching experience for those who had the wit to learn.

*From Huston Smith, *The Religions of Man* (New York: Harper & Row, 1958), pp. 236–38.

Finally, history was important because its opportunities did not stream forth on an even plateau. Events, all of them important, were nevertheless not of equal importance. It was not the case that anyone, anywhere, at any time could turn to history and find awaiting him an opportunity equivalent to any other. Each opportunity was unique but some were decisive. "There is a tide in the affairs of men which, taken at the flood, leads on to fortune."[1] One must, therefore, attend to history carefully, for when opportunities pass they are gone.

This uniqueness in events is epitomized in the Hebraic notions (a) of God's direct intervention in history at certain critical points and (b) of a chosen people as recipients of his unique challenges. Both are vividly illustrated in the epic of Abraham. This epic is introduced by a remarkable prologue, Genesis 1–11, which describes the steady deterioration of the world from its original goodness. Disobedience (eating the forbidden fruit) is followed by murder (Cain of Abel), promiscuity (the sons of God and the daughters of men), incest and homosexuality (the sons of Noah) until a flood is needed to sluice out the mess. In the midst of this corruption God is not inactive. Against its backdrop, in the last days of the Sumeric universal state, God calls Abraham. He is to go forth into a new land to establish a new people. The moment is decisive. Because Abraham seizes it, he ceases to be anonymous. He becomes the first Hebrew, the first of "the chosen people."

Many people have seen themselves as victims of history. In Judaism, as Huston Smith continues,

. . . history is in tension between its divine potentialities and its present frustrations. There is a profound disharmony between God's will and the existing social order. As a consequence, more than any other religion of the time, Judaism laid the groundwork for social protest. As things are not as they should be, revolution in some form is to be expected. The idea bore fruit. It is in the countries that have been affected by the Jewish perspective on history, which was taken over by Christianity and to some extent by Islam, that the most intensive movements for social reform have occurred. The prophets set the pattern. "Protected by religious sanctions," Professor William Albright has written, "the prophets of Judah were a reforming political force which has never been surpassed and perhaps never equalled in subsequent world history." Passionately convinced that things were not as they ought to be, they created in the name of the God for whom they spoke an atmosphere of reform that "put Hyde Park and the best days of muckraking newspapers to shame."[2]

---

[1] William Shakespeare, *Julius Caesar,* Act IV, Sc. 3, Line 217.
[2] W. F. Albright in *Approaches to World Peace* (New York: Council on Science, Philosophy and Religion, 1943), p. 9.

READING 6
Covenants and Meaning

A. Definition of Covenant*

COVENANT (Heb. *berit*): An agreement by which two contracting parties freely enter into a special kind of relationship (e.g., of solidarity, friendship, obedience, etc.). A covenant could be made between man and his fellow or between man and God and was usually confirmed by some kind of ritual symbolizing the union of the partners. . . .

The covenant which God made with Abraham and subsequently confirmed to Isaac and Jacob is fundamental to the theological understanding of the development of Judaism. The original covenant with the patriarchs was renewed, this time with the whole people, at Sinai (Exod. 24) where the people accepted the obligations of the law ("the two tablets of the covenant"; cf. Exod. 31:18; 32:15 ff.). The covenant was renewed again by Ezra. God's eternal fidelity to his covenant, in spite of Israel's backsliding, is a major theme in Aggadah and liturgy (cf. also Lev. 26:42–45). Outward signs serve to testify to the permanent validity of a covenant (e.g., circumcision—*berit milah,* the *"berit" par excellence*—for the covenant of Abraham; the Sabbath, Exod. 31:16–17). Other, more specific, covenants conferred the priesthood upon the House of Aaron (Num. 25:12–13) and kingship upon the House of David (Ps. 132). A covenant involving mankind as a whole, and indeed the entire natural order, was made with Noah (Gen. 9:12–15); according to Jeremiah (33:19–21, 25–26) the specific covenants with Israel and David are

A stylized version of the tablets of the Law of Moses.

*From R. J. Zwi Werblowsky and Geoffrey Wigoder, eds. *The Encyclopedia of the Jewish Religion* (New York: Holt, Rinehart and Winston, 1965), pp. 100–101.

everlasting. The traditional idea of a covenant between God and His people is presupposed by the prophets and forms the background of their preaching.

B. The Covenant with Noah

Genesis 6:9–22*

This is the line of Noah.—Noah was a righteous man; he was blameless in his age; Noah walked with God.—Noah begot three sons: Shem, Ham, and Japheth.

The earth became corrupt before God; the earth was filled with lawlessness. When God saw how corrupt the earth was, for all flesh had corrupted its ways on earth, God said to Noah, "I have decided to put an end to all flesh, for the earth is filled with lawlessness because of them: I am about to destroy them with the earth. Make yourself an ark of gopher wood; make it an ark with compartments, and cover it inside and out with pitch. This is how you shall make it: the length of the ark shall be three hundred cubits, its width fifty cubits, and its height thirty cubits. Make an opening for daylight in the ark, and terminate it within a cubit of the top. Put the entrance to the ark in its side; make it with bottom, second, and third decks.

"For My part, I am about to bring the Flood—waters upon the earth—to destroy all flesh under the sky in which there is breath of life; everything on earth shall perish. But I will establish My covenant with you, and you shall enter the ark, with your sons, your wife, and your sons' wives. And of all that lives, of all flesh, you shall take two of each into the ark to keep alive with you; they shall be male and female. From birds of every kind, cattle of every kind, every kind of creeping thing on earth, two of each shall come to you to stay alive. For your part, take of everything that is eaten and store it away, to serve as food for you and for them." Noah did so; just as God commanded him, so he did.

Genesis 9:1–17

God blessed Noah and his sons, and said to them, "Be fertile and increase, and fill the earth. The fear and the dread of you shall be upon all the beasts of the earth and upon all the birds of the sky—everything with which the earth is astir—and upon all the fish of the sea; they are given into your hand. Every creature that lives shall be yours to eat; as with the green grasses, I give you all these. You must not, however, eat flesh with its life-blood in it. But for your own life-blood I will require a reckoning: I

*This and the following passages from Genesis are from *The Torah: The Five Books of Moses* (Philadelphia: The Jewish Publication Society of America, 1962).

will require it of every beast; of man, too, and I will require a reckoning for human life, of every man for that of his fellow man!

Whoever sheds the blood of man,
By man shall his blood be shed;
For in His image
Did God make man.

Be fertile, then, and increase; abound on the earth and increase on it."

And God said to Noah and to his sons with him, "I now establish My covenant with you and your offspring to come, and with every living thing that is with you—birds, cattle, and every wild beast as well—all that have come out of the ark, every living thing on earth. I will maintain My covenant with you: never again shall all flesh be cut off by the waters of a flood, and never again shall there be a flood to destroy the earth."

God further said, "This is the sign that I set for the covenant between Me and you, and every living creature with you, for all ages to come. I have set My bow in the clouds, and it shall serve as a sign of the covenant between Me and the earth. When I bring clouds over the earth, and the bow appears in the clouds, I will remember My covenant between Me and you and every living creature among all flesh, so that the waters shall never again become a flood to destroy all flesh. When the bow is in the clouds, I will see it and remember the everlasting covenant between God and all living creatures, all flesh that is on earth. That," God said to Noah, "shall be the sign of the covenant that I have established between Me and all flesh that is on earth."

C. The Covenant with Abraham

Genesis 17:1-21

When Abram was ninety-nine years old, the Lord appeared to Abram and said to him, "I am El Shaddai. Walk in My ways and be blameless. I will establish My covenant between Me and you, and I will make you exceedingly numerous."

Abram threw himself on his face; and God spoke to him further, "As for Me, this is My covenant with you: You shall be the father of a multitude of nations. And you shall no longer be called Abram, but your name shall be Abraham, for I make you the father of a multitude of nations. I will make you exceedingly fertile, and make nations of you; and kings shall come forth from you. I will maintain My covenant between Me and you, and your offspring to come, as an everlasting covenant throughout the ages, to be God to you and to your offspring to come. I give the land you sojourn in to you and your offspring to come, all the land of Canaan, as an everlasting possession. I will be their God."

God further said to Abraham, "As for you, you and your offspring to come throughout the ages shall keep My covenant. Such shall be the covenant between Me and you and your offspring to follow which you shall keep: every male among you shall be circumcised. You shall circumcise the flesh of your foreskin, and that shall be the sign of the covenant between Me and you. And throughout the generations, every male among you shall be circumcised at the age of eight days. As for the homeborn slave and the one bought from an outsider who is not of your offspring, they must be circumcised, homeborn and purchased alike. Thus shall My covenant be marked in your flesh as an everlasting pact. And if any male who is uncircumcised fails to circumcise the flesh of his foreskin, that person shall be cut off from his kin; he has broken My covenant."

And God said to Abraham, "As for your wife Sarai, you shall not call her Sarai, but her name shall be Sarah. I will bless her; indeed, I will give you a son by her. I will bless her so that she shall give rise to nations; rulers of peoples shall issue from her." Abraham threw himself on his face and laughed, as he said to himself, "Can a child be born to a man a hundred years old, or can Sarah bear a child at ninety?" And Abraham said to God, "Oh that Ishmael might live by Your favor!" God said, "Nevertheless, Sarah your wife shall bear you a son, and you shall name him Isaac; and I will maintain My covenant with him as an everlasting covenant for his offspring to come. As for Ishmael, I have heeded you. I hereby bless him. I will make him fertile and exceedingly numerous. He shall be the father of twelve chieftains, and I will make of him a great nation. But My covenant I will maintain with Isaac, whom Sarah shall bear to you at this season next year."

D. Circumcision*

CIRCUMCISION: Removal of the foreskin in an operation performed on all male Jewish children on the eighth day after birth, and also upon male converts to Judaism. Circumcision was imposed by God upon Abraham and his descendants (Gen. 17:10–12) and has always been regarded as the supreme . . . sign of loyalty and adherence to Judaism. As the sign of the covenant (*berit*) "sealed in the flesh", circumcision came to be known as *berit milah* or the "covenant of our father Abraham".

Circumcision implements from Germany, eighteenth to nineteenth century. The cups are for ceremonial wine; the clamp, knife, and scissors are surgical instruments; the vial is for depositing the foreskin; and the flask was used in earlier days to hold a healing and coagulant substance.

*Adapted from Werblowsky and Wigoder, eds., *Encyclopedia of the Jewish Religion*, p. 90.

E. Israel's Selection*

ISIDORE EPSTEIN

In the third month of their departure from the land of Egypt the Israelites arrived at Sinai, which, in the judgment of many scholars, is located just east of the Gulf of Aqaba. This burning desert, with its overhanging cliffs and volcanic mountains, was the scene of the ever-memorable Covenant which made YHWH the God of Israel, and Israel the people of YHWH. The Sinaitic Covenant had its roots in God's covenant with Abraham which in turn had its antecedents in the divine covenant with Noah. This Noachic covenant . . . forms an important moment in the process of universal history as unfolded in the opening chapters of the Bible; and it is within the framework of this universal history that the significance of the Sinaitic Covenant is to be found.

The story begins with the creation of the world by God and the formation of man in His image. But this creative process did not cease when the world and man had been made, for that which had been created had to be developed and fostered. This task God entrusted to man. Made in the image of God, man must conform to the character of God, and because God creates, man must also create. He must work and cooperate with God in maintaining and developing the work He had committed to man's care.

The basis of this creative cooperation is obedience to the Creator, which must express itself in obedience to the moral law. This moral law falls into two classes: (1) Justice, which is concerned with recognition of human rights; (2) Righteousness, which stresses acceptance of duties.

The first precept of the law of Justice was communicated to mankind through Noah when, after the Deluge, God entered into a covenant with him, wherein He enjoined respect for the sanctity of human life. Furthermore, in order to enforce this respect, He forbade, on the one hand, the consumption of animal blood, blood being the symbol of life and as such to be treated as sacred, and, on the other, prescribed the death penalty for the wilful shedding of human blood.

These Noachic precepts were obviously offered as a *modus vivendi* [compromise] to a society which had to be re-created, after having broken down badly, in consequence of 'violence' (Gen. 6:11), and were by no means intended to constitute the whole content of the law of Justice. But Justice, however widened in scope, inasmuch as it seeks merely to safeguard human rights, is but the negative aspect of the moral law. Justice, therefore, is only regulative, not creative. Creativeness alike in man and the Divine enters into full activity only when prompted by Righteousness. This is a truth which was first perceived and acted upon by

*Adapted from Isidore Epstein, *Judaism* (New York: Penguin Books, 1959), pp. 19–20.

Abraham. God in consequence entered into a covenant with him claiming him and his descendants as instruments for making known to mankind 'the way of the Lord to do Righteousness and Justice' (Gen. 18:19), and thereby performing the universal service for which he and his seed had been chosen.

It was in ratification of the Covenant with Abraham, in all its implications, that God's Covenant with Israel at Sinai was made. Fundamental to this Covenant was the divine exhortation 'And ye shall be unto me a kingdom of priests, and a holy nation' (Ex. 19:6). The charge thus conveyed was both national and universal. As a 'kingdom of priests' Israel[ites] were to render service to the universality of mankind, whilst as a 'holy nation' they were to follow a particular way of life—a life of holiness—which was to mark them off as a distinct people among the nations of the world.

F. The Covenant with Moses

Exodus 19*

On the third new moon after the Israelites had gone forth from the land of Egypt, on that very day, they entered the wilderness of Sinai. Having journeyed from Rephidim, they entered the wilderness of Sinai and encamped in the wilderness. Israel encamped there in front of the mountain, and Moses went up to God. The Lord called to him from the mountain, saying, "Thus shall you say to the house of Jacob and declare to the children of Israel: 'You have seen what I did to the Egyptians, how I bore you on eagles' wings and brought you to Me. Now then, if you will obey Me faithfully and keep My covenant, you shall be My treasured possession among all the peoples. Indeed, all the earth is Mine, but you shall be to Me a kingdom of priests and a holy nation.' These are the words that you shall speak to the children of Israel."

Moses came and summoned the elders of the people and put before them all the words that the Lord had commanded him. All the people answered as one, saying, "All that the Lord has spoken we will do!" And Moses brought back the people's words to the Lord. And the Lord said to Moses, "I will come to you in a thick cloud, in order that the people may hear when I speak with you and so trust you ever after." Then Moses reported the people's words to the Lord, and the Lord said to Moses, "Go to the people and warn them to stay pure today and tomorrow. Let them wash their clothes. Let them be ready for the third day; for on the third day the Lord will come down, in the sight of all the people, on Mount Sinai. You shall set bounds for the people round about, saying, 'Beware of going

*The passages from Exodus are from *The Torah: The Five Books of Moses.*

up the mountain or touching the border of it. Whoever touches the mountain shall be put to death: no hand shall touch him, but he shall be either stoned or shot; beast or man, he shall not live.' When the ram's horn sounds a long blast, they may go up on the mountain."

Moses came down from the mountain to the people and warned the people to stay pure, and they washed their clothes. And he said to the people, "Be ready for the third day: do not go near a woman."

On the third day, as morning dawned, there was thunder, and lightning, and a dense cloud upon the mountain, and a very loud blast of the horn; and all the people who were in the camp trembled. Moses led the people out of the camp toward God, and they took their places at the foot of the mountain.

Now Mount Sinai was all in smoke, for the Lord had come down upon it in fire; the smoke rose like the smoke of a kiln, and the whole mountain trembled violently. The blare of the horn grew louder and louder. As Moses spoke, God answered him in thunder. The Lord came down upon Mount Sinai, on the top of the mountain, and the Lord called Moses to the top of the mountain and Moses went up. The Lord said to Moses, "Go down, warn the people not to break through to the Lord to gaze, lest many of them perish. The priests also, who come near the Lord, must purify themselves, lest the Lord break out against them." But Moses said to the Lord, "The people cannot come up to Mount Sinai, for You warned us saying, 'Set bounds about the mountain and sanctify it.'" So the Lord said to him, "Go down, and come back together with Aaron; but let not the priests or the people break through to come up to the Lord, lest He break out against them." And Moses went down to the people and spoke to them.

Exodus 20

God spoke all these words, saying:

I the Lord am your God who brought you out of the land of Egypt, the house of bondage. You shall have no other gods beside Me.

You shall not make for yourself a sculptured image, or any likeness of what is in the heavens above, or on the earth below, or in the waters under the earth. You shall not bow down to them or serve them. For I the Lord your God am an impassioned God, visiting the guilt of the fathers upon the children, upon the third and upon the fourth generations of those who reject Me, but showing kindness to the thousandth generation of those who love Me and keep My commandments.

You shall not swear falsely by the name of the Lord your God; for the Lord will not clear one who swears falsely by His name.

Remember the sabbath day and keep it holy. Six days you shall labor and do all your work, but the seventh day is a sabbath of the Lord your God; you shall not do any work—you, your son or daughter, your male or female slave, or your cattle, or the stranger who is within your settlements. For in six days the Lord made heaven and earth and sea, and all that is in them, and He rested on the seventh day; therefore the Lord blessed the sabbath day and hallowed it.

Honor your father and your mother, that you may long endure on the land which the Lord your God is giving you.

You shall not murder.

You shall not commit adultery.

You shall not steal.

You shall not bear false witness against your neighbor.

You shall not covet your neighbor's house; you shall not covet your neighbor's wife, or his male or female slave, or his ox or his ass, or anything that is your neighbor's.

All the people witnessed the thunder and lightning, the blare of the horn and the mountain smoking; and when the people saw it, they fell back and stood at a distance. "You speak to us," they said to Moses, "and we will obey; but let not God speak to us, lest we die." Moses answered the people, "Be not afraid; for God has come only in order to test you, and in order that the fear of Him may be ever with you, so that you do not go astray." So the people remained at a distance, while Moses approached the thick cloud where God was.

The Lord said to Moses:

Thus shall you say to the Israelites: You yourselves saw that I spoke to you from the very heavens: With Me, therefore, you shall not make any gods of silver, nor shall you make for yourselves any gods of gold. Make for Me an altar of earth and sacrifice on it your burnt offerings and your sacrifices of well-being, your sheep and your oxen; in every place where I cause My name to be mentioned I will come to you and bless you. And if you make for Me an altar of stones, do not build it of hewn stones; for by wielding your tool upon them you have profaned them. Do not ascend My altar by steps, that your nakedness may not be exposed upon it.

Exodus 24

Then He said to Moses, "Come up to the Lord, with Aaron, Nadab and Abihu, and seventy elders of Israel, and bow low from afar. But only Moses shall come near the Lord. The others shall not come near; and the people shall not come up with him at all."

Moses went and repeated to the people all the commands of the Lord and all the rules; and all the people answered with one voice, saying, "All the things that the Lord has commanded we will do!" Moses then wrote down all the commands of the Lord.

Early in the morning, he set up an altar at the foot of the mountain, with twelve pillars for the twelve tribes of Israel. He designated some young

Moses holding the tablets of the Ten Commandments.

men among the Israelites, and they offered burnt offerings and sacrificed bulls as offerings of well-being to the Lord. Moses took one part of the blood and put it in basins, and the other part of the blood he dashed against the altar. Then he took the record of the covenant and read it aloud to the people. And they said, "All that the Lord has spoken we will faithfully do!" Moses took the blood and dashed it on the people and said, "This is the blood of the covenant which the Lord now makes with you concerning all these commands."

Then Moses and Aaron, Nadab and Abihu, and seventy elders of Israel ascended; and they saw the God of Israel: under His feet there was the likeness of a pavement of sapphire, like the very sky for purity. Yet He did not raise His hand against the leaders of the Israelites; they beheld God, and they ate and drank.

The Lord said to Moses, "Come up to Me on the mountain and wait there, and I will give you the stone tablets with the teachings and commandments which I have inscribed to instruct them." So Moses and his attendant Joshua arose, and Moses ascended the mountain of God. To the elders he had said, "Wait here for us until we return to you. You have Aaron and Hur with you; let anyone who has a legal matter approach them."

When Moses had ascended the mountain, the cloud covered the mountain. The Presence of the Lord abode on Mount Sinai, and the cloud hid it for six days. On the seventh day He called to Moses from the midst of the cloud. Now the Presence of the Lord appeared in the sight of the Israelites as a consuming fire on the top of the mountain. Moses went inside the cloud and ascended the mountain; and Moses remained on the mountain forty days and forty nights.

A Yemenite Jew holds the Torah scroll.

READING 7
Israel—Its Torah*
HAYIM HALEVY DONIN

The Jewish faith does not stop with "And God created the heavens and the earth." It starts there. It continues to acknowledge that "I am the Lord your God who took you out of the land of Egypt." He is a living God, who continues to play a role in the universe He created. He is a sovereign God, who is concerned about the behavior of the people He created, and to that end has found ways to make His will known to mankind. In His own inscrutable ways, He continues to judge the behavior of all men, rewarding and punishing either in this world or in the spiritual world to come.

Judaism insists that there is no practical distinction between one who entirely denies the existence of God and the one who admits to the existence of God and even to His role in Creation but denies that God has anything more to do with this world. The distinction between such views is purely academic, for there are no differentiating implications for human life. In either case, there are no compelling reasons to worship Him or to follow in His ways.

Central to the belief in a living God is the Jewish belief that in some spiritual fashion He communicated His will and His commandments to the creature whom He endowed with free will, but whom He called to be His obedient servant. The very essence of Judaism rests upon the acceptance of a spiritual-historical event in which our ancestors participated as a group, as well as upon acceptance of subsequent spiritual revelations to the Prophets of Israel. The extraordinary historical event I refer to is the promulgation of the Ten Commandments at Mount

*From Rabbi Hayim Halevy Donin, *To Be a Jew* (New York: Basic Books, 1972), pp. 24–27.

Sinai seven weeks following the exodus of the children of Israel from Egypt. God's will was also made manifest in the Written Torah, written down by Moses under Divine prophecy during the forty-year period after the exodus. Side by side with the Five Books of Moses (Pentateuch), we believe that God's will was also made manifest in the Oral Tradition or Oral Torah which also had its source at Sinai, revealed to Moses and then orally taught by him to the religious heads of Israel. The Written Torah itself alludes to such oral instructions. This Oral Torah—which clarifies and provides the details for many of the commandments contained in the Written Torah—was transmitted from generation to generation until finally recorded in the second century to become the cornerstone upon which the Talmud was built.

Non-traditionalists regard the Torah as the inspired writing of great men, as a record of man's attempt to reach out to God. According to this view, there is nothing eternal about the Torah and nothing Divine about it. It is subject to the errors that men, even great men, are capable of making. If this is the case, why indeed should it be treated as any more authoritative a guide to behavior or as any more the embodiment of Truth, than say, the ethics of Aristotle, or Kant, or Spinoza? If it is only a set of man-made tribal laws, anyone is indeed justified in eliminating what no longer suits him, changing or amending it as it strikes the fancy of each generation or religious leader. This is precisely the rationale used by non-traditionalists to justify the far-reaching changes in Jewish practices that they have introduced.

However one chooses to visualize or understand or comprehend the specific nature of God's revelation to Israel and the Prophets, what stands out is that if the Torah means anything at all, it is a record of God reaching out to man, and not vice versa. If it possesses any enduring value and truth, the Torah must be seen as a record not of man's spiritual genius, but of God's will communicated to mortal and finite man. No interpretation of Judaism is Jewishly valid if it does not posit God as the *source* of Torah.

What is Torah? Technically it refers to the Five Books of Moses. This is the Written Torah (*Torah SheBiktav*). The scroll upon which it is written and which is kept in the Holy Ark of the synagogue is called a scroll of the Torah (*Sefer Torah*). In a sense, this is the constitution of the Jewish people. But this constitution was promulgated not by men, but revealed by God. By Torah is also meant the Oral Truth (*Torah She-B'al Peh*) "which Moses received at Sinai, and transmitted to Joshua, and Joshua to the Elders, and the Elders to the Prophets, and the Prophets to the Men of the Great Assembly . . ." (Ethics of the Fathers 1:1).

The Oral Torah included the finer points of the commandments, the details of the general principles contained in the Scriptures and the ways by which the commandments were to be applied. For example, the Torah forbids "work" on the Sabbath. What constitutes "work"? How shall "work" be defined for purposes of the Sabbath? Except for several references to such tasks as gathering wood, kindling fire, cooking and baking, the Written Torah does not say. The Oral Torah does.

The Written Torah commands that animals needed for food be killed "as I have commanded thee." How shall this slaughtering take place? What regulations govern such slaughtering? The Written Torah does not say. The Oral Torah does.

The Written Torah commands us to "bind them as a sign upon your hands and as frontlets between your eyes." This reference to *tefillin* leaves us in the dark as to how they were to be made up, what they were to consist of, how they were to be donned. The Written Torah does not say. The Oral Torah does.

The Written Torah prescribes capital punishment for various crimes. What legal rules and procedures had to be followed before such a verdict could be handed down? What were the limitations? The Written Torah does not say. The Oral Torah does.

Synagogue service in Israel.

Ultimately, this Oral Torah was reduced to writing. During the second century C.E., it was incorporated into the Mishna, which in turn became the cornerstone for the Gemara which consists of the monumental records and minutes of the case discussions and legal debates conducted by the Sages. Mishna and Gemara together make up the Talmud.

The Torah, whether Written or Oral, is the teaching that directs man how to live. Although it speaks primarily to Israel, it also has directives for all men. It is concerned with every aspect of human life. Ritual laws, generally thought of as "religious observances," are only part of the total complex of commandments. The commandments of the Torah, its statutes and regulations, cover the entire range of human and social behavior. It asserts its jurisdiction in areas of behavior which in other religions are generally thought of as belonging to the ethical or moral domains or to the jurisdiction of secular civil and criminal codes of law. Even its non-legal and non-statutory sections stress spiritual truths and convey insight into the still finer extra-legal ethical and moral norms of behavior.

The rest of the books of the Hebrew Bible, written over a period of many centuries, consist of the Prophets (*Neviim*) and the Sacred Writings (*Ketuvim*). These books convey the teachings of the Prophets in the context of Israel's history over a period of about seven hundred years. They tell of the Prophets' visions of God and of their ongoing struggles to promote greater allegiance among the people to the teachings of the Torah; of their struggles against the many false prophets and priests who so often misled the people and turned them away from God and the Torah. Among these books is the inspirational Psalms that reflects man's deepest religious sentiments.

The Torah, with the Neviim and the Ketuvim are together referred to as *Ta Nakh.* (This is what non-Jews call the "Old Testament," but which to the Jew has always been the *only* Testament). In the broadest sense, however, the study of Torah refers not only to the Scriptures and the Oral Torah, but also to the entire body of rabbinic legislation and interpretation based upon the Torah that developed over the centuries. For the Torah was always a living law, constantly applied by a living people to real conditions that were often changing. Though these are obviously the result of human efforts, they are an integral part of the entire body of religious jurisprudence to which the Torah itself grants authoritative status: "And you shall observe and do according to all that they shall teach you. According to the law which they shall teach you and according to the judgment which they shall tell you, you shall do" (Deut. 17:10–11).

Torah is the embodiment of the Jewish faith. It contains the terms of his Covenant with God. It is what makes a Jew a Jew.

READING 8
Law in Judaism and Applied Idealism*
MILTON STEINBERG

LAW IN JUDAISM

The Jewish religion contains a body of law, not only ecclesiastical, which would be readily understandable, but civil and criminal also.

What is more, law in Judaism is not some half-forgotten detail tucked away in a corner. Quite the contrary, it stands out in the open, looming large. It is the theme of an extensive literature, including some of the greatest texts of the Tradition; it was the first interest of many of the most brilliant minds and noblest spirits among medieval Jews; it is widely studied and cultivated to this day. . . .

Law is present in Judaism first of all because it is present in the Torah-Book. Of and by itself this circumstance suffices to make it a permanent element of the Tradition.

Law is part of Judaism in the second place because the Jews are more than members in a religious communion, being also fellows in a historic people. For about a millenium and a half that people lived its own life on its own soil and in conformity with its own political and moral principles. Quite understandably, it amassed in the process a sizable body of juridical materials.

What is more, even after the dispersal of the Jews they continued in greater or lesser measure to regulate themselves by their national code. All through the Middle Ages down to the nineteenth century Jewish communities were autonomous, at least in internal affairs. To be sure, there had been written into the Tradition the dictum of Mar Samuel, distinguished legal scholar of the third century, to the effect that the civil

*Adapted from Milton Steinberg, *Basic Judaism* (New York: Harcourt, Brace & World, 1947), pp. 143–48.

law of the land, so long as it was consistent with essential Judaism, was to be regarded by Jews as binding on themselves. Nevertheless, Jews commonly preferred their own courts for the settlement of disputes. Which means that as recently as a century ago Jewish law still functioned as a social instrument.

Also, law persists in the Tradition because the study of it, like any other mental occupation, can be pleasurable, as many Jews in each generation have discovered to their delight. To this purpose it does not matter in the least whether the subject matter is or is not operative. It may still pique men's curiosity and elicit from them the resolve toward understanding and mastery. It becomes a pure science, a pursuit engaged in not for tangible advantage but for intellectual joy. Always there has been something of this spirit in the study of Jewish law, a temper made all the keener because all through the Middle Ages the world allowed Jews so few other outlets for their energies.

Law is an element in Judaism, last of all, because of the intense Jewish preoccupation with ethics, and because of the historic Jewish insistence that ideals need to be put to work. If they be personal they must be translated into habits and disciplines. If they be social they must be incarnated in institutions, folkways, and law. Otherwise, their cogency and content will evaporate, and they will be left in the end empty vessels.

Persuaded of this truth, the Tradition has refused to permit its social values to go unapplied. Steadfastly, passionately, it has struggled for their utilization as guiding rules for the social process.

This then is the final and climactic reason for the presence of law in Judaism. It could not be otherwise, Judaism being what it is: a religion impelled by a vigorous social idealism and determined to put this idealism to use.

APPLIED IDEALISM

Characteristically enough, the Torah-Book, the earliest formulation of Jewish ideals, contains also their first implementation.

Is man made in the image of God? Then, to take illustrations at random, the stranger may not be oppressed; and the wages of a hired servant may not be withheld; and the slave girl shall be protected against abuse by her master; and no man shall bear the penalties of another's offenses; nor may a creditor enter a debtor's house to claim payment; the slaying of a slave is as much murder as the killing of a free man; and when the bondman goes free, his term of service concluded, he shall be well compensated by way of severance.

Are all men equal before God? Then there must be but one law for the Israelite and the stranger in his gates, and justice may not be perverted whether out of deference toward the rich or out of sympathy for the poor.

A Torah reading in an Israeli synagogue.

Are men brothers, owing one another fraternal solicitude? Then let a tithe be taken up for the poor; the needy may lawfully claim for their own the corners of fields, the gleanings, and anything overlooked in the harvesting. Therefore, too, anyone who requires it may enter a field and eat, except that he may carry nothing away. Hence also the accepting of interest is prohibited, nor may a millstone or cloak be taken as security for a loan.

Are the world's goods a trust imparted by God to mankind? Then, loans shall be canceled every seventh year so that no one may forever be sunk in debt; and bondman may not, except at his explicit request, be indentured for more than six years; nor may the land be perpetually sold but shall be returned every fifty years to the descendants of its original owners so that the impoverished may have fresh access to the soil from which they have been dispossessed.

The Biblical precedent of high ideals courageously applied carries over into post-Biblical Judaism. The *Mishnah* and the *Talmuds* are as passionate and determined to implement justice and mercy as were the prophets. In effect, the rabbis picked up where Scripture left off, enacting legislation extraordinary for humanity and liberalism.

First in human history, they challenged capital punishment, virtually abolishing it in their courts.

They guarded the person and rights of the slaves; in fact they all but did away with Hebrew slavery.

They guaranteed the right to strike.

They established a legal presumption in favor of labor in disputes between workers and their employers.

They instituted universal compulsory education.

Orientals though they were, they protected zealously the rights of women and improved their status.

They worked out the first systematic philanthropy in human history.

But what of the crucial issues of the day?

Where does Judaism stand on these? Which of the conflicting ideologies, what specific social reforms does it endorse?

To these questions there can be no detailed answers. The prophets and rabbis who were the chief architects of the Tradition lived in an age other than ours when ideologies such as the democratic, totalitarian, capitalist, socialist, and communist had not yet been conceived, and when our social dilemmas did not exist, at least not in their present form.

Yet the Tradition is so clear in its basic social outlook that deductions can with confidence be drawn from it for contemporary problems. These deductions, like all inferences, carry with them some element of risk. And they take the form not of specific conclusions, but of general principles.

But the risk is not so great nor the principles so abstract as to deprive the Tradition of social relevance. On the contrary, a fairly compact outlook can be extracted from it readily and with high assurance, as is attested by the pronouncements in recent years of the various rabbinical bodies. These associations are separated by all sorts of theological and ritualistic differences, yet each of them has proclaimed a quite concrete social program, and all the programs coincide on all important themes, clear evidence that the Tradition is still capable of investing Jewish social thought with unity and particularity.

On the evidences of the past and of the modern rabbinate, Judaism stands these days:

—For the fullest freedom, political, economic, and social, for every individual and group, which includes among other things, maximal civil liberties, trade unionism, the equality of all;

—For the social use of wealth, though whether this involves social *ownership* and if so to what extent is disputed among contemporary interpreters of Judaism;

—For a society based on co-operation as its root rule rather than competition;

—For international peace guaranteed by a world government, the notion of the absolute sovereignty of the national state having always been an obscenity in the eyes of the Tradition.

What does all this add up to in the prevailing parlance?

Quite clearly to political democracy, to a modification of capitalism in the direction of economic democracy, and to a world state.

This sum total is not as exact as might be desired, but neither is it so vague as to be mistakable.

READING 9

The Dietary Laws and Their Meaning*
HERMAN WOUK

A TOUCHY TOPIC

The Jewish diet discipline cuts sharply across general manners and ideas. It is one of the stress points where observance tends first to break down, and so it is a sore subject. A detached picture is not likely to please anybody. The nonobservant dig in their heels at the whole idea. The devout, on the other hand, who have to work pretty hard at keeping up the diet, expect to be praised, and they want to see the nonobservant excoriated [severely denounced]. The purpose here is only to tell what the dietary laws are. The reader will have to supply the moral judgments; from his emotional bias if he approaches the topic with one, otherwise from his common sense.

We are looking at a detail of a symbol system that stamps all the customary acts of life. This is the stamp on eating: an act that all people perform several times a day, given the choice. People may neglect work, play, prayer, and love-making, but they seldom forget to eat. All religions include grace over food. Many religions go farther and set a mark on what one eats and how one eats. Often such austerities are reserved for the monk, the nun, the priest, the ascetic, the lama. Judaism's disciplines are relatively mild, but they are for everybody.

The Torah gives only one brief reason for the laws: they will help discipline Israel to holiness. My agnostic friend . . . thought that declining to eat lobsters was no answer to the threat of hydrogen war. I think he has something there; but neither is getting married, or building a home, or

*From Herman Wouk, *This Is My God* (New York: Doubleday & Co., 1959), pp. 126–35.

having children, or doing a day's work. There is nothing I can think of that does not look pitifully absurd under the threat of a hydrogen holocaust, except possibly the quest for God. If the diet laws have some structural purpose in a major religion, we ought to try to find what that may be.

We will get into guesswork. The sages of Jewry have offered varying opinions on the laws. The great trap is to notice a visible effect of the diet in one's own time, and to assume that that was the whole cause of the laws when they were given in the Sinai desert. But let us see what the laws are and how they operate.

THE DIET

There is no limit on food that grows from the ground; the disciplines deal only with sentient life. The Bible gives us physical tokens of the creatures that may be eaten.

For animals, the two marks are a split hoof and cud-chewing. In effect this admits a small class of beasts that live on grass and leaves, and shuts out the rest of animal life: beasts of prey, rodents, reptiles, swine, horses, pachyderms, and primates, most of which have been eaten at one time or another by various peoples. It is sometimes argued that the ban on pigs was meant only for hot countries in the olden days. Obviously the range of excluded animals puts that argument out of court. We cannot eat polar bears either. The pattern has nothing to do with climate. It seems to be formal; in logic it almost has to be. If the diet were only an advanced health notion of the brilliant Moses, the world would have in time caught up with his wisdom, and the Jewish forms would have vanished in universal observance.

Of the creatures in the sea, Jews eat those with fins and scales. This rule eliminates the shellfish so popular in America—shrimps, oysters, and lobsters; also a number of French delicacies—sea urchins, snails, mussels, frogs, octopuses, squids, and the like. I have read attempts to defend this discipline on the ground that octopuses and lobsters are revolting, while fish are not, but I think this resembles the debater's point about pork in hot countries. To anyone who eats octopuses, I am sure that a well-cooked one is an attractive sight, tentacles, suckers, and all. The fact is that within the Hebrew formal diet lie many excellent fish, and outside it—as in the case of animals—lie creatures which some folks esteem as delicacies.

There are no specific marks for birds. The Torah lists a large number of proscribed ones, all birds of prey or carrion [eaters of dead flesh]. In general Jews and non-Jews eat the same fowl. The difference is in the kosher slaughtering. Insects are wholly out. Few insects show up as food in America, but now and then at a cocktail party one has to forgo such tidbits as chocolate-covered ants.

A delicatessen catering to the tastes of the Jewish community.

KOSHER RULES

"Kosher means pure," runs the slogan of a major manufacturer of such products.

It is pleasant to see the advertising mind strike such a round blow for Judaism, but as usual it speaks to simple intelligences, at some sacrifice of exactness. The concept is in all truth a hard one to pin down. "Kosher" is a late Hebrew word that does not occur in the Books of Moses. Perhaps the nearest English word is "fit," in the sense of proper or suitable. But the fitness, it must be clear, is mostly ceremonial. Kosher preparation of food does result in a high degree of hygienic fitness. But a hog could be raised in an incubator on antibiotics, bathed daily, slaughtered in a hospital operating room, and its carcass sterilized by ultra-violet rays, without rendering kosher the pork chops that it yields. "Unclean" in Leviticus is a ceremonial word. That is why the Torah says of camels and rabbits, "They are unclean *for you,*" limiting the definition and the discipline to Israel. Chickens and goats, which we can eat, are scarcely cleaner by nature than eagles and lions, but the latter are in the class of the unclean.

All this being understood, "kosher means pure" may perhaps stand as a statement of fact. There is a general ban against eating carrion: defined as the flesh of an animal that dies of old age or of disease, or that is torn to death by beasts of prey, or that meets any other violent death. The assurance that no such meat can be sold as kosher is certainly of hygienic value, even today. In less civilized times and places it has given the Jewish diet a vast margin of sanitary excellence. This law supplies a word that Jews extend to all unfit food: *trefe,* or torn.

The Torah has four main rules for preparing meat. Commentators variously take them as humane regulations and as sanitary laws. Without forcing logic, one can perhaps find both aims in the rules. At any rate, breaking any one of the four renders the meat "torn" and inedible under Hebrew law.

The first rule, the only law of diet in the Bible for all mankind, is clearly humane in intent. It bars the eating of flesh cut from a live creature—"the limb of the living." If the reader shrinks from horror at the thought, he is not familiar with ancient killing and cooking practices that still survive in primitive communities, and in some not considered primitive.

The second law forbids the drinking of blood, on the ground that "the blood is the life." The use of blood in sophisticated cookery is common, especially for sauces. Jewish law not only bans this, but it excludes the meat itself unless most of the circulatory blood is removed. The impression is widespread that for this reason one cannot get a decent kosher steak. Since we barbecue pretty good rare steak in my home— sometimes to the stunned surprise of Jewish guests—I can testify otherwise. Enough juice remains in the tissues to make perfect steaks. But in the old country, Jewish housewives fried steaks gray-brown. They brought the style with them. The so-called Jewish steak is therefore done to death by the standards of American cookery, but it need not be. Out West on the farm one usually encounters the Jewish-style steak fried clear through. It is a matter of regional taste, nothing more.

The third rule stems from the bizarre prohibition repeated three times in the Torah in identical words: "You shall not boil a kid in the milk of its mother." The repetition suggested to Maimonides [Spanish-born Jewish philosopher (1135–1204)] that in Mosaic times this was a common rite of idolatry. However that may be, the strong emphasis led long ago to complete separation of flesh and dairy food in the Hebrew diet. Food from the ground or from the sea is eaten with meat meals or dairy meals. Meat and milk, or their products, never appear together on the table. In observant homes, there are separate utensils and crockery for the two types of meals. In Israeli army kitchens and navy galleys, this dual equipment is standard.

The fourth rule bans suet, the hard fat formed below the diaphragm. The regulations separating suet from edible fat are complex and help make butchery of kosher meat a work for skilled and learned men. Prohibited fats are identical with those specified for the altar in the Book of Leviticus.

The Genesis tale of Jacob's wrestling with a mysterious stranger [Gen. 32:22–32] accounts for another ban in Jewish diets: the sciatic nerve of the hindquarter. Jacob was injured in the nerve of his thigh, we are told, and left the battle with a limp. The story has all the marks of a mystic vision. The encounter occurs the night before he meets his vengeful brother Esau after a separation of twenty years; it goes on till dawn; and Jacob's successful struggle against the stranger results in the change of his name from Jacob to Israel, "because you have contended with God and with men and have prevailed." The Torah adds, at the end of the tale, that in memory of the event the children of Israel do not eat the sciatic nerve.

It seems like a small deprivation. It could be small, but today it is not. The complete removal of the nerve from the hindquarters of an animal is a difficult point of butchery. It is simpler, and evidently less costly, to sell the hindquarters of kosher-slaughtered cattle to the general packers. Observant Jews therefore forgo some excellent cuts of meat. This is a remediable situation, and with a rise in demand it may be remedied.

SLAUGHTER

The bans against drinking blood and against "the limb of the living" determine the rigid, indeed sacred, method of taking animal life under Hebrew law. There is only one way: a single instantaneous severance of the carotid arteries in the neck. The blood pours out; the supply to the brain is at once cut off; the animal's consciousness vanishes. The rest is muscular reflexes, to which the beast is as oblivious as a man in a coma, and swift death. This is what the animal physiologists tell us. Scientific testimony, gathered when this mode of slaughter has been under attack, shows that it is a death as merciful as any that humans can visit on animals, and far more merciful than most.

Stringent conditions to endure a painless death are part of our law. If one of these precautions is omitted, the meat is called torn, and we cannot eat it. The death stroke must be a single slash. Even one sawing motion disqualifies, let alone a second stroke, a stunning blow, or any other inflicting of pain. The edge of the knife must be ground razor-sharp and smooth; one detectable nick causes rejection of the meat. The animal must be motionless at the instant of the death stroke, so that the knife may cut true. Skilled professional slaughterers, who undergo qualifying examinations for dexterity and technical knowledge, do this work. Equally knowledgeable inspectors watch each move. The guilds of slaughterer and inspector (the Hebrew terms are *shohet* and *mashgiah*) are ancient and strong. Often the office, with the complete training, passes from father to son.

The inspectors study the carcass for certain traces of disease which for thousands of years have rendered meat non-kosher. This part of our procedure is unquestionably sanitary, centuries in advance of its time. Over the generations it has helped create the exceptional health statistics of Jewish communities. As the meat passes to the consumer, there are further procedures for draining the residue of blood. These were once the province of the housewife, and mothers handed the knowledge to their daughters, but more and more today the mass distributor of kosher food performs these last steps and sells meat ready for the pot. He assumes the responsibility for getting a rabbinic opinion of doubtful symptoms.

DEGREES OF OBSERVANCE

In former times this was not so. The housewife did most of her own inspection, especially of poultry. She bought a chicken slaughtered before her eyes, took it home, and in cleaning it checked the viscera for signs of disease and internal injury known to her since childhood. In doubtful cases she brought the meat to her rabbi. Friday morning was always the busiest time of the week for my grandfather, in his twenty-three years of ministry in the Bronx. The stream of housewives with *shailas,* religious queries, on bloody new-killed fowl was almost continuous. If he and I were studying together that morning we did not get far.

Nowadays answering shailas on fowl does not loom large in the Jewish ministry; not nearly so large as raising funds, making amusing speeches, writing persuasive brochures, and so forth. New times, new tasks. Old-fashioned people look askance at the change and hint that young rabbis today are mere affable ignoramuses. The fact is that the orthodox seminarists still get an exhaustive training, and have to pass a searching test, in the laws of meat inspection. Nineteen out of twenty seldom use the knowledge. They hardly can, unless they go into the kosher-meat-packing industry. . . .

In the old country a pious man either did his own slaughtering or he worshipped side by side with the town shohet and knew his piety, skill, and intelligence at first hand. In the United States we must rely on seals of eminent rabbis, guaranteeing proper slaughter, inspection, and handling. There are devout people who cannot bring themselves to trust the guarantees. Such control of industrial processing seems too loose, too liable to error. To them the most remote risk of eating defiled meat—let alone the flesh of banned creatures or a fragment of their products—is unacceptable. My grandfather during his twenty-three years in the United States did not eat the flesh of cattle. His Sabbath meat was a fowl killed under his own supervision. He did not ask the rest of the family to follow his example. He ate in my mother's home and in mine, but he would not eat our meat. Yet even he had to rely to some extent on seals and signatures. The milk and butter he used bore guarantees of rabbinic supervision. He did not see the milking and the churning himself because he could not.

My grandfather was such a cheerful and jovial man that it never occurred to us that he was an ascetic; as indeed he was, a rather extreme one. Few people are able to forgo beef and lamb for half an adult lifetime as he did, on a point of ritual. The exceptionally pious today eat flesh called *glat kosher,* carrying special guarantees. Some members of Hasidic sects eat only meat which has been canned by other members of their sect under the seal of their own chief rabbi. If they travel, they carry enough of such provisions to last them the journey. If they run out, they subsist on raw vegetables and fruit. They will not use the utensils of public dining places. So the degrees of observance shade upward, or leftward if you will, to strictness, scruples, and self-denial, which some consider extravagant and which others regard as minimal compliance with the law.

An important point in this matter of shades of observance, it seems to me, is to avoid calling one's own practice the only true Judaism; to label anything stricter mere fanaticism, and anything less strict mere pork-eating. One can fall into such an attitude because the old stability and uniformity of practice do not at the moment exist. People who eat ham or shrimps, or steaks from electrocuted or poleaxed cattle, are clearly not following the law of Moses. People who never eat or drink in public restaurants surely run less risk of accidental deviation from the diet than those who do. The exigencies of an active life may make this strictness difficult. The observant follow conscience under guidance of teachers they trust. They all hold to the same disciplines; the variations are in detail.

READING 10
History of the Jews

A. A Four-Thousand-Year History

JEREMY N. GOTTSTEIN

INTRODUCTION

Throughout their history, the Jews have searched for meaning as a people. Yet while engaged in this search, Jews have also had an incalculable influence on the rest of the world. Both Christianity and Islam were profoundly influenced by Judaism. In the modern age, Jews such as Karl Marx, Sigmund Freud, and Albert Einstein had a tremendous impact on the world. Although Jewry consists of only .5 percent of the world's population, Jews have received 12 percent of the Nobel prizes in physics, chemistry, and medicine.

This article is intended to give a few specific examples of the Jewish historical experience so one can understand how Jews find meaning in their past. It may also lead to better understanding of the influence Jewish ideas have had on humankind.

BIBLICAL PERIOD (ca. 2500–300 B.C.E.)

The most basic Jewish belief to emerge from the biblical period was the belief in one God (monotheism). This was a revolutionary idea in its time, for it led to the ideas that people are governed by laws and not by men, and that morality and politics should not be separate.

Abraham is considered the father of the Jewish people. He introduced to the world the idea that there was only one God. This idea suggested

A model of ancient Jerusalem.

that if God is the Father of us all, then all men must be brothers—that since we all come from the same ancestor, we all must be equal. This idea of equality challenged the notion, so prevalent throughout human history, that some people are superior to others.

Moses added the idea of freedom to that of equality by liberating the Jews from slavery in Egypt. This event is celebrated each Passover season.

The Jewish patriarchs—Abraham, Isaac, and Jacob—revealed the will of God to humankind. Moses continued this tradition. The Word of God was revealed to the Jewish people at Mt. Sinai through the Ten Commandments and the Torah (the first five books of the Bible). The Bible has been translated into the vast majority of the world's languages. Both Christianity and Islam accept the "Old Testament" as an authoritative Word of God.

After Moses brought the Jews out of Egypt, they wandered forty years in the desert until they reached the land of Canaan. Today this land is called Israel. For the next two hundred years the Israelites were governed by what the Bible has called Judges. At the end of this time, Saul established a kingdom. His successor, David, built a strong and united nation from Saul's beginnings. The third king, Solomon, son of David, built the Temple in Jerusalem as the center of the Jewish world.

Solomon was the last king of a united Israel. After his death (in 925 B.C.E.), the kingdom was divided into two parts, Israel in the north and Judah in the south. This began what is known as the age of the Prophets.

The prophets were men chosen by God to expand on the Law and show the people how it should be put into action in everyday life. The writings of the prophets urged the loyalty of the Jewish people to the ways of God and Torah, and emphasized the teachings of morality.

The northern Kingdom of Israel was destroyed by the Assyrians in 722 B.C.E. This left Judah as the sole bearer of Jewish ideals. Prophets such as Micah, Isaiah, and Jeremiah continually exhorted the people of Judah to follow the commandments of Torah, or else disaster would strike.

But in 586 B.C.E., the Babylonians captured Jerusalem, destroyed the Temple, and sent the Jews into a fifty-year exile known as the Babylonian Captivity. Only when Babylonia was conquered by the Persians were the Jews allowed to return to their homeland. There, under the leadership of the prophets Ezra and Nehemiah, the Temple was reconstructed.

A mosaic showing the Babylonian Captivity.

The biblical period introduced the ideas of freedom, equality, and ethical behavior into all aspects of government and society. The influence these ideals have had can be seen by reading the words engraved on the Statue of Liberty: "Proclaim Liberty throughout the land unto all the inhabitants thereof." This quote is from Leviticus 25:10, one of the five books of the Torah.

THE HELLENISTIC AGE (ca. 300 B.C.E.–135 C.E.)

After Alexander the Great of Greece conquered Palestine in 332 B.C.E., Jewish culture began to be influenced by that of the Greeks. While the empires of Syria and Egypt, which succeeded Alexander, allowed the Jews religious freedom, many Jews accepted Greek ideas and ways of living—that is, they became *Hellenized.*

But not all Jews became assimilated into Greek culture. Many fought to retain their own identity and religion.

Thus, in 168 B.C.E., when the Syrian ruler Antiochus IV ordered a ban on Jewish religious practices, there was trouble. Antiochus forbade the observance of the Sabbath, study of the Torah, and circumcision. He also ordered all Jews to make sacrifices to Greek gods. A group of Jews called the Maccabees fought the Syrians and defeated their armies. The victory of the Maccabees won the Jews the right to practice their religion.

This triumph is still celebrated in the holiday of Chanukah. It is interesting to note that Chanukah is the first recorded event documenting a battle fought in the name of religious freedom. Religious freedom today is guaranteed in the Constitution of the United States and other constitutions around the world.

There was also considerable tension between the Romans and the Jews. Under the pressures of foreign occupation two major parties developed within Judaism. The Pharisees valued the oral traditions of Judaism and a broad interpretation of the Torah. The Sadducees, on the other hand, insisted on the importance of the Temple and opposed the broad interpretations of the Pharisees. Other sects, such as the Zealots, the Herodians, and the Essenes, also were important during the first century C.E.

It is important to note that the birth of Jesus took place during this time. At first, Christianity was merely one of the many Jewish sects. However, it soon established itself as a separate religion.

In 66 C.E., the Jews revolted against the Romans. This revolt ended with the destruction of the Temple in 70. The Jews, however, continued to fight against the Romans, and they were not finally defeated until 135.

TALMUDIC PERIOD (ca. 135–600)

After the final destruction of the Jewish state by the Romans in 135 C.E., the Jews had no king, no temple, and no formal government organization to hold them together. In this time of hardship the Talmud was created.

The Talmud is a book of laws governing every aspect of Jewish life. It has two parts, the Mishnah and the Gemarah. Its development spanned nearly six hundred years.

The Mishnah is a collection of sayings and decisions of past rabbinical scholars covering such topics as agriculture, festivals, marriage and divorce, property laws, and ritual purity. The Mishnah also includes the judgments and decisions made on these laws. The names of the rabbis who made them, their reasoning, and differing opinions from the majority judgments are included. The Mishnah went beyond the Torah, expanding and clarifying the law.

The wars with the Romans seemed to have drained the strength of the Jews of Palestine. As a result, Jewish learning centered in Babylonia, where great academies developed. These academies made scholarship available to everyone, not just an elite priesthood. The commentaries of these academies on the Mishnah were gathered together in a book called the Gemarah, the second part of the Talmud.

The practice and study of the Torah and the Talmud were to prove more powerful in uniting the Jews, now spread all over the world, than the land they had lost.

JUDEO-ISLAMIC AGE (Seventh to Thirteenth Centuries)

The ideas of Muhammad, the founder of Islam, developed where a large Jewish population had prepared the groundwork for acceptance of monotheism. Because the Muslims considered them a "People of the Book," the Jews were tolerated in the Islamic empire.

In Spain, the Christians had persecuted the Jews. But under Muslim rule, the Jewish and Islamic communities were well integrated. Jews even reached positions of importance in government. As a result of this tolerant attitude, there was a tremendous outburst of Jewish creativity—a Golden Age.

Jews in Spain were active in the professions: medicine, astronomy, and philosophy. A great scholar and rabbi, Moses Maimonides, wrote a great philosophical work, the *Guide for the Perplexed.* Another great scholarly rabbi, Rashi, produced a commentary to the Bible and most of the Talmud. Rashi's work has remained a model of biblical scholarship to this day. The Golden Age in Spain also saw the development of Jewish mysticism—the *Kabbalah.*

During the slow Christian reconquest of Spain, the Church tried to convert the Jews. This led to persecutions in 1391 and ultimately to the torture chambers of the Inquisition. In 1492, a decree ordered the Jews either to accept the Christian faith or to leave the country. Many Jews pretended to convert but retained their Jewish traditions in secret.

The contributions of the Jewish philosophers and poets during this period helped to maintain learning in the Church and provided a basis for some of its theology. For example, the great Christian scholastic philosopher St. Thomas Aquinas was greatly influenced by the work of Maimonides. Another example is a philosophic work by the Jewish poet Ibn Gabirol called "The Fountain of Life." The scholars of the Church who took up this book over the years forgot its Jewish origins and claimed it was written by a monk named Avicebron. Not until the nineteenth century did they find out that this popular book of religious philosophy was the work of an eleventh-century Jewish poet.

The contributions of Jewish physicians, mathematicians, and natural scientists in the Judeo-Islamic age were outstanding and served to spark the rebirth of science in the West.

A final distinction of this period is worth noting. Two divisions of Jews emerged, the Sephardim (of Spain and the Mediterranean) and the Ashkenazim (of Germany and Eastern Europe). One can still see this division in the way prayers are said and in the symbols of worship.

THE EUROPEAN AGE (Thirteenth to Eighteenth Centuries)

The Middle Ages in Europe was a dark period for the Jewish people. It was a constant fight against persecution and extinction. Most nations conquered in the name of Christianity were converted to Christianity. The Jews, however, were able to keep their faith and emerged from this period spiritually and culturally alive.

The period of the Crusades was a particularly difficult time. It brought much suffering to the Jews and other non-Christians. In 1215, Pope Innocent III wrote: "The Jews are doomed to wander about the earth as fugitives and vagabonds." In order to ensure that no one would mistakenly offer kindness to a Jew, Pope Innocent ordered Jews to wear distinctive garments. In Vienna it was a peculiar hat; in France it was a wheel of yellow cloth sewn on the breast and back.

Aside from the Crusades, the Jews faced other dangers. They were barred from owning land and from the professions. Money lending provided one of the only opportunities open to Jews because the Church forbade Christians to lend money for interest. The Black Death killed at least a third of the population of Europe in 1348. Jews were falsely accused of poisoning the wells and causing the plague. The blood libel, by which Jews were falsely accused of killing Christian children to use their blood for ritual purposes, also became widespread.

In the Middle Ages, the Jews were expelled from England, France, and the German states. Also, the Church declared that the books of the Jews, particularly the Talmud, blasphemed against Jesus. This charge led to a number of public trials and the burning of these books—and in many cases to the death of the individual who owned or used them. The dreaded Inquisition ordered Jews to convert under penalty of torture, including the rack, thumbscrew, hot lead, and even burning people alive. Yet, Jewish society showed its great resilience. Communities were often reconstructed on the very spot where a massacre had taken place.

The Arab port of Damietta, on the Mediterranean, was frequently attacked by the Crusaders, as shown in this sixteenth-century French woodcut.

THE MODERN AGE (Eighteenth Century to the Present)

The suffering of the Jews in Western and Central Europe stimulated a migration into Eastern Europe. However, Jewish communities in Eastern Europe were not free from persecution either.

In Eastern and Western Europe, Jews were forced to live in restricted areas called ghettos. A sense of community and peoplehood caused them to hold tightly to things they were persecuted for, such as the Torah, Talmud, learning, and religious observances. In the Jewish communities, education was emphasized. Hundreds of Yeshivot (academies for higher rabbinic studies) flourished, producing countless outstanding scholars. Among them was Joseph Caro, a Spanish Jew who wrote a book called *The House of Joseph.* It was a work of such tremendous scholarship that Caro was called the greatest rabbi since Maimonides. Caro's book led to the *Schulehan Aruch,* or *Prepared Table,* which simplified knowledge of the law.

In the beginning of the eighteenth century, a Jewish movement called Hasidism emerged in Russia and Poland. Hasidism emphasized religious fervor and ecstasy rather than intellectualism. This movement was a major force, giving new hope to the masses of Jewish people.

The nineteenth century saw changes in conventional attitudes toward the Jews in Western and Central Europe. In 1806 the Emperor Napoleon convened a council which attempted to deal with Jewish emancipation. This had some positive results: Jews were later granted citizenship in some German states, in France, and in Prussia.

With the fall of Napoleon, however, conditions worsened for the Jews once again. However, the liberal reform movement of 1848 permitted the Jewish people to play an active role in European affairs. In England, several prominent Jews were knighted. The Rothschild family became the outstanding bankers in Europe.

As the movement for Jewish emancipation grew in Europe, such writers as Moses Mendelssohn stressed secular education. This movement was known as Haskalah. One of its results was the Reform movement, which brought Jewish rituals more in tune with the times. Another result of the Haskalah was the scientific study of Judaism and of Jewish history.

Although the Haskalah movement was active in Eastern Europe, it did not gain much support from the non-Jewish population. The Jews of Czarist Russia continued to suffer from persecution and discrimination. They were forced to live in ghettos called pales, or shtetls, and suffered from pogroms, or murderous riots. Nevertheless, great Jewish contributions to literature began to emerge. Yiddish became a literary language, partly as a result of the work of one famous writer, Sholom Aleichem. Many of the younger Jews, however, were determined to learn the language of their country.

Zionism—the idea that the Jewish people should have a homeland—gained strength under the leadership of an Austrian Jew named Theodore Herzl. The two World Wars and the Holocaust strengthened the desire for a Jewish homeland in Palestine. Finally, in 1948, the United Nations created Israel as an independent Jewish nation. Yet to this day, many of Israel's neighbors and other countries fail to recognize Israel's right to exist as an independent state.

CONCLUSION

The four-thousand-year history of the Jews has been marked both by tremendous creative activity and by persecution. By looking at the history of the Jews, one may develop a greater understanding not only of Jewish thought and history, but of the meaning of history itself and its influence in answering the question: "Who am I and what made me the way I am?"

B. Jewish Migrations to the United States*
LEE J. LEVINGER

Jews of America have not only their Jewish life, but, like all other American citizens, contribute to American life in general. They belong to various political parties, in which they vote and sometimes hold office. They have their inventors, their writers, their musicians and artists. In time of war they send their full quota to fight for America. They have their business leaders in many lines of endeavor. In other words, the Jews of America are complete partakers in American life, and at the same time possess certain Jewish institutions, too. They combine in themselves the age-old Jewish tradition of worship and loyalty, and the newer American life of progress and freedom. Their Judaism and their Americanism reinforce each other.

WHERE THE AMERICAN JEWS CAME FROM

These Jews came to the United States from every land under the sun, for the Children of Israel dwell everywhere. They came for the same reasons that our other immigrants have come since the very discovery of the New World. Some came, like the French or Spanish, for love of adventure or desire for colonialization. Some came, like the Germans and Irish, because they were very poor in the Old World and wanted to establish homes where they could provide a better livelihood for their families. Above all, the vast majority of them came like the Quakers and the Pilgrim Fathers as refugees from religious persecution, seeking a land

*From Rabbi Lee J. Levinger, *A History of the Jews in the United States,* 4th rev. ed. (New York: Union of American Hebrew Congregations, 1949), pp. 7–15.

where they might worship God in their own way. As a modern writer, herself a Jewish immigrant, has said: "Every immigrant ship is another Mayflower, and Ellis Island is just a new name for Plymouth Rock" (Mary Antin: *They Who Knock at Our Gates*).

The first Jews who came to America were from Spain and Portugal, some of them coming to this country directly, and others after wandering to several other lands on their weary search for a permanent home. Since the year 1492 these Jews had been fugitives, trying to find a place of security east or west, north or south. Naturally some of them tried the New World, so that the first and for a long time the only Jewish immigrants to America were Spanish Jews. Another factor that led these people to America was the colonizing activity of the Spanish and Portuguese at that early date. It was natural that people from these lands should come to America, first because there they would find colonists whose language they spoke, and secondly, because of the comparative ease of obtaining passage.

Now and then a wanderer came from England, Germany, or even Poland, but fully half of the early Jews were of Spanish origin. Then came a change, and from 1815 on the Jewish immigration came largely from Germany and other countries of central Europe. For this was the time of the great German immigration to America, when thousands of Germans of all religions fled their native land for the New World. It was the time when the revolt of 1848 had been repressed and those who wanted freedom had to seek it in a foreign land. It was also a period of great poverty in Germany, when multitudes desired a fresh start in a new home. Hence the German Jews came to America, along with other Germans, seeking opportunity, freedom, and above all liberty to worship according to the dictates of their conscience.

During all this time, there were very few immigrants from eastern Europe. But this immigration increased in 1881 when the terrible May Laws were promulgated by the Czar of Russia. Since that time persecutions have piled up in eastern Europe, taking the form of discriminatory laws against the Jews, anti-Semitic parties in politics and mob violence. Since then great masses of Jews have fled from Russia, Austria, Roumania and nearby lands, of whom the greatest number fled to the United States. They, too, came for a chance to make a living, for freedom from tyranny, and most of all for liberty to be themselves and to live as Jews. At the same time the Jews were not the only new arrivals from eastern Europe. Large numbers of peasants also, especially of the different minority nationalities, came for the same reasons. Tyranny was heavy on them all, poverty was bitter to them all, but both poverty and tyranny bore most terribly on the Jews.

One might think of Jewish history in America in terms of certain figures, showing the increase of the numbers of Jews in this country. After the

Revolution there were 3,000 Jews in the new nation. In 1840 there were 15,000; in 1881, a quarter of a million; and in 1928, there were 4,200,000 all together. They increased much like a series of steps, each one immensely larger than the one before. With many individual exceptions, these steps roughly represent different countries from which the Jews came.

The first fifteen thousand represented largely the Sephardim, the Jews from Spain and Portugal; the next two hundred thousand or more are the German Jews; the next three and a half million are the Jews from eastern Europe. Thus the descendants of the earliest settlers form the smallest group of Jews in the United States, the next largest is formed by the descendants of the German Jews, while the largest of all is composed of the latest to arrive, those from eastern Europe, and their children. Of course, there are also small bodies of Jews from Persia, Turkey and all sorts of countries, who have sent a few of their representatives to this great gathering-place of the nations, America.

CHARACTERISTICS OF THE THREE MIGRATIONS

Naturally, each of these three groups of immigrants had its own characteristics, depending on the sort of Jewish life these people had led, the kind of national surroundings they had known in their former homes. The first migration, that of the Spanish Jews, consisted of a few families, drifting in from time to time. They were chiefly merchants; some of them were wealthy merchants, engaged in commerce with other lands. They settled in the thirteen original colonies in a few leading commercial cities, and had five congregations in all at the time of the Revolution. They were strictly observant Jews, and most of their institutions were for their religious life. The typical community began with a cemetery when a few families came to a town; as soon as there were ten men in the community for services, they established a synagogue; finally they organized to help the poor, and to help each other in time of sickness or death.

The German Jews who arrived next were very different in several respects. Most of them were poor when they first came. They usually began in the new land as peddlers wandering from house to house and from farm to farm, often with their entire stock of goods on their backs. By industry and courage they overcame the obstacles of poverty, a strange language, and the natural suspicion for unknown foreigners. Many a one started by buying a horse and wagon with which to carry on his peddling, then a little store, then a larger business of one kind or another. The result is that many of the very old men who are leaders in business, in charity, and in public work among American Jews today were among these pioneers, while a surprising number of the active middle-aged Jews of the present—judges, physicians and bankers—are their sons, reared and educated in America.

An Orthodox Jewish cemetery.

Comparatively few of these German immigrants were scholars or professional men in their old homes, but many of them had a certain amount of both German and Jewish culture, due to the fine schools in Germany during their youth. Many of these men read books and had modern ideas. Some of them had belonged to the rising new reform movement in Germany. Thus it came about naturally that liberal Judaism in America was fathered by these poor immigrants from Germany. They originated, likewise, social institutions, such as the B'nai B'rith and the Young Men's Hebrew Association. They founded philanthropic institutions—orphan asylums, homes for the aged, hospitals, and relief societies. All these, of course, were very small in their beginnings; all of them were needed by some element in the growing Jewish community. They organized nation-wide Jewish institutions, notably the Union of American Hebrew Congregations, and through it the Hebrew Union College, in Cincinnati, the oldest seminary for training rabbis in America. They grew steadily in wealth, education, Jewish influence and public standing.

The distribution of the German immigrants was different from that of the Spanish. They did not stay in a few cities on the Atlantic seaboard, for they found a great continent just opening up to settlement. So they went ahead with the pioneers into every part of the growing nation. Naturally, they went largely to the same cities and sections where their non-Jewish comrades from Germany were settling. In this way Cincinnati became one of the most important Jewish centers in the United States, because it was a center of German settlement. These Jews settled in remote sections of the west and south; most of the Jewish communities of the country were founded during this period by some of these German immigrants.

Finally there came the great mass of immigration from eastern Europe. The Jews from Russia, Poland, Austria, Roumania and related lands came neither as scattered individuals nor as family groups. They represent the transplanting of practically entire communities, rich and poor, learned and ignorant together. The German immigrants had been chiefly the poor or the dissatisfied, for those with advantages at home hesitated to leave. So were the early immigrants from Russia. But after 1881 in Russia few Jews could be safe or prosperous; whole settlements were often ordered out of the villages where they had lived for generations, and driven to strange cities where they had no homes and no means of livelihood. This new migration was different, not only in its vastly greater numbers, but also in its nature. The new wave of migration centered in New York City, and spread out from that center. There are now Russian Jews in many other cities as well, but a great body of them still remains in that tremendous Jewish community.

These east European Jews were, for the most part, either orthodox or Zionists; or socialists and not religious at all. Very few of them belonged to reform synagogues, although very soon a milder modification of orthodoxy, called conservative Judaism, arose among them. They possessed a great deal of Jewish culture, as their rabbis and also many laymen were learned in the Bible and the Talmud; but they had fewer scholars in Russian or other modern tongues. This was due to the lack of public schools in Russia and the exclusion of Jews from many of the private schools, so that they had to rely entirely on their own Jewish schools and their own Jewish learning. Their culture, then, was either Yiddish or Hebrew. The Yiddish newspapers and theaters, the Zionist sentiment and organizations, the Hebrew schools and Talmud Torahs, owe their origin to the Russian Jews, exactly as the reform synagogues and their religious schools, charities and lodges, originate with the German Jews, and as the first orthodox synagogues originate with the Spanish Jews.

THE MINGLING OF ELEMENTS IN AMERICAN JEWRY

American Jewry represents all these three, not as separate groups, but as they now live intermingled and largely united. The differences pointed out are historical only, and exist now only in small part. Jews of Russian origin have a great influence through their overwhelming numbers, which Jews of German origin often equal because they came to America first, and consequently have acquired more wealth and are better adjusted to conditions in this country. Meanwhile the little Spanish community has largely been absorbed into the greater masses, retaining its separate identity in only a few cities.

Construction of a kibbutz in Israel. Kibbutzim (collective settlements) are usually agricultural and are owned or leased and managed by the members.

READING 11
The Concept of Man

A. Man, the Crown of Creation*

How manifold are Thy works, O Lord!
In wisdom hast Thou made them all.
   O Lord, our God,
   How glorious is Thy name in all the earth!
When I behold the heavens, the work of Thy fingers,
The moon and the stars which Thou hast established;
   What is man that Thou art mindful of him,
   And the son of man that Thou thinkest of him?
Yet hast Thou made him
But little less than divine,
And hast crowned him with glory and honor.
   Thou hast made him to have dominion
   Over the works of Thy hands;
   All things hast Thou put under his feet.
Beloved of Thee is man, Thine own creation,
Fashioned in Thine image.
   Thou hast given him understanding and insight,
   And hast shown him what is good and what is evil.
Thou hast revealed to him what is good;
Thou hast given him to choose between right and wrong.
   Thou hast given him a mind,
   That he might use his blessings wisely;

*From *Sabbath and Festival Prayer Book* (New York: The Rabbinical Assembly of America and The United Synagogue of America, 1946), p. 329.

A heart hast Thou given him, and free will,
That he might consider his ways
And live according to Thy will.
  We are mindful of all the great gifts
  Which Thou, O Lord, hast given us;
  May we use them wisely that they may not be in vain.
You have been told, O man, what is good,
And what the Lord requires of you:
  To do justly, to love mercy,
  And to walk humbly with your God.

[Based on Psalm 8]

B. Man: His Dignity, Possibilities, and Responsibility*

ARTHUR HERTZBERG

> When God resolved upon the creation of the world, He took counsel with the Torah—that is Divine Wisdom. She was skeptical about the value of an earthly world on account of the sinfulness of man, who would be sure to disregard her precepts. But God dispelled her doubts. He told her that Repentance had been created long before and sinners would have the opportunity to mend their ways. Besides good work would be invested with atoning power and Paradise and Hell were created to dispense reward and punishment. Finally, the Messiah was appointed to bring salvation, which would put an end to all sinfulness.

The preceding quotation is from the *Sefer Raziel,* a volume of secret mystic writings of uncertain date and authorship. The themes mentioned above are the major foci of doctrinal concern in Judaism. It should be added here again, for emphasis, that Judaism knows no accepted catechism. It is nonetheless untrue to maintain that the Jewish religion is a set of legal commandments divorced from faith. Jewish faith is indefinable in Western theological categories, which are alien to its essence, and by nature it permits variation in belief. There is, however, an immanent logic of its own that will appear to the careful reader of this volume and especially of the selections that follow in this section.

MAN: HIS DIGNITY AND POSSIBILITIES

Man is created in the image of God—this is the essential Biblical doctrine of man. God loves justice and mercy; man must therefore be true to his divinely ordained character by practicing these virtues. To be like God in the Jewish view means to be His partner in ruling the world and in

*From Arthur Hertzberg, ed., *Judaism* (New York: George Braziller, 1961), pp. 177–85.

carrying forward the work of making order, i.e., a just order, in the world. Man can descend to great depths, but he is not by nature irretrievably sinful. There are temptations to evil in the world but the path of piety is not in the renunciation of the world of the here and now. Man's task is to hallow life, to raise the workaday world in which he eats, labors and loves, to its highest estate so that his every act reflects the divine unity of all being. Note in particular the last three selections in this section [pages 61–62], by Judah Halevi and Nahman of Bratslav.

God created man in his own image, in the image of God He created him. (Gen. 1:27)

Thus says the Lord: "Let not the wise man glory in his wisdom, let not the mighty man glory in his might, let not the rich man glory in his riches; but let him who glories glory in this, that he understands and knows Me, that I am the Lord who practices kindness, justice, and righteousness in the earth; for in these things I delight, says the Lord." (Jer. 9:22–23)

When I look at Your heavens, the work of Your fingers, the moon and the stars which You have established, what is man that You are mindful of him, and the son of man that You care for him? Yet You have made him but little lower than the angels, and have crowned him with glory and honor. You have made him to have dominion over the works of Your hands; You have put all things under his feet. . . . (Ps. 8:4–7)

Long ago when the world with its inhabitants was not yet in existence, You conceived the thought, and commanded with a word, and at once the works of creation stood before You. You said that You would make for Your world man an administrator of Your works, that it might be known that he was not made for the sake of the world, but the world for his sake. (Syriac Baruch 14:17)

How are the witnesses admonished in capital cases? They would bring them in and admonish them as follows: Perhaps you will offer mere assumption or hearsay or second hand information; or you might say to yourselves that you heard it from a man that is trustworthy. Or perhaps you do not know that we shall test your statements with subsequent examination and inquiry. Know, therefore, that capital cases are not like civil cases. In civil cases, a man may make atonement by paying a sum of money, but in capital cases the witness is answerable for the blood of any person that is wrongfully condemned and for the blood of his descendants that would have been born to him to the end of time. For thus have we found it to be with Cain, who slew his brother. It is written, "The bloods of your brother cry to Me from the ground" [Gen. 4:10]. It says not "the blood of your brother" but "the *bloods* of your brother"—his blood and the blood of his descendants.

Therefore a single man was first created in the world, to teach that if any man causes a single soul to perish, Scripture considers him as though he had caused an entire world to perish; and if any man saves a single soul, Scripture considers him as though he had saved an entire world.

And a single man was first created for the sake of peace among mankind, that no man could say to another, "My father was greater than yours."

And a single man was first created to proclaim the greatness of the Holy One, praised be He, for man casts many coins with one die and they are all alike, while the King of kings, the Holy One, praised be He, patterns every man after Adam and every man is unique. Therefore every man is obliged to say: For my sake was the world created. (Mishnah *Sanhedrin* 4:5)

Man is dear to God, for he was created in the divine image. Man is especially dear to God in that he has been made aware that he was created in the divine image, as it is written, "In the image of God He made man" [Gen. 9:6]. (Mishnah *Avot* 3:14)

Let all your deeds be for the sake of heaven. They once asked Hillel where he was going. He answered, "I am going to perform a religious act (*mitzvah*)." "Which one?" "I am going to the bath house." "Is that a religious act?" "Yes. . . . Those who are in charge of the images of kings which are erected in theaters and circuses scour them and wash them and are rewarded and honored for it. How much more should I take care of my body, for I have been created in the image of God, as it is written, 'In the image of God He created man'" [Gen. 5:1]. (*Avot of Rabbi Nathan,* Version b, Chap. 30)

Why was man created on the sixth day [after the creation of all other creatures]? So that, should he become overbearing, he can be told "The gnat was created before you were." (*Sanhedrin* 38a)

"Consider the work of God; who can make straight what He has made crooked?" [Eccles. 7:13]. When the Holy One, praised be He, created Adam, he showed him all of the trees in the Garden of Eden, telling him "Behold, My works are beautiful and glorious; yet everything which I have created is for your sake. Take care that you do not corrupt or destroy My world." (*Ecclesiastes Rabbah* 7:13)

Rabbi Simon said: When the Holy One, praised be He, was about to create Adam, the angels were divided into two different groups. Some said, "Let him not be created," while others said, "Let him be created." "Love and Truth met together; Righteousness and Peace kissed each other" [Ps. 85:10]. Love said, "Let him be created, for he will do loving deeds" but Truth said, "Let him not be created, for he will be all lies." Righteousness said, "Let him be created, for he will do righteous deeds" but Peace said, "Let him not be created, for he will be all argument and discord." What did the Holy One, praised be He, do? He seized Truth and cast it to the ground, as it is written, "Truth was cast down to the ground" [Daniel 8:12]. Then the angels said to the Holy One: Lord of the Universe! How can You despise Your angel Truth? Let Truth rise from the ground, as it is written, "Truth will spring up from the ground" [Ps. 85:11]. (*Genesis Rabbah* 8:5)

One day Elijah the prophet appeared to Rabbi Baruka in the market of Lapet. Rabbi Baruka asked him, "Is there any one among the people of this market who is destined to share in the world to come?" . . . Two men appeared on the scene and Elijah said, "These two will share in the world to come." Rabbi Baruka asked them, "What is your occupation?" They said, "We are merry-makers. When we see a man who is downcast, we cheer him up. When we see two people quarreling with one another, we endeavor to make peace between them." (*Ta'anit* 22a)

When the Holy One, praised be He, was about to create men, the angels said, " 'What is man, that You are mindful of him?' [Ps. 8:5]. Why do you need man?" The Holy One, praised be He, answered, "Who, then, shall fulfill My Torah and commandments?" The angels said, "We shall." God answered, "You cannot, for in it is written 'This is the law when a man dies in a tent . . .' [Num. 19:14], but none of you die. In it is written 'If a woman conceives, and bears a male child . . .' [Lev. 12:2], but none of you give birth. It is written 'This you may eat . . .' [Lev. 11:21], but none of you eat." (*Tanhuma Buber, B'hukotai* 6)

According to our view a servant of God is not one who detaches himself from the world, lest he be a burden to it, and it to him; or hates life, which is one of God's bounties granted to him. . . . On the contrary, he loves the world and a long life, because it affords him opportunities of deserving the world to come. The more good he does the greater is his claim to the next world. . . .

Israeli soldiers in prayer during the Yom Kippur War of October, 1973.

The pious man is nothing but a prince who is obeyed by his senses, and by his mental as well as his physical faculties, which he governs corporeally, as it is written, "He who rules his spirit is better than he who takes a city" [Prov. 16:32]. He is fit to rule, because if he were the prince of a country he would be as just as he is to his body and soul. He subdues his passions, keeping them in bonds, but giving them their share in order to satisfy them as regards food, drink, cleanliness, etc. (Judah Halevi, *Kuzari,* Part III)

The capacity to see is a high and lofty power. The eyes always see great and marvelous things. If man would only attain the merit of having pure eyes, he would know important things by the power of his eyes alone. His eyes are always seeing but they do not know what they are seeing. (Rabbi Nahman of Bratslav)

There are unbelievers who maintain that the world is eternal, but this view is baseless. The truth is that the world and all that it contains can exist, but it need not necessarily; only God *must* exist and He creates all the worlds *ex nihilo* [out of nothing]. When Israel obeys the will of God, it becomes rooted in the Highest Source which is eternal and thereby the whole world is raised into the realm of eternal existence.

Man can become part of God's unity, which is eternal, only by forgetfulness of self; he must forget himself completely in order to partake of the Divine Unity. One cannot reach such an estate except in aloneness. By withdrawing into intimate dialogue with God, man can attain the complete abandonment of his passions and evil habits, i.e., he can free himself from the claims of his flesh and return to his Source. The best time for such withdrawal is at night, when the world is free of the claims of earthly existence. During the day men chase after the concerns of this world. This atmosphere is disturbing even to the man who is personally detached from such concerns, for the worldly bustle of others makes it harder for him to attain to the state of self-forgetfulness. Such withdrawal is best attained in a place which people do not pass by.

When man attains this level, his soul becomes an existential necessity, i.e., he ascends from the realm of the possible to that of the eternal. Once he himself has become eternal, he sees the whole world in the aspect of its eternity. (Ibid.)

MAN'S RESPONSIBILITY

God is omnipotent and yet man is responsible. Everything is foreseen and yet man has free will. These are the classic contradictions of theistic faith, and they appear very early in Judaism. There is no attempt at philosophic resolution, only the assertion that man knows that he has choices to make and that he is morally responsible for those choices. He cannot help but know that there is a God who judges him and upon whom he cannot place the responsibility for his own misdeeds.

Man is not responsible for himself alone. He is responsible to society for the well-being of all men. There must therefore be law in society and respect for government, unless society itself transgresses the moral law. The rights of individuals are absolute, for every man is created in the divine image. Each has his particular virtue and capacity for service.

Man's proper response to life is piety and reverence not only before God but before other men.

> I call heaven and earth to witness against you this day, that I have set before you life and death, blessing and curse; therefore, choose life, that you may live, you and your descendants. (Deut. 30:19)

> Behold, I set before you this day a blessing and a curse: A blessing if you obey the commandments of the Lord your God which I command you this day; a curse if you do not obey the commandments of the Lord your God, but turn aside from the way which I command you this day, to go after other gods, which you know not. (Deut. 11:26–28)

>> There are six things which the Lord hates,
>> Seven which are an abomination to Him:
>> Haughty eyes, a lying tongue,
>> Hands that shed innocent blood,
>> A heart that devises wicked plots,
>> Feet that are swift to run to mischief,
>> A false witness that utters lies,
>> And one that sows discord among brethren. (Prov. 6:16–19)

> Hasten to perform the slightest commandment, and flee from sin; for the performance of one commandment leads to another and one transgression leads to another. The reward of a commandment is another to be fulfilled and the reward of one transgression is another. (Mishnah *Avot* 4:2)

Everything is foreseen by God, and freedom of choice is given to man; the world is judged with goodness, and all depends upon the preponderance of good or evil deeds. (Mishnah *Avot* 3:15)

Everything is in the hands of heaven, except the fear of heaven. (*Megillah* 25a)

The world is judged according to the preponderance of good or evil, and the individual is judged in the same way. Therefore, if a man fulfills one commandment, he is truly blessed, for he has tipped the balance to the side of merit for himself and for the entire world. However, if he commits one transgression, woe is he, for he has tipped the balance to the side of guilt for himself and for the entire world, as it is said, "One sinner destroys much good" [Eccles. 9:18]. One sin of an individual destroys much good for himself and for the entire world. (*Kiddushin* 40b)

"And the Lord spoke to Moses and Aaron, saying, 'Separate yourselves from this congregation, that I may consume them in a moment.' And they fell upon their faces and said, 'O God, the God of the spirit of all flesh, shall one man sin and will you be wroth with all the congregation?'" [Num. 16:20-22]. Rabbi Simeon ben Johai said: Several men were sitting in a boat. One of them began boring a hole beneath him with an auger. His companions said, "What are you doing?" He replied, "What business is it of yours? Am I not boring a hole under myself?" They answered, "It is our business because the water will come in and swamp the boat with all of us in it." (*Leviticus Rabbah* 4:6)

For two and one half years the Schools of Hillel and Shammai debated the question whether it would have been better had man never been created. Finally they agreed that it would have been better had man not been created. However, since man had been created, let him investigate his past deeds, and let him give due consideration to what he is about to do. (*Erubin* 13b)

When Rabbi Johanan ben Zakai was ill, his disciples visited him. . . . They said to him, "Bless us, master!" He said to them, "May it be His will that the fear of heaven be as great to you as the fear of flesh and blood." His disciples asked, "Only as great?" He answered, "If it only *would* be as great! You know that when a man commits a sin he says, 'No one will see me.'" (*Berakhot* 28b)

"You make men like the fish of the sea" [Hab. 1:14]. Just as in the sea the larger fish swallow up the smaller fish, so it is among men. Were it not for fear of the government, every man greater than another would swallow him up. This is what Rav Hanina said: Pray for the welfare of the government, for were it not for fear of the government, a man would swallow up his neighbor alive. (*Avodah Zarah* 4a)

Rabbah bar bar Hana had a litigation against some laborers who, during their work, broke a cask of wine. He took away their clothing, whereupon they complained against him to Rav, who told him to return their clothing to them. When Rabbah asked "Is this the law?" Rav answered "Yes, as it is written 'That you may walk in the way of the good'" [Prov. 2:20]. He returned their clothing to them. The laborers then said "We are poor men and have worked all day and have nothing to eat." Rav said "Pay them their wages." When Rabbah asked again "Is this the law?" Rav answered "Yes, as it is written, 'Keep the path of the righteous'" (*ibid.*). (*Baba Metziah* 83a)

C. Freedom of Will*

MOSES MAIMONIDES

Man has been given free will: if he wishes to turn toward the good way and to be righteous, the power is in his own hands; if he wishes to turn toward the evil way and to be wicked, the power is likewise in his own hands. Thus it is written in the Torah: "And the Lord God said, Behold, the man is become as one of us, to know good and evil." This means that in regard to this matter, the species of man became single of its kind in this world, and that no other species is like it. Man knows good and evil out of himself, out of his intelligence and reason. He does what he wishes to do, and there is none to restrain his hand from doing either good or evil. And because this is so, he could even "put forth his hand, and take also of the tree of life, and eat, and live forever."

Moses Maimonides (1135–1204).

Do not open your mind to what the fools among peoples of the world and most of the untutored in Israel say, namely, that the Holy One, blessed be He, determines even at the very creation of every man, whether he shall be righteous or wicked. It is not thus. For indeed every man can become a righteous man like Moses our master, or wicked like Jeroboam, he can be wise or foolish, merciful or cruel, base or noble, and so on in regard to all qualities. But there is none who forces him, none who determines him, none who draws him toward the one or the other of the two ways. It is he himself who, out of his own volition, turns to the path he wishes to take. That is what Jeremiah said: "Out of the mouth of the Most High proceedeth not evil and good." What he means is that the Creator does not determine whether a man is to become good or evil.

And since this is so, it must be concluded that he who sins does harm unto himself alone. And so it is quite right that he should weep and lament his sins and that which he has done to his soul in doing evil. And therefore it is written: "Wherefore doth a living man complain? Because of his sins!" Furthermore, because we have the power over our actions in our own hands and have done this evil, knowing what we were doing, it is right that we should turn about and forsake our wickedness, just because the power is in our own hands. About this it is written: "Let us search and try our ways, and return to the Lord." This is a mighty root and pillar of the Torah and of the commandments—as it is said: "See, I have set before

*From Nahum N. Glatzer, ed., *A Jewish Reader: In Time and Eternity,* 2d rev. ed. (New York: Schocken Books, 1961), pp. 65–68.

thee this day life and good, and death and evil." And it is written: "Behold, I set before you this day a blessing and a curse." This means that the power is in your hands and that everything a man may do of the actions that men do, he will do, whether it be good or evil. And so it is said: "Oh that they had such a heart as this alway, to fear Me, and keep all My commandments." This means: The Creator does not compel man, he does not determine him to do good or evil, but he leaves it all to him.

If God determined whether a man were to be righteous or wicked, or if there were something inherent in man that inexorably drew him to one way among many ways, to a particular kind of knowledge, to a particular view, to a particular deed—as foolish astrologers have conceived in their own fancy—why then did the prophets bid us: Do this and do not do that! Mend your ways and leave off transgressing! Why would they say this if, from the moment of his creation, everything about man were determined, or if his inner law forced him to something from which he could not withdraw? What reason would there then be for the entire Torah? And by what right would God punish the wicked and reward the righteous? "Shall not the Judge of all the earth do justly?"

And do not be astonished and say: How is it possible that man should do as he pleases, or that what he does is left entirely to him; can anything in the world be done save through the permission of its Master, and against his will? For the Scriptures say: "Whatsoever the Lord pleased, that hath He done, in heaven and in earth." But be advised that all is done according to his will, even if our actions are left to us ourselves. How this can be? Just as it is the will of the Creator that fire and air rise but water and earth sink down, and that the wheel turns around and around, and that the other creatures in the world are according to their fashion as it was his will, so also he wished man to have the power over his actions in his own hands and that what he does be left to him, and that none compel him or draw him this way or that. Out of himself and with the knowledge that God has given him, he is to do all those things which man can do. And that is why he can be judged according to his doing: if he has done what is good, all shall be well with him, and if he has done what is evil, all shall be ill with him. It is this the prophet says in the words: "This hath been of your doing"; "They have chosen their own ways." And about this, Solomon said: "Rejoice, O young man, in thy youth . . . but know thou, that for all these things God will bring thee into judgment." This means: Know that the power to do is in your own hands, but that at some future time you will be called to account.

Perhaps you will say: The Holy One, blessed be He, knows all that will come to pass before it has come to pass. And so, does He or does He not know if a man will be righteous or wicked? If he knows that a certain man will be righteous, it is not well possible that this man will not be righteous. But if you say that he does know a man will be righteous, and that it is still possible for this man to become wicked, why then he does not know for certain? Know that the reply to this question is "longer than the earth and broader than the sea," and many mighty roots and many mountains hang thereby. But you must know and understand what I am about to tell you: The Holy One, blessed be He, does not know with a knowledge that is outside of him, as men who are not one with their knowledge. In the case of God, blessed be He, name and knowledge are one and the same thing. The knowledge of man cannot grasp this quite fully; and just as man has not the power to discover and to grasp the truth of the Creator—for it is said, "Thou canst not see My face, for man shall not see Me and live"—so man has not the power to discover and to grasp the knowledge of the Creator. That is what the prophet says: "For My thoughts are not your thoughts, neither are your ways My ways." And since this is so, we have not the power to know the nature of the knowledge of the Holy One, blessed be He, his knowledge of all creatures and of their doing. But we do know beyond a doubt that the doing of man is in his own hands, that the Holy One, blessed be He, does not draw him this way or that, or determine him to do thus and so. And we know this not only through clear reasoning from the teachings of wisdom. And so it has been said in the spirit of prophecy that man is judged for what he does according to his doing, whether it be good or evil. And this is a principle on which all the words of the prophets depend.

READING 12
The Concept of Man and Life

A. Is There a Jewish View of Life?*

ALBERT EINSTEIN

There is, in my opinion, no Jewish view of life in the philosophic sense. Judaism appears to me to be almost exclusively concerned with the moral attitude in and toward life.

Judaism I believe to be rather the content of the life-approach of the Jewish people than the contents of the laws laid down in the Torah and interpreted in the Talmud. Torah and Talmud are for me only the most weighty evidence of the governing concepts of Jewish life in earlier times.

The essence of the Jewish concept of life seems to me to be the affirmation of life for all creatures. For the life of the individual has meaning only in the service of enhancing and ennobling the life of every living thing. Life is holy; i.e. it is the highest worth on which all other values depend. The sanctification of the life which transcends the individual brings with it reverence for the spiritual, a peculiarly characteristic trait of Jewish tradition.

Judaism is not a faith. The Jewish God is but a negation of superstition and an imaginative result of its elimination. He also represents an attempt to ground morality in fear—a deplorable, discreditable attempt. Yet it seems to me that the powerful moral tradition in the Jewish people has, in great measure, released itself from this fear. Moreover, it is clear that "to serve God" is equivalent to serving "every living thing." It is for this that

*From *Opinion: A Journal of Jewish Life and Letters*, vol. II, no. 17–18 (Sept. 26, 1932), p. 7.

the best among the Jewish people, especially the Prophets including Jesus, ceaselessly battled. Thus Judaism is not a transcendental religion. It is concerned only with the tangible experiences of life, and with nothing else. Therefore it seems to me to be questionable whether it may be termed a "religion" in the customary sense of the word, especially since no "creed" is demanded of Jews, but only the sanctification of life in its all-inclusive sense.

There remains, however, something more in the Jewish tradition, so gloriously revealed in certain of the psalms; namely, a kind of drunken joy and surprise at the beauty and incomprehensible sublimity of this world, of which man can attain but a faint intimation. It is the feeling from which genuine research draws its intellectual strength, but which also seems to manifest itself in the song of birds. This appears to me to be the loftiest content of the God-idea.

Is this, then, characteristic of Judaism? And does it exist elsewhere under other names? In *pure form* it exists nowhere, not even in Judaism where too much literalism obscures the pure doctrine. But, nevertheless, I see in Judaism one of its most vital and pure realizations. This is especially true of its fundamental principle of the sanctification of life.

It is noteworthy that in the Commandment to keep the Sabbath holy the animals were also expressly included—so strongly was felt as an ideal the demand for the solidarity of all living things. Far more strongly yet is expressed the demand for the solidarity of all humankind; and it is no accident that the socialistic demands for the most part emanated from Jews.

To how great an extent the consciousness of the sanctity of life is alive in the Jewish people is beautifully illustrated by a remark once made to me by Walter Rathenau: "When a Jew says he takes pleasure in the hunt, he lies." It is impossible to express more simply the consciousness of the sanctity and the unity of all life as it exists in the Jewish people.

B. Life*

LIFE: Life is considered God's supreme blessing, and it is hence often identified with the good as such—cf. Deut. 30:19: "I have set before you life and death, blessing and curse; therefore choose life, that both you and your seed may live." The *Torah* itself is a "Tree of Life," and the purpose of its commandments is "that men shall live by them" (Lev. 18:5), a phrase to which the rabbis added "and not die by them" (*Yoma* 85b). Hence all laws—with the exception only of the cardinal sins of idolatry, bloodshed, and adultery—are liable to suspension in case of danger to

*From R. J. Zwi Werblowsky and Geoffrey Wigoder, eds., *The Encyclopedia of the Jewish Religion* (New York: Holt, Rinehart and Winston, 1965), pp. 239–40.

Hasidim dancing in Meron, Israel. The devotion and exaltation of the Hasidim are expressed in spontaneous dancing.

life (*Sanh.* 74a). As long as there is life there is hope, and a "living dog is better than a dead lion" (Ecc. 9:4). The biblical emphasis on life in this world as a supreme value (see Ps. 115:17 "The dead praise not the Lord, neither any that go down into silence") was generally maintained in Jewish tradition, in spite of the increasing importance of belief in an afterlife. Death is regarded as the principal source of impurity, and priests, Nazirites, or anyone wishing to enter the Temple were forbidden to defile themselves by contact with the dead (Lev. 21:1; Num. 5:2 ff.; 6:6). The infinite value of every human life is solemnly affirmed in the court's instruction to witnesses in capital trials: "Whoever destroys one life is as if he destroyed a whole world, and whoever preserves one life is as if he preserved a whole world" (*Sanh.* 4:5). Hastening death even by one minute is considered tantamount to bloodshed, and rabbinic law prohibits euthanasia. The motif of life is particularly conspicuous in the additional prayers of the period between New Year and the Day of Atonement. Many of the biblical references to life have later been interpreted as meaning the immortality of the soul or the resurrection of the dead.

READING 13
The Sabbath: The Cycle of the Week*
HAYIM HALEVY DONIN

Judaism carries with it a rich heritage of holidays and traditional religious observances. These important events mark high points in the Jewish historical experience. They also teach the participants much about who they are and what their heritage is.

Perhaps the most beloved of all observances is the "Shabbat," or Sabbath. In his book To Be a Jew, *Rabbi Donin gives interesting insight to the Sabbath and its meaning.*

THE SABBATH AS A MEMORIAL TO THE CREATION OF THE WORLD

What lesson is derived from such a memorial? What does it testify? Besides, what does the Torah mean to teach us when it says that "God rested"? Is He human that He tires and needs physical rest? It is to teach us that just as God stopped creating physical things on the seventh day, so is man to stop creating on this day. Man is to stop making things, to stop manipulating nature. He is to let all things run by themselves. By desisting from all such labors, we not only acknowledge the existence of a Creator, but also emulate the Divine example.

By desisting from all work on the seventh day, we testify that the world is not ours; that, not we, but God is the Lord and Creator of the universe. The fish and the animals that we don't catch, the plants or the flowers that we don't cut or pluck, the grass that we don't water on this day, the goods

*From Rabbi Hayim Halevy Donin, *To Be a Jew* (New York: Basic Books, 1972), pp. 65-69, 70-88.

that we refrain from fashioning or cutting—all this inaction on the part of the individual is a demonstration of homage to the Lord, of returning all things, as it were, to His domain. On the other hand any constructive interference by man with the physical world constitutes "work," according to the Biblical definition. Any act, however small, that involves man in physically creative acts and shows his mastery over the world constitutes *work.* It is this underlying motif which may help to explain some of the whys of the Sabbath laws. This is why acts which may not even require any physical effort, such as plucking a flower or striking a match, are still called *work.* To desist from this work on the seventh day is equivalent to recognizing God as the Creator of the world.

Samson Raphael Hirsch, in his monumental work, *Horeb,* sums up the meaning of the Sabbath laws thus:

> How, above all, does man show his domination over the earth? In that he can fashion all things in his environment to his own purpose—the earth for his habitation and source of sustenance; plant and animal for food and clothing. He can transform everything into an instrument of human service. He is allowed to rule over the world for six days with God's will. On the seventh day, however, he is forbidden by Divine behest to fashion anything for his purpose. In this way he acknowledges that he has no rights of ownership or authority over the world. Nothing may be dealt with as man pleases, for everything belongs to God, the Creator, Who has set man into the world to rule it according to His word. On each Sabbath day, the world, so to speak, is restored to God, and thus man proclaims, both to himself and to his surroundings, that he enjoys only a borrowed authority.

> Therefore even the smallest work done on the Sabbath is a denial of the fact that God is the Creator and Master of the world. It is an arrogant setting-up of man as his own master. It is a denial of the whole task of the Jew as man and as Israelite, which is nothing but the management of the earth according to the will of God. . . . On the other hand, every refraining from work on the Sabbath is in itself a positive expression of the fact that God is the Creator and Master of the world; that it is He who has set man in his place; that He is the Lawgiver of his life; it is a proclamation and acknowledgment of our task as men and Israelites.

> Thus, doing no work on the Sabbath is an *ot,* an expressive *symbol* for all time. The Sabbath expresses the truth that the Only God is the Creator and Master of all and that man, together with all else, has been called to the service of the Only God. It is *moed,* a *time-institution,* a day singled out from other days, a summons to the ennoblement of life. It is *kodesh,* a *holy* time: if, during the six working days, man forgets that Almighty God is the Source of all power and his Lawgiver, then the Sabbath comes to elevate him by directing him once again towards his Creator. It is *brit,* a *covenant,* the only contract and basis of every relationship between God and the Jew, both as man and as Israelite. For if you consider the world and yourself as God's property, and regard your power over the earth as lent to you by God for the fulfillment of your task in life, then will your life be lived in accordance with

the Torah. But if you regard the world as your own and yourself as its master, then the contract is torn up, and you are just making sport of the Torah. Finally, it is *brakha,* a *blessing;* if you thus renew your covenant with God every Sabbath, and dedicate yourself as God's servant, then on every Sabbath God will give you renewed enlightenment of the spirit, enthusiasm and strength for the fulfillment of this great task. In this way you will realize how God really calls you to an elevated state of life which is especially experienced on Sabbath. Our Sages describe this elevated state of the soul by saying that the Sabbath provides the Jew with an "extra soul" or a "super-soul."

The *melachah* which is forbidden on Sabbath is conceived as the execution of an intelligent purpose by the practical skill of man. Or, more generally, production, creation, transforming an object for human purposes; but *not* physical exertion. Even if you tired yourself out the whole day, as long as you have *produced* nothing within the meaning of the term *melachah;* as long as your activity has not been a constructive exercise of your intelligence, you have performed no *melachah* or work. On the other hand, if you have engendered, without the slightest exertion, even the smallest change in an object for human purposes, then you have profaned the Sabbath, flouted God, and undermined your calling as a Jew. Your physical power belongs to your animal nature; it is with your technical skill which serves your spirit that you master the world—and it is with this that, as a human being, you should subject yourself to God on Sabbath.[1]

THE SABBATH AS A MEMORIAL TO THE EXODUS FROM EGYPT

This motif beckons us to remember our slavery, the better to cherish freedom. If the Sabbath on the one hand emphasizes our servitude to God, it also stresses our *freedom from servitude to human masters.* It emphasizes the freedom of the human soul, the freedom of mind and of body. In this context it is important to note that the Torah forbids work to be carried on "by thy man-servant, nor thy maid-servant, nor thy cattle, nor thy stranger that is within thy gates." To be free of servitude on this day was not only for the landowner, the master, the free man—but even in those ancient, primitive times was also intended for the stranger, the servant, and the toiling beast.

Sabbath is thus a weekly-recurring divine protest against slavery and oppression. Lifting up his Kiddush cup on Friday night, the Jew links the creation of the world with man's freedom, so declaring slavery and oppression deadly sins against the very foundations of the universe. Can one be surprised that tyrants of all times did not permit Israel to celebrate the Sabbath?[2]

Synagogue stained glass depicts the Hebrews' slavery in Egypt.

[1]Samson Raphael Hirsch, *Horeb: A Philosophy of Jewish Laws and Observances* (London: Soncino Press, 1962), pp. 63–64.

[2]I. Grunfeld, *The Sabbath* (New York: Feldheim, 1959), p. 10.

But slavery doesn't only consist of doing forced labor for which one doesn't get paid or gets paid very little. Slavery is not only a situation in which cruel taskmasters stand over you and tell you that you can't stop, that you must finish the assigned task before you go home and rest. Have you ever stopped to think that you yourself can be your own cruelest taskmaster, that you are capable of driving yourself in a manner that no slavemaster ever drove his slaves?

You've got to finish the job. You can't stop. There are deadlines to meet, there are obligations to fulfill, there are things which must be taken care of. There are conferences, there are business commitments. There is house cleaning, laundry, shopping, the need to get ready for an evening out. We drive ourselves day in and day out, and we think we are *free!*

Even when contemporary man doesn't actually go to his job, what does he do? He plays just as hard. He transfers the same tension, the same competitive spirit, the same frenzy and the same pressure on his nervous system, which takes such a great toll of human life, from the business office to the ball field, the golf course, the highways of our land, to mowing the lawn, and fixing the house. He thinks he's not working! He may not be getting paid for any of it. He may even enjoy some of it more than what he does for a living. He may even be having a good time. All that, yes! But the mental and emotional and physical rest, the tranquillity of mind and soul—this he doesn't have. Lewis Mumford saw the problem a little more clearly when he wrote:

> In our Western culture the day of rest has now become another day of busy work, filled with amusements and restless diversions not essentially different from the routine of the work week, particularly in America. From the Sunday morning scramble through the metropolitan newspapers, to the distracting tedium of the motor car excursion, we continually activate leisure time, instead of letting all work and routine duties come serenely to a halt.[3]

How many, in the midst of all their pressing obligations and commitments, their worries and concerns, business and personal, can just stop everything and say: "Yes, I have so many things to do. But for the next twenty-four hours, I am a free man. I will cut myself off from the world, and all its concerns, and do nothing or limit myself to spiritual pursuits"? How many can deliberately and consciously say—not "I have really finished, therefore I can rest"—but "though I have not finished, it is as though I have. I now stop for there is no such thing as *must* do"?

The Sabbath observer can and does! He has no taskmasters. For twenty-four hours, he is free. Nothing interferes with his rest, his tranquillity of mind and of soul, unless it be a matter of life and death in which he must play a decisive role. And it is precisely because the

[3]Lewis Mumford, *The Conduct of Life* (New York: Harcourt Brace & Co., 1951), pp. 258-59.

Sabbath recurs as often as every seven days, that it is the refreshing pause that a Sabbath-observant Jew finds it to be. It is not only a matter of not working physically. It is also not working emotionally. And from the positive side, it is the engendering of a completely new and different spirit. Our tradition refers to it as the additional soul, the *neshama y'tairah.* This is an attitude, a state of mind. . . .

PREPARING FOR THE SABBATH

To properly honor the Sabbath and to capture its beauty and spiritual delight, it is necessary to prepare for its coming.

The preparations in a household should be no less elegant than the preparations the same family might make to receive a distinguished and beloved guest.

What might a family do if a very honored guest was coming for dinner?

- A man would plan on getting home from work in plenty of time to shave, bathe, and get dressed.
- A mother would see to it that she and her children were washed and dressed in clean, fresh clothes.
- The dining table would be set in advance as on a special festive occasion; one's best dishes and tableware would be used.
- Dinner would not only be prepared in advance, but the menu would be a little more elaborate than that served at a daily meal. In a poor home, meat and fish would be reserved for the Sabbath meals. But even where meat or fish is on a family's daily menu, there are still many distinctions that a hostess makes when serving a special festive meal, both in types of dishes as well as in the number of courses.
- A house would be thoroughly cleaned, or at least straightened up.
- Every member of the family would take care of the most pressing chores before the guest arrives.
- One can also imagine that members of a household might warn friends, neighbors and business associates not to interrupt by telephone calls while their guest is visiting with them. It would not only be rude to the visitor but disturbing to all if there were constant interruptions.

All this is done *before* the honored guest arrives. This is also what must be done to prepare properly for the Sabbath.

It is unlikely that the Sabbath spirit can be captured or made meaningful even where a festive meal is served, if the children are permitted to come to a table in their play clothes or jeans; if adults sit down in their weekday workclothes, or if the necessary personal and household preparations are omitted.

THE SABBATH EVE

The Sabbath Candles

Lighting of the Sabbath candles formally ushers in the Sabbath for the members of the household.

It is the obligation of the wife to fulfill this religious duty. Unless a woman had been living alone, she starts to observe it on the first Sabbath after her marriage. . . .

The Sabbath candles are lighted approximately twenty minutes before sundown. In the absence of a Jewish calendar listing candlelighting time for a particular geographic area, the time of sundown can be found in the daily local newspaper and the candlelighting time determined accordingly. Once the time of sundown passes, the candles may no longer be lit.

It is permissible for the candles to be lit somewhat earlier. This is often done in the summer months when the day is particularly long and the Sabbath might be ushered in an hour or so earlier.

The minimum number of candles lighted is two. They symbolically represent the two forms of the fourth commandment: *Zachor—Remember* the Sabbath day to keep it holy (Exodus 20:8), and *Shamor—Observe* the Sabbath day to keep it holy (Deut. 5:12). . . .

Although proper ritual procedure requires that the recitation of a blessing always precedes the performance of the mitzvah, in this instance *the candles are lighted first and the benediction is recited afterward.* The reason is obvious. Recital of the blessing formally ushers in the Sabbath after which it is forbidden to light a flame. The procedure is to close one's eyes or cover them with the hands while the benediction is recited. When eyes are opened after the blessing, the sight of the Sabbath lights brings forth the delight that is actually regarded as the culmination of the mitzvah.

The Sabbath celebration involves every member of the family.

The blessing recited for the Sabbath candles is:

> Blessed art Thou Lord our God King of the universe, who has sanctified us with His commandments and commanded us to kindle the Sabbath lights.

After the candles are lit, it is proper to greet the others in the household with the words *Shabbat Shalom.* Everyone responds likewise.

The Sabbath candles should be lighted on the table where the Sabbath meal is eaten. If this is impractical, it should at least be done in the same room. . . .

A beautiful table setting makes the Sabbath even more special.

The Sabbath Table

The table set for the Sabbath should contain, in addition to the candles, the following special items set at the head of the table:

- Two unsliced Sabbath loaves known as *hallah.* They are covered by a napkin or cloth. (Specially decorated hallah covers are available and are recommended for use because they help beautify the Sabbath table.)
- A Kiddush Cup.

The Evening Services

The Friday evening service is known as Welcoming the Sabbath, or *Kabbalat Shabbat.* It is generally scheduled to begin in synagogues shortly after the Sabbath candles are lighted at home.

Although women are not obliged to attend these services, (and after arduous preparations for the Sabbath they may be tired and deserving of the "breathing spell" between the candlelighting and dinner time) the Sabbath spirit is enhanced if the women too welcome the Sabbath with the appropriate prayers at home. Many attend the services if they can.

The male members of the household as well as all the children should make every effort to attend the synagogue for these Friday evening services, which begin prior to sundown. These services usually last between forty and fifty minutes and possess a spiritual quality that is unique. In many synagogues, these services are conducted with much congregational singing and provide an inspiring atmosphere in which to usher in the Sabbath. . . .

Illness, extremely foul weather, or great distance from the synagogue are legitimate reasons for not attending the services. In such instances, the Sabbath prayers must be said at home. . . .

The custom of "Late Friday Evening Services" has become widespread in the United States. These are generally scheduled for about 8:30 in the evening—after dinner, from late fall to early spring. There is no objection to these "Services" if they are intended to serve as an *Oneg Shabbat* gathering where some traditional Sabbath songs are sung; where an address of a religious or educational nature or any appropriate message is heard from a guest speaker or the rabbi; where refreshments are served during a social hour. Depending upon the community and the locality, there is a place and sometimes even a need for such a program, especially in the winter months when the evenings are long.

These "Services" must not, however, serve as a substitute for the authentic sundown service which ushers in the Sabbath in the year, nor for the regular Sabbath morning services.

But if the Sabbath is ushered in on time with due regard to the Sabbath laws and the Sabbath day is also properly observed, the late Friday evening hours may be made as spiritually rewarding by the pursuit of activities other than a "late service."

The Home Ritual and Kiddush

Upon returning home from the synagogue following the Friday evening *Kabbalat Shabbat* and *maariv* service (or upon concluding these prayers at home), it is customary for the family to gather about the Sabbath table to sing the traditional *Shalom Aleichem.*\

It is then customary for the father to bless his children. The mother may also perform this rite. The ritual is a simple one. The father places both his hands on the bowed head of a child (or where two children are simultaneously being blessed—one hand on the head of each child) and says:

> To a son(s): May God make you as Ephraim and Menasheh.
> To a daughter(s): May God make you as Sarah, Rebecca, Rachel, and Leah.
> Followed by:
> May the Lord bless you and protect you. May the Lord shine His countenance upon you and be gracious to you. May the Lord favor you and grant you peace.

The Sabbath Kiddush (Sanctification) is then recited by the male head of the household while holding a full cup of wine in his hands. It should be his intention to say the Kiddush on behalf of all those present. Different customs prevail on whether everyone stands or sits during the Kiddush. Either way is correct.

It is a Torah (Biblical) requirement to sanctify the Sabbath with a verbal declaration, for it is written "Remember the Sabbath day to sanctify it" (Exodus 20:8). Our Sages taught that this "remembering" requires the recitation of a declaration of Sanctification (Kiddush) at the beginning of the Sabbath, and a declaration of Separation or Division (Havdalah) at the conclusion of the Sabbath.

The Sages ruled that this "remembrance" (recitation of Kiddush and Havdalah) preferably be over a cup of wine, the traditional symbol of joy and of a festive occasion. . . .

> It was evening and it was morning.
> On the sixth day the heavens and the earth and all their hosts were completed. For by the seventh day God had completed his work which he had made, and he rested on the seventh day from all his work which he had made. Then God blessed the seventh day and hallowed it, because on it he rested from all his work which God had created to function thenceforth.
> Blessed art Thou Lord our God King of the universe, who creates the fruit of the vine.

> Blessed art Thou Lord our God King of the universe, who hast sanctified us with thy commandments and hast been pleased with us; in love and favour hast given us thy holy Sabbath as a heritage, a memorial of the creation—that day being also the first among the holy festivals, in remembrance of the exodus from Egypt. Thou hast chosen us and hallowed us above all nations, and in love and favour hast given us thy holy Sabbath as a heritage. Blessed art Thou, O Lord, who hallowest the Sabbath.

After the recitation of the Kiddush, those present respond with "Amen." The one who recited it should drink from the wine and then give some of it to all those present. The others need not recite the blessing.

Following the Kiddush, everyone ritually washes for the meal. This is done by filling a glass, cup, or other vessel with water and pouring the water over the right hand, then over the left hand.

Before the hands are wiped dry with a towel, the following benediction is said:

> Blessed art Thou Lord our God King of the universe, who has sanctified us with His commandments and commanded us concerning the washing of the hands.

Without further talk or interruption, the ritual washing is immediately followed by sitting down to the table. The head of the household uncovers the two hallot, lifting them momentarily while reciting the blessing over the bread:

> Blessed art Thou Lord our God King of the universe, who brings forth bread from the earth.

The hallah is then cut and slices distributed to all at the table. The others need not repeat the blessing over the bread if they responded "Amen" when they heard it and if the head of the household had them in mind. . . .

It is customary to brighten the Sabbath dinner by the singing of *zmirot* between the courses of the meal. The zmirot are poems, most of them written during the Middle Ages, that rhapsodize the Sabbath rest and the Sabbath glory. Numerous melodies for each of these songs are extant and they lend an added dimension of cheer to the Sabbath meal. One need not limit himself to these "official" zmirot, but may choose from among many songs and melodies which have some religious or spiritual theme.

It is obligatory to give thanks to God after having eaten, in fulfillment of the Torah requirement that "You shall eat and be satisfied and bless the Lord" (Deut. 8:10). The grace after meals (*birkat hamazon*) for which popular chants have developed should climax the meal. Unlike the rest of the week when the *birkat hamazon* is likely to be said in haste and without song, on the Sabbath it should be chanted and said without haste. Even the preschool child will soon enough learn the words of the prayer and heartily join in.

It is religiously praiseworthy to do those things on the Sabbath which delight the soul and which provide a measure of pleasure and joy, as long as they do not constitute a violation of the Sabbath. Violations of the Sabbath, in spirit or in deed, can never be justified on the grounds that "they are a delight to me"; "they give me pleasure"; or "I enjoy them." Such rationalizations invite the dissipation of the unique spiritual qualities connected with the Sabbath. Since different people enjoy doing different things and favor a wide range of recreational pursuits, such rationalizations are tantamount to the total secularization of this "day of rest," and in effect, destroy the Sabbath.

Activities that "give pleasure" on the Sabbath must take place within the framework of the spiritual purposes of the Sabbath, and in consideration of the special and distinct *holiness* of the day. Such activities must not trespass into the tasks forbidden on the Sabbath by the Torah or rabbinic legislation. It is inevitable that in disregarding the halakhic discipline of the Torah, the special "Sabbath joy" and the unique "Sabbath spirit" will invariably dissipate.

LEISURE ACTIVITIES FOR THE SABBATH

. . . Depending upon the time of the year and one's area of residence, one or more of the following activities may also occupy the time of different members of a family during those few leisure Sabbath hours that are left after attending the synagogue and enjoying the Sabbath meal:

- Reading and/or studying.
- Discussing and/or reviewing with children the things they have been studying and doing all week.
- Leisure stroll.
- Socializing with neighbors or nearby friends or family.
- Attending lectures, forums, or study groups organized by a synagogue or other organization.
- Getting extra hours of sleep and rest by getting to bed earlier than usual or by enjoying a Sabbath afternoon siesta.
- Home games such as chess or checkers and similar activities are permitted. Children who study all week should be permitted to devote some time to such games.
- In many communities, activities in the Sabbath spirit are organized for the children or young people. Group singing, Israeli or other folk dancing, discussion groups, refreshments and socializing are typical programs enjoyed. These are usually sponsored by youth organizations.

These same activities are also suitable for the Sabbath afternoon hours, following the services and the Sabbath meals.

A father spends time with his children on the Sabbath.

Rather than feeling bored, as though one's activities are restricted, a Sabbath observer should find that the day thus spent is a tranquil delight, and that the hours at his disposal, even given the limited choice, are too few.

THE SABBATH DAY

The Morning Services

The Sabbath morning services at the synagogue are the most elaborate as well as the lengthiest of the week, and participating in them is important to the day's observance.

The length of the Sabbath service is due to several factors:

- The reading of the weekly portion of the Torah is a central feature of the Sabbath service.
- The delivery of a message or sermon by the rabbi is a commonplace and widely followed practice in most synagogues.
- It is a widespread and laudable practice for the congregation to sing many of the prayers.
- Though it enhances the enjoyment of the main service of the week, where a cantor and choir officiate, their liturgical renditions also tend to lengthen the service.
- Special ceremonies and honors sometimes accompany the observance of a Bar-Mitzvah in the synagogue.

In the United States most traditional congregations begin their Sabbath services sometime between 8:30 A.M. and 9:00 A.M. They usually last about three to three and a half hours, till about noon. In Israel, most synagogues begin their Sabbath morning services at about 8:00 A.M. and they usually last about two to two and a half hours.

In some communities in the United States and Israel, some people prefer to attend an early morning Sabbath service at 6:30 A.M. which usually lasts till about 8:30 A.M. . . .

The Three Sabbath Meals

It is a special mitzvah to eat three meals (*shalosh seudot*) on the Sabbath. Since one meal is on Friday evening, the other two are taken during the day. In communities where the Sabbath services last most of the morning, the second main Sabbath meal is eaten at about noon or shortly thereafter. The third meal, known as the *seudah shlishit,* is then eaten in the very late afternoon, before sundown. This meal is usually a simple meal, but should include bread or *hallah.*

The same procedure for washing, breaking bread (two Sabbath loaves), zmirot, reciting grace, etc., that were followed at the Friday evening meal are also followed for the other two Sabbath meals.

CONCLUDING THE SABBATH

The Ending of the Day

The Sabbath day ends, not at sundown when the sun sets, but at nightfall when the stars come out. *Nightfall* begins when at least three stars are visible in the heavens. Calculations have, however, long replaced the visual method of determining the onset of nightfall.

The time between sundown and nightfall is traditionally neither day nor night. In Hebrew it is called "between the suns." Since its status is doubtful, it is automatically attached to the Sabbath, so that there shall be no question of Sabbath violation. . . .

Havdalah

Just as the recitation of Kiddush is required for Friday evening so the recitation of Havdalah is required to mark the conclusion of the Sabbath.

Havdalah, which means Division or Separation, may be said any time after nightfall. In the synagogue, it follows the brief evening (*maariv*) service. It should also be said at home for the benefit of those members of the household who hadn't heard it.

The Havdalah is said over a cup of wine, with additional blessings recited for fragrant spices (*b'samim*) and light (*ner*). The symbolic significance of the fragrant spices is that the sweet smell—regarded in rabbinic sources as a delight for the soul, rather than for the body—refreshes in some small way, making up for the loss of the "additional soul" which takes leave at the end of the Sabbath and for the loss of spiritual strength this entails.

As for the light, since it is not permitted to be kindled on the Sabbath, it was considered proper that its very first use after the Sabbath be for a religious purpose. It also symbolizes—as the first act of the week—the first act of creation which marked the first day of the week when God said, "Let there be light."

If wine is unavailable for Havdalah, other beverages such as beer or liqueurs may be substituted.

Special fragrant spice mixtures for use at Havdalah are available at Jewish religious supplies stores. The spices are generally kept in decorative and artistically designed containers of silver, brass, chromium, or wood. These containers are referred to as *b'samim boxes*.

The Havdalah candle is a special candle that is made of two or more braided wicks, since the flame of a torch is required and not a regular candle. They come in various sizes and colors. If a special Havdalah candle is not available, two ordinary candles may be used if they are held in an upside down v shape, like this Λ so that the flames of the two candles come together, providing a torchlike effect.

The candle is given to one member of the household to hold (usually a child) while the Havdalah is recited.

After filling the cup with wine (or other beverage) to the brim and lighting the Havdalah candle, the head of the household raises the cup of wine in his right hand and says:

> Blessed art Thou Lord our God King of the universe, who creates the fruit of the vine (by whose will all things exist).

The b'samim box is then picked up and the following blessing recited:

> Blessed art Thou Lord our God King of the universe, who creates diverse spices.

As this blessing is concluded, the fragrant spices are smelled.

Turning back to look at the flame of the Havdalah candle, the following blessing is then recited:

> Blessed art Thou Lord our God King of the universe, who creates the light of the fire.

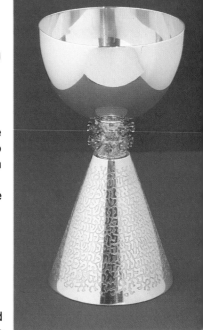

As this blessing is concluded, it is customary to momentarily examine one's hands or at least the right hand by the light of the flame so as to derive some immediate use from the light, that the blessing not be said in vain.

The cup of wine is then picked up again and the essence of the Havdalah prayer is said:

> Blessed art Thou Lord our God King of the universe, who makes a division between the sacred and the secular, between light and darkness, between Israel and the other nations, between the seventh day and the six working days. Blessed art Thou, Lord, who makes a distinction between the sacred and the secular.

The Siddur contains an introductory paragraph composed of selected Biblical verses that is customarily recited prior to the blessing over the wine. If one is proficient in Hebrew, this paragraph beginning with the words *Hinei ayl yeshuati* should be included in the Havdalah.

The blessing over wine is engraved on the stem of this silver Sabbath cup.

READING 14

The Cycle of the Year

A. How the Years Are Counted*

HAYIM HALEVY DONIN

The point of reference for the counting of years differed in antiquity from people to people and from nation to nation, based as it was on some significant historical event. Usually the reign of a new king marked year One in the reign of so and so, and thus the count continued until a new king arose and the clock was turned back to the beginning. These years were used to date official documents and record historical events. The Bible offers many examples of such usage.

Early Christians also based the counting of their years on the reign of the one they regarded as their "spiritual king," considering the year of his birth to have been year One. The dominance of Christian civilization in world affairs has resulted in the Christian count's becoming the world's most widely used dating system. While Christians use the intrinsically religious postscript B.C. and A.D., Jewish texts generally substitute the notation B.C.E. and C.E., meaning *Before the Common Era* and *Common Era.*

The Jews for many centuries used as their point of reference in counting the years the exodus from Egypt, in addition to using the reign of the current ruler. Thus, by the beginning of the Christian era the Jews were already into their fourteenth century of counting years. Had they continued on that basis, we would today be in the midst of our thirty-fourth century, or at approximately the year 3350.

*From Donin, *To Be a Jew,* pp. 242–43.

However, after the destruction of the Jerusalem Temple in the seventieth year of the common era and the dispersion of the Jews, we find the use of the exodus as a point of reference for counting years being displaced by other focal points. The destruction of the Temple served as one such basis, and dates based upon that event are found in documents well into the early medieval period. However, the system that gained the widest popularity among Jews and which is still in use today is one based not on an event or symbol whose significance is limited to our own faith or people, but on a theme of universal significance and applicability, namely the Creation of the world.

The number of years since Creation was arrived at by the Sages by going back over all the records then in existence, reviewing the Biblical record in terms of personal life spans, equating the years mentioned in early chapters of Genesis as equivalent to our own, and regarding the seven days of Creation as days like our own. That those seven "days" of Creation may in fact have been time periods of extremely long duration, that they correspond to "stages" rather than days similar to our own twenty-four-hour day, does not detract from the spiritual or ethical significance of the Creation as the conceptual basis of the Jewish year. It is what the number 5733 stands for and what it implies—God's sovereignty over the universe—that is important, not the technical or scientific accuracy of the count, for no exact figure is possible.

B. The Calendar and Holidays*

CALENDAR OF JEWISH HOLIDAYS					
	1974–75 (5735)	1975–76 (5736)	1976–77 (5737)	1977–78 (5738)	1978–79 (5739)
†Rosh Hashanah (1st day)	Sept. 17	Sept. 6	Sept. 25	Sept. 13	Oct. 2
Yom Kippur	Sept. 26	Sept. 15	Oct. 4	Sept. 22	Oct. 11
†Sukkot (1st day)	Oct. 1	Sept. 20	Oct. 9	Sept. 27	Oct. 16
Hoshana Rabba	Oct. 7	Sept. 26	Oct. 15	Oct. 3	Oct. 22
Shemini Atzeret	Oct. 8	Sept. 27	Oct. 16	Oct. 4	Oct. 23
Simchat Torah	Oct. 9	Sept. 28	Oct. 17	Oct. 5	Oct. 24
Chanukah	Dec. 9–16	Nov. 29–Dec. 6	Dec. 17–24	Dec. 5–12	Dec. 25–Jan. 1
Hamishah Asar Bishvat	Jan. 27	Jan. 17	Feb. 3	Jan. 23	Feb. 12
Purim	Feb. 25	Mar. 16	Mar. 4	Mar. 23	Mar. 13
†Passover (1st day)	Mar. 27	Apr. 15	Apr. 3	Apr. 22	Apr. 12
†Passover (7th day)	Apr. 2	Apr. 21	Apr. 9	Apr. 28	Apr. 18
Lag B'Omer	Apr. 29	May 18	May 6	May 25	May 15
†Shavuot (1st day)	May 16	June 4	May 23	June 11	June 1
Tisha B'Av	July 17	July 5	July 24	Aug. 13	Aug. 2
†Orthodox and Conservative congregations celebrate two days, Reform one day only.					

*The calendar of Jewish holidays and brief descriptions are from "The Jewish Holidays," a brochure produced by the Anti-Defamation League, Minnesota-Dakotas Regional Office, Minneapolis.

THE JEWISH HOLIDAYS

Sabbath

> "Remember the Sabbath day, to keep it holy. Six days you shall labor, and do all your work; but the seventh day is a Sabbath to the Lord your God." (Exodus 20:8–10)

Of all the Jewish holidays and festivals, Sabbath is the only one mentioned in the Ten Commandments. Set apart by God as a day of calm retreat and reflection, the Sabbath is considered the most important of all holy days by Jews. The Sabbath begins at Friday sunset and lasts until nightfall on Saturday. Today, Jews observe Sabbath in different ways. Orthodox Jews will not ride on the Sabbath, nor will they kindle a light. Work, the exchange of money, financial activity of any kind are forbidden. Conservative and Reform Jews, who interpret the Biblical injunctions more liberally, do not restrict their actions to the same degree. Some Jews go to the synagogue or temple services on Friday evenings before supper, some after supper. Others attend services on Saturday morning. But for all Jews, the inner meaning of Sabbath is the same: it is a time for physical relaxation and spiritual renewal.

Rosh Hashanah

Rosh Hashanah, which in Hebrew means "first of the year," comes early in the fall. Rosh Hashanah is the beginning of the ten-day period called the "Ten Days of Penitence," or the "Days of Awe." Yom Kippur, the "Day of Atonement," concludes this holy period.

Yom Kippur

Yom Kippur (the Day of Atonement) is the last day of the "Ten Days of Penitence" which, according to the Jewish tradition, is a time for repentance, prayer and charity. On this solemn and important day Jewish men and women are bidden to refrain from eating and drinking, and even young children try to fast for at least a part of the day. The Bible (Leviticus 16:29–31, 23:26–32; Numbers 29:7) also requires that Jews do no manner of work on Yom Kippur. The people spend the entire day in prayer and worship.

Sukkot

Five days after the solemnity of Yom Kippur comes the most joyous of Jewish holidays, Sukkot, a festival celebrating the time when the ancient Israelites gathered in their fruit harvest and offered thanks to God for His goodness to them. In many ways it is similar to the American Thanksgiving, and some scholars believe that the Pilgrim fathers were inspired to hold their first Thanksgiving by the Sukkot festival about which they read in the Bible.

Shemini Atzeret

The eighth day of Sukkot, called Shemini Atzeret (the eighth day of assembly), is celebrated as a festival. On this day, no matter how stormy the weather outside, the congregation offers a special prayer for rain. This prayer may be traced back to ancient Israel, where Sukkot marked the end of the annual dry season and the people would pray for rain and good crops in the coming year.

Simchat Torah

On the ninth and final day of Sukkot, the year's reading of the Pentateuch is completed. This day is known as Simchat Torah, a full-fledged holiday in itself—and a most happy one—for it celebrates the end of the year's reading and the beginning of the new.

On Simchat Torah eve, a section from the closing chapter of the Book of Deuteronomy, the very last part of the Torah (the five books of Moses), is read aloud. This event is heralded by a procession in which the sacred scrolls are carried around the synagogue while the children merrily follow with banners and songs. The next morning another procession takes place and the Scripture reading begins with the last chapter of Deuteronomy and concludes with the first chapter of Genesis.

Chanukah

In December of every year, Jews observe the festival of Chanukah. It is a joyous holiday, celebrating the first great victory for religious freedom, won by Jews, more than two thousand years ago.

In those days, the Jews of Palestine were dominated by the rule of Antiochus IV, a Syrian-Greek emperor who demanded that everyone in his empire follow his ways of worship. The Jews, however, refused to give up their faith in the One God. For three years, under the leadership of Judah Maccabee, they fought the army of Antiochus. The account of this struggle is recorded in the Books of the Maccabees. After the Jews defeated Antiochus, they cleansed and purified the Temple in Jerusalem of every pagan object that had been brought into it. It is told in Jewish legend that when Judah's men were cleaning out the Temple, they found just a single jar of holy oil—only enough to keep the Eternal Light before the Holy Ark burning for one day. Miraculously, this one jar burned for eight days and eight nights, allowing the priests of the Temple enough time to prepare a sufficient supply of oil so that the Eternal Light could remain lit without interruption.

Judah Maccabee then proclaimed an eight-day holiday to celebrate the rededication of the Temple of God. Thus, the festival received its name, for Chanukah means "dedication." Every night of the festival, candles are lit in a special candelabrum called a *menorah*—one candle the first night, two the second, and so on until eight candles are lit on the eighth night.

Children traditionally play with dreydels *(tops) on Chanukah. The Hebrew letters on the sides of the* dreydel *mean "The great miracle took place there* [*in Palestine*]*."*

Purim

The story of Purim, as told in the Book of Esther, reads like a fairy tale. It takes us back some twenty-four hundred years to the land of Persia, ruled by a king named Ahasuerus, where there lived a wicked man named Haman who tried to exterminate the Jewish people.

At that time, the Queen of Persia was Esther, a Jewish lady who had been brought up by a cousin named Mordecai. Together, Esther and Mordecai were instrumental in overcoming Haman's evil plan.

On Purim eve in the synagogue, it is traditional to read the Book of Esther (in Hebrew, the Megillah). At every mention of Haman's name, the children stamp, clap and make all manner of noise with their Purim greggers (noisemakers). In this fashion, they symbolically blot out Haman's name and the memory of his evil. The next morning when the reading is concluded, the Jewish people, with prayers of thanksgiving, express their gratitude that faith proved triumphant over hatred.

Passover

To find the beginnings of the story of Passover (Pesach, in Hebrew), we must travel back thousands of years to the land of Egypt. There, the Book of Exodus tells us, the Jews were enslaved by a heartless Pharaoh. Taking pity on His people, God chose Moses to lead the Jews out of slavery. Moses implored Pharaoh to let the Jews worship God in freedom. But Pharaoh refused.

The Eternal One then sent one plague after another upon the Egyptians until they reluctantly allowed the Hebrews to leave. He then commanded the Red Sea to open so that the Hebrew slaves might escape the pursuing Egyptians and go on to a new life. Once safely encamped on dry land, the thankful Jews offered up praise to God for their deliverance. Having tasted the bitterness of slavery, they thrilled at the challenge of liberty.

So important is the emancipation story that the whole Passover ceremony is built around it. Among Orthodox and Conservative Jews, the Seder (which means "order" in Hebrew) is held on both the first and second nights of the eight-day holiday. Reform Jews, who observe a seven-day Passover, hold their one Seder on the first evening. Many synagogues now also conduct a Seder for the entire congregation.

Shavuot

Arriving just as spring is about to turn into summer (late May or early June), Shavuot (the Festival of Weeks) is a holiday of three-fold joy and pleasure. First celebrated in Biblical days as the conclusion of the grain harvest, in later years Shavuot was identified as the holiday commemorating the revelation of the Ten Commandments to Moses at Sinai. Still more recently, Shavuot has been established by Reform and Conservative Jews as the day for the holding of confirmation ceremonies.

C. The New Year and Yom Kippur*

HAYIM HALEVY DONIN

WHY THE FIRST OF TISHRAI
IS CELEBRATED AS THE NEW YEAR

The Torah refers to the month of Nisan (when Passover occurs) as the *first month* of the year in the Jewish calendar, and makes no reference to a day to be known as Rosh Hashana, the New Year. The first day of Tishrai (the seventh month, according to the Bible) is mentioned in the Torah as the holy day of the Day of Remembrance (*Yom Hazikaron*) and the Day of Sounding the Shofar (*Yom Teruah*).

*From Donin, *To Be a Jew,* pp. 243–49.

Based on a tradition of hoary antiquity which assigned the event of Creation to the first of Tishrai, this holy day also became known as Rosh Hashana, the New Year, especially after Creation was made the point of reference for counting the years. It is the Mishna (Rosh Hashana 1:1) which first refers to Rosh Hashana, but to four different New Year days: (a) the first of Nisan, as the New Year day for Kings, according to which date Israel's kings calculated the years of their reign. (No matter when they assumed the throne, the first of Nisan was the cut-off point when the second year of the reign began.) This was also the New Year day for figuring the festivals, so that Passover counted as the year's first festival; (b) the first of Tishrai, as the New Year for Years, by which the years were counted, and from which day the Sabbatical and Jubilee years were calculated. This is the day we observe as Rosh Hashana; (c) the first of Elul as the New Year for the tithing of animals; and (d) the fifteenth of Shevat as the New Year for Trees.

Those of us who are used to working with fiscal years that differ from calendar years can understand the distinctions.

In the prayer book, the holy day that we call Rosh Hashana is still referred to by its Biblical names, although the tradition of this day's being the anniversary of the world's Creation and the concomitant idea of God's sovereignty over the universe are dominant themes of the prayers. Among the masses, however, the name *Rosh Hashana* (New Year) is the most popular and best known. The term *High Holydays* developed in English usage as a reference to Rosh Hashana and Yom Kippur. There is no equivalent Hebrew term. In Hebrew, these days have traditionally been called *Yamim Noraim* which means *Days of Awe*.

ROSH HASHANA

In the seventh month, on the first day of the month, you shall observe a day of rest, a memorial proclaimed with the blast of the horn, a holy convocation. You shall not do any servile work. . . . (Lev. 23:24–25)

In the Torah and in the prayer book this sacred day is called the Day of Remembrance (*Yom Hazikaron*) and the Day of Sounding the Shofar (*Yom Teruah*). It marks the start of a ten-day period of spiritual self-examination and repentance which culminates with Yom Kippur, the Day of Atonement. Inasmuch as the years are reckoned from the first of Tishrai, however, this day became known throughout the Jewish world as Rosh Hashana, the New Year.

Intensive prayer is the central mood of this day. Acknowledgment of God's sovereignty over the world and His rulership over mankind are the major themes of the prayers.

The special Biblical precept that is most identified with Rosh Hashana is the blowing of the shofar. It is a religious duty on this day to listen to the shofar sounds.

The one who blows the shofar recites the blessing: "Blessed art Thou, Lord our God, King of the universe who has sanctified us with His commandments and commanded us to hear the sound of the shofar." The congregation responds with *Amen.* During the course of the Rosh Hashana service, a total of 100 notes are sounded.

Ancient tradition has handed down three distinct shofar-notes: a long drawn-out sound (*tekiah*), a broken, plaintive sound (*shevarim*), a series of sharp, staccato sounds (*teruah*).

People confined to their homes who cannot be in the synagogue to listen to the shofar should try to obtain the services of someone who can stop by to blow the shofar for them.

The sound of the shofar has been regarded from time immemorial as a call to penitence and as a reminder of the shofar sound at Sinai. According to Maimonides, the Scriptural precept to blow the shofar on this day has profound meaning. It tells us, he says:

> Awake, ye sleepers from your sleep . . . and ponder over your deeds; remember your Creator and go back to Him in penitence. Be not of those who miss realities in their pursuit of shadows and waste their years in seeking after vain things which cannot profit or deliver. Look well to your souls and consider your acts; forsake each of you his wrong ways and improper thoughts and return to God so that He may have mercy upon you (Hil. Teshuvah 3:4).

Blowing the shofar on the High Holidays.

If Rosh Hashana falls on the Sabbath, the shofar is not blown on that day.

At the conclusion of the evening service, the proper greeting to extend to one another is:

> May you be inscribed and sealed for a good year.

A number of symbolic customs have evolved concerning the holy day's dinner meals. The most widespread is that of dipping a piece of hallah or a slice of apple into honey and saying before eating it:

> May it be the Lord's will to renew for us a year that will be good and sweet.

The entire period from Rosh Hashana through Yom Kippur is known as the Ten Days of Repentance, or *aseret y'mai teshuvah.* It is marked by special penitential prayers that are recited each day in the synagogue.

The Sabbath which falls during this ten-day period is known as Shabbat Teshuvah, the Sabbath of Repentance, or as Shabbat Shuvah, the Sabbath of Return. The latter word is taken from the opening of the chapter from the Prophets read on this Sabbath: *Shuvah Yisrael,* "Return O Israel unto the Lord, your God" (Hosea 14:2).

The proper greeting to extend during the period following Rosh Hashana is *gmar hatimah tovah,* "May the final seal be for good." The greeting reflects the belief that Rosh Hashana and Yom Kippur are Days of Judgment (*Yom Hadin*) for all people.

YOM KIPPUR

The Lord spoke to Moses saying: ". . . the tenth day of this seventh month is the Day of Atonement: It shall be a holy convocation to you, and *you shall afflict your souls;* . . . You shall do no work throughout that day; for it is a day of atonement . . . For whoever does not afflict his soul throughout this day, shall be cut off from his people. And whoever does any work on that day, that person will I cause to perish from among his people. Do no work whatever; it is a law for all time throughout the generations in all your settlements. It shall be a Sabbath of complete rest for you and *you shall afflict your souls;* on the *ninth day of the month at evening, from evening until evening,* shall you rest on your Sabbath." (Lev. 23:26–32)

The day before Yom Kippur is a day of preparation for the fast:

- Charity money should be set aside and brought to the synagogue prior to the evening services for distribution to various religious and social welfare institutions.
- Since Yom Kippur does not atone for sins committed against one's fellow man unless the grieved party has been pacified and has agreed to forgive the wrongdoer, this day should be regarded as a deadline date for reconciliation, for expressing regrets and asking forgiveness. It matters not whether the wrong committed was in material things or by verbal insult. God does not forgive unless the grieved party has first forgiven.

  Where attempts to pacify take place, the grieved party must feel it incumbent upon himself to extend forgiveness with a full heart. If he stubbornly persists in refusing to be pacified, he is regarded as cruel, as himself behaving evilly and not as a worthy son of the Israelite people.
- The meal in the late afternoon prior to the fast should be a festive meal. One should not, however, overeat, or eat anything that might cause thirst as it will make the fasting more difficult.
- Before leaving for the synagogue it is customary for the father to bless his sons and daughters.

The Torah specifies that the fast is to begin on the *ninth* day, so that the fasting on Yom Kippur actually begins *before sundown* while it is still light. It does not conclude till the *evening* of the next day. By "the evening" is not meant sundown, but rather nightfall when the stars appear, which is somewhat later. How much later depends on the geographical latitude. (In northern parts of the United States it generally occurs about forty minutes after sundown.)

The Biblical commandment to "afflict your souls" is observed by a complete and total fast, by abstaining from all *eating* and *drinking* for the entire period (approximately twenty-five hours).

With regard to work, the Day of Atonement follows the same rules as the weekly Sabbath, with similar exceptions where life is endangered. Whatever is forbidden on the Sabbath is forbidden on Yom Kippur.

It is forbidden to fast on a Sabbath day because it would detract from the delight which the day should provide, and all other fasts which coincide with the Sabbath are either postponed to Sunday or moved back to Thursday. But if Yom Kippur falls on a Sabbath day, it is still required to fast and "afflict the soul." Some offer the explanation that fasting *for the purpose of atonement* does not clash with the Sabbath requirement of *oneg* or delight. Others simply regard the Yom Kippur requirement as taking precedence and base their view on the fact that Yom Kippur is called *Shabbat Shabbaton,* implying a Sabbath of Sabbaths.

The Oral Torah teaches us that in addition to prohibiting eating and drinking, "to afflict your souls" also involves, though with less severe sanctions, prohibitions against washing and bathing, anointing one's body, wearing of shoes (applies only to shoes made of leather), and sexual relations.

The washing that is forbidden is that which is done for pleasure, or to help one feel more comfortable and pleasant (*shel ta'anug*). But that which is done to wash away dirt, or upon rising in the morning, or after taking care of one's needs is permitted (*k'darko tamid*).

A person who is ill or whose feet pain him is permitted to wear shoes normally.

Children under the age of nine should not be permitted to fast at all, as it may be injurious to their health. From the age of nine, they should be gradually trained to fast for longer and longer periods. Girls from the age of twelve and boys from thirteen years must fast as any adult.

The Yom Kippur fast may be broken only for reasons of critical illness. The sick person's expressed wish or the opinion of physicians may be the determining factor in granting the dispensation. A rabbi's decision in any such case should be sought.

A woman in childbirth (from the moment she begins to feel birthpains) and for the first three days following birth is not permitted to fast at all, even if she insists upon it. From the third through the seventh day she may fast if she wants to, but is permitted to break the fast if she feels the need.

The service which introduces Yom Kippur is called *Kol Nidre* (All Vows) from the name of the historically meaningful and moving prayer that is then recited. The concluding service of Yom Kippur on the next day is called *Neilah* which means "the Closing" (of the Gates). Except for the time when one goes home to sleep or rest, the entire period is spent in prayer.

The wearing of white on Yom Kippur—white clothes, white robe (*kitel*), white skullcap—is a time-honored custom intended to recall the white robes (*takhrikhim*) in which the dead are buried, and thus to mellow the heart of the worshipper. White also represents purity and symbolizes the Prophetic promise: "Though your sins be as scarlet, they shall be as *white* as snow" (Isaiah 1:18).

The conclusion of Yom Kippur is marked by a single long blast of the shofar. It is symbolic of "when the ram's horn sounded long . . ." which marked the conclusion of the Revelation at Sinai (Exodus 19:13). It also commemorates the blowing of the shofar on Yom Kippur in ancient times to signify the start of the Jubilee Year.

Following Yom Kippur, one should begin to prepare for the festival of Succot, four days later, by building a succah and acquiring a lulav and etrog.

A wedding ceremony in Beersheba, Israel.

READING 15
The Life Cycle

We have noted that each week is marked by the Sabbath, and that the cycle of annual holidays gives special meaning to each year of life. These cycles of the week and year are important aspects of what it means to be Jewish. The life cycle itself poses special occasions which Judaism affirms in religious ways. To highlight this fact we shall briefly examine marriage, birth, circumcision, bar mitzvah and bat mitzvah, and death. In all aspects of life the Jew strives to serve God and observe His commandments.

The family, which begins with each marriage, is one of the most sacred aspects of Jewish life.

A. The Wedding Ceremony*
HAYIM HALEVY DONIN

Jewish wedding ceremonies are made up of two parts:

• Betrothal or Sanctification (*Kiddushin*), during which the bride is betrothed to the groom as he places a ring upon her finger and says to her: Be sanctified (betrothed) to me with this ring in accordance with the law of Moses and Israel.

With this statement, and the bride's consent, she becomes his wife. This part requires the presence of two qualified witnesses.

*From Donin, *To Be a Jew*, pp. 287–89, 271.

- Marriage (*Nisuin*), is the consummation of the betrothal. It is symbolized by the bride and groom standing beneath the covering (*hupah*) while the Seven Benedictions (*Sheva Brakhot*) are recited. The recitation of these benedictions requires the presence of a minyan.

The blessings appropriate for these two parts of the ceremony are said over a cup of wine by those officiating. The bride and groom drink from the wine.

Since a wedding contract (*ketuba*), which obligates the husband to support his wife, must be drawn up prior to the ceremony, it is customary for this ketuba to be read during the wedding ceremony between the Kiddushin and the Nisuin.

The custom is not to use rings with diamonds or other precious stones for the ceremony. This is related to the age-old desire to avoid any possibility of fraud which would legally invalidate the marriage. (If the bride's consent to the marriage was motivated by the value of the gift that she was getting and the "precious" stones turned out to be fake, or of far less value than she assumed, grounds for invalidating the marriage would exist.) If a ring with precious stones is used and the bride is aware of its value, there is no question as to the validity of the marriage ceremony.

Aramaic blessings are the decorative framework of this ketuba *from Isfahan, Persia, made in 1872. The lions are Persia's national symbols.*

The ring that is given to the bride at the ceremony may not be borrowed, but *must* belong to the groom. The ring is regarded as a gift to the bride and not just as an object used in a symbolic act. One cannot give away something that one has only borrowed and does not himself own.

If there is a family heirloom which possesses a sentimental value and the couple wants to use it for the ceremony, it may be done if the groom acquires it from its legal owner as a gift or through purchase. Then he is free to give it to his bride. The ring becomes hers to do with as she wishes.

It is customary to break a small glass at the conclusion of the wedding ceremony to recall the destruction of the ancient Temple in Jerusalem in 70 C.E. by the Romans. "Breaking a glass" and similar practices on other occasions is called for by the Mishna to recall the destruction.

Though the Jewish State was reestablished in 1948 and Jewish sovereignty over the Temple Mount returned in 1967, the Temple itself has not yet been restored. Thus, the broken glass continues to symbolize the incompleteness of the religious restoration of Israel.

The *hupah* covering symbolizes the consummation of the marriage. This is also indicated by having the bride and groom retire to a room by themselves for a short period of privacy immediately following the ceremony.

The festive meal that follows the ceremony is classified as a seudat mitzvah, a religious feast. The *Sheva Brakhot* that were said at the wedding ceremony are repeated at the conclusion of the wedding dinner as well.

It is a great mitzvah to "make the groom and bride merry." Music, dancing, and expressions of great joy traditionally accompany all Jewish wedding ceremonies.

Wedding ceremonies may not take place on the Sabbath nor on the festivals (even the Intermediate days of Pesach and Succot), nor during the three weeks from the seventeenth of Tammuz through Tish b'Av, nor during a thirty-day period during Sefira, nor on a regular fast day.

Marriage brings the potential of new life in the birth of children. Rabbi Donin provides some basic insights into the importance of such an event:

Those who bring a child into the world must recognize the basic obligation they have toward providing for the infant the loving care it craves and physical attention it needs. And they must recognize the obligation they have for providing the moral guidance the child should have. There is no more important role in life than raising a child to responsible adulthood.

At birth, man is pure, free of all sin. The daily morning prayer taken from the Talmud (Berakhot 60b) says it succinctly: "O my God, the soul which you gave me is pure, you created it, you fashioned it, you breathed it into me." "Blessed shall you be in your coming in" (Deut. 28:6) is interpreted as meaning also "in your coming into this world" (Baba Mezia 107a). It is only in the course of life that acts contrary to God's will accumulate, weighing down the soul. The course set for a child by its parents during his first days and early years is worth the most serious reflection and attention.

B. Naming of Children*
HAYIM HALEVY DONIN

A male child is named during the ceremony of the Covenant of the Circumcision (brit milah); a female child is named in the synagogue the week following her birth when the father is called up to the Torah and a prayer (*mi she-bierakh*) is made for the health of the mother and the newborn infant.

The full Hebrew name as used for all religious purposes and Hebrew legal documents is: *name* ben (son of) *father's name,* or *name* bat (daughter of) *father's name.* If the father is of Priestly or Levitical descent, the title Ha-Kohen or Ha-Levi is appended to the name. (Aside from those who are identified as descendants of the tribe of Levi and of the Kohen class, all other Jews are classified simply as *Yisrael,* Israel.)

*From Donin, *To Be a Jew,* pp. 271–73.

There are no other religious or halakhic guidelines pertaining to the naming of Jewish children, although in the United States, the rabbis are probably asked more questions about what is and is not permissible in this area than about any other single area of ritual, moral, or ethical conduct.

In the Diaspora, where children are generally given gentile names in the civil birth records, the giving of an additional Yiddish or Hebrew name provides an important identification with the Jewish people and the Hebrew faith. It is this Hebrew or Yiddish name that is given at the brit or in the synagogue, as the case may be, which is thereafter used for all religious purposes, religious documents and prayers. It is by this name that a person is called up to the Torah and that one uses in offering prayers for one's health, in drawing up a wedding contract, etc.

If the Hebrew name given at birth is never referred to by a family and is never used in the synagogue, it obviously loses all significance, and the so-called "naming" was, in retrospect, a futile and meaningless exercise. In this instance, the *real* name of the person—even for religious documents—is the name by which he is actually called, be it an Anglo-Saxon, French or German name.

There is a widespread custom among Jews, particularly those of Ashkenazic background, to name a child after a closely deceased relative whose memory they wish to honor and perpetuate.

Although there is no religious obligation to do so, most seem anxious to follow this time-honored custom. It is a noble and worthy custom, but young parents should not deceive themselves. The custom loses all meaning and no one's memory is really honored if the name that the child is given is never used, is forgotten by all, and the child is actually called by another name. Similarly, the custom has little significance if the only relationship between the child's name and the name of the deceased is a common first letter.

The formal naming of a child is *not* a mystical rite through which the child is introduced into Judaism. In other words, "giving a Jewish name" does not by itself provide status as a Jew if the other requisites of Jewishness are absent. Are there not many gentiles whose names are thoroughly Hebraic or Biblical?

On the other hand, the absence of a "formal naming" either at the brit or at the synagogue, or the absence of a distinctively Hebraic name, does not detract from one's Jewish status, *if* all other requisites are present. (There have been occasions in Jewish history when at the "formal naming," the child was given a distinctively non-Jewish or non-Hebraic name. Alexander, taken from Alexander the Great, is one such example of a name that has come down in Jewish families as a "Jewish" name.)

The revival of Hebrew language and culture, the reestablishment of the State of Israel, and the desire to identify as Jews on the part of Diaspora

Jewry should encourage young parents to use Biblical and Hebraic names, both classical and contemporary, not only for the "formal naming" and for religious purposes, but also as the *legal* name of the child to be recorded in the civil birth records, the name by which he or she will *really* be known to all.

C. Three Rites of Passage*
JACOB NEUSNER

The three rites examined in this reading are circumcision, bar mitzvah, and death. Bar mitzvah, as well as bat mitzvah, is described more fully in the reading that follows.

The covenant between God and Israel is not a mere theological abstraction, nor is it effected only through laws of community and family life. It is quite literally engraved on the flesh of every male Jewish child through the rite of circumcision, *brit milah,* the covenant of circumcision.

Circumcision must take place on the eighth day after birth, normally in the presence of a quorum of ten adult males. Elijah is believed to be present. A chair is set for him, based upon the legend that Elijah complained to God that Israel neglected the covenant (I Kings 19:10–14). God therefore ordered him to come to every circumcision so as to witness the loyalty of the Jews to the covenant. The *mohel,* or circumciser, is expert at the operation. The blessing is said, "Praised are You . . . who sanctified us with Your commandments and commanded us to bring the son into the covenant of Abraham our father." The wine is blessed, "Praised are You, Lord our God, who sanctified the beloved from the womb and set a statute into his very flesh, and his parts sealed with the sign of the holy covenant. On this account, Living God, our portion and rock, save the beloved of our flesh from destruction, for the sake of his covenant placed in our flesh. Blessed are You . . . who makes the covenant."

The advent of puberty is marked by the *Bar Mitzvah* rite, at which a young man becomes obligated to keep the commandments; *bar* means "son, or subject to," and *mitzvah* means "commandment." The young man is called to pronounce the benediction over a portion of the Torah lection in the synagogue and is given the honor of reading the prophetic passage as well. In olden times, it was not so important an occasion as it has become in modern America.

Only when a Jew achieves intelligence and self-consciousness, normally at puberty, is he expected to accept the full privilege of *mitzvah,* commandment, and to regard himself as *commanded* by God. Judaism

A boy reading from the Torah at his bar mitzvah.

*From Jacob Neusner, *The Way of Torah: An Introduction to Judaism,* 2d ed. (Encino, Calif.: Dickenson Publishing Co., 1974), pp. 41–42.

perceives the commandments as expressions of one's acceptance of the yoke of the kingdom of heaven, submission to God's will. That acceptance cannot be coerced, but requires thoughtful and complete affirmation. The *Bar Mitzvah* thus represents the moment that the young Jew first assumes full responsibility before God to keep the commandments.

At the onset of death, the dying Jew says a confession:

My God and God of my fathers, accept my prayer. . . .
Forgive me for all the sins which I have committed in my lifetime. . . .
Accept my pain and suffering as atonement and forgive my wrong-doing for against you alone have I sinned. . . .
I acknowledge that my life and recovery depend on You.
May it be Your will to heal me.
Yet if You have decreed that I shall die of this affliction,
May my death atone for all sins and transgressions which I have committed before You.
Shelter me in the shadow of your wings.
Grant me a share in the world to come.
Father of orphans and Guardian of widows, protect my beloved family. . . .
Into your hand I commit my soul. You redeem me, O Lord God of truth.
Hear O Israel, the Lord is our God, the Lord alone.
The Lord He is God.
The Lord He is God.[1]

The corpse is carefully washed and always protected. The body is covered in a white shroud, then laid in a coffin, and buried. Normally burial takes place on the day of death or on the following day. Once in the grave, three pieces of broken pottery are laid on the eyes and mouth, as signs of their vanity. A handful of dirt from the land of Israel is laid under the head. The family recites the *kaddish,* a . . . prayer of sanctification of God's name. In it no reference to death occurs. The prayer expresses the hope that the Messiah will soon come, "speedily, in our days," and that "he who brings harmony to the heavens will make peace on earth." The mourners remain at home for a period of seven days and continue to recite the memorial *kaddish* for eleven months.

D. Bar-Mitzva and Bas-Mitzva*

HERMAN WOUK

BAR-MITZVA

Bar-mitzva means "son of the commandment." The ceremony is the next milestone in a Jewish child's days; his entrance into a responsible religious life.

[1] *A Rabbi's Manual,* ed. Jules Harlow (New York: Rabbinical Assembly of America, 1965), p. 96.

*From Herman Wouk, *This Is My God* (New York: Doubleday & Co., 1959), pp. 142–47.

In my novel, *Marjorie Morningstar,* I did my best to portray a bar-mitzva with accuracy and affection. I thought I succeeded pretty well, but for my pains I encountered the most bitter and violent objections from some fellow Jews. I had, they asserted, made a sacred occasion seem comical. There were comic touches in the picture, of course, but I believe these lay in the folkway as it exists, not in the imagination of the writer.

It is a sad people that does not have humorous excess as part of its life on one occasion or another. The Dickensian Christmas is the nearest thing in literature I know to an American bar-mitzva. It has in much the same degree the fantastic preparations, the incredible eating, the enormous wassailing, the swirl of emotions and of family mixups, all superimposed with only partial relevance on a religious solemnity. Christmas in the books of Dickens bursts with extravagant vitality, and so does our bar-mitzva. We Jews are a folk of great natural gusto. In the freedom of the United States, where for the first time in centuries we have known equality of opportunity, we have made of the bar-mitzva a blazing costly jubilee. I do not see that there is anything wrong with that. The American coming-out party is not too different. If the religious occasion really held its own, and retained its meaning, all would be well. My reservation about the American bar-mitzva is much the same as the doubts of some Christian clergymen about the department-store Yuletide. The risk exists that the mere machinery of pleasure can work to obliterate the meaning of the event, leaving the celebration a tuneful and colorful hurricane whirling about an empty center.

The event itself is both moving and important.

Like any other way of life, Judaism requires training, beginning when intelligence appears in the infant. A child does not develop the mind to grasp the concepts, nor the stability to hold to the disciplines, until the age of thirteen. The father then formally gives up the burden of his son's religious duties. The boy takes them on himself. He begins to pray in phylacteries, and on the Sabbath nearest his birthday he receives an *aliya,* a call to the Torah, to speak the blessing over a part of the weekly reading, a privilege of male adults. This call marks his new status.

The most honorific call in the popular view is the last, the *maftir,* because it includes reading the weekly piece from the Prophets. The custom long ago arose in the European communities to give the maftir to a boy on his bar-mitzva Sabbath. That is what we do still.

But of course this custom took hold in a time of general compulsory Hebrew education. For the ordinary European Jewish boy, chanting a maftir in its special melody was no harder than for an American boy of thirteen to pick up a newspaper and read it aloud. All this changed completely when the main body of Jewry shifted to the United States, with a catastrophic drop in Hebrew culture. The American Jewish boy who could read a page of Hebrew prophecy aloud without stumbling was exceptional. One who could translate it at sight, or could chant it without long painful practice, was almost a freak.

Nevertheless the existing custom was to give the boy a maftir. And so during two generations in the United States countless boys who barely knew the Hebrew alphabet were schooled to parrot foreign words in a strange musical mode, by dint of coaching stretched over a year or more. This uninforming and disagreeable process was, for the majority of them, the sum total of their exposure to Judaism.

The damage was great. The boys could see—and the sages were quite right in turning over religious responsibility to boys of thirteen, for they can perceive and evaluate very sharply—the phoniness of what they were doing. The bored coaches who for pay drove them through dreary chanting sessions every night for a year, the crutches of transliterated Hebrew and recordings, did not escape their satiric eyes. They judged that they were being drilled to palm themselves off as something they were not—properly trained young Hebrew scholars.

And yet how inevitable it all was, and is! Which parents would be first to admit that their children were unskilled in Hebrew, when the custom was to go through a pretense that they were skilled? Human nature being what it is, the choice for the parents of ill-educated boys was to give them the customary bar-mitzva or none at all. For a long time the American rabbis were overborne by the momentum of the custom. The rationale was, "Better this than nothing." At last the evil results became too evident to ignore. Now a new and long-overdue procedure is gaining ground.

What is happening is that educators are harnessing the custom instead of being stampeded and trampled by it. Since parents and children alike have been regarding the bar-mitzva as a graduation, the rabbis have begun to treat it as such; and to require, as in any graduation, satisfying evidence of knowledge before conferring the diploma. The rote maftir under this rule no longer answers. The lad has to pass serious examinations in Hebrew, in the classics, in the laws of the faith, and in the history of Jewry. If he cannot, the rabbis do not permit the family to take over the synagogue for an empty ceremony. This means serious training has to start, at the latest, by the age of eight or nine. Judaism cannot be crammed into a boy in a year, though a maftir can be.

This policy takes courage in the rabbi and firm backing by his trustees. But since it is the obvious alternative to a continuing disaster in education, it is emerging year by year into more general use. As it takes hold, the Jewish faith stands some chance of being judged by the new generation—even if on the very simplest terms—for what it truly is. Our religion has its hard points, but it is colorful and powerful, and for four thousand years it has been interesting. It is not a chant of gibberish, which is all that the most sublime chapter in Isaiah can be to an insufficiently trained boy.

Some people of late, in a reaction to the extravagance of the American bar-mitzva, have dropped the public gala, appropriating the cost of it either as a gift to charity or as a fund to send the boy in later years on a trip to the Holy Land. This austerity seems commendable, but I wonder if it will become a rule. There is a time for everything. To provide a grand feast at such a turning point in life is an old and strong human impulse. Fireworks in season are always welcome, though they blaze and die at high cost in a short time.

When the overburdened bar-mitzva boy used to say in his memorized speech (a vestigial gesture at a scholarly discourse, now on the wane), "Today I am a man," he was of course speaking metaphorically, as his small stature, pink smooth cheeks, and breaking voice usually indicated. The manhood conferred by this event is ceremonial. The father does not expect him to start earning a living, or go to sleep at night without being ordered to, or do his schoolwork with enthusiasm, or begin reading the *Wall Street Journal*. Judaism simply holds that the boy is bright enough and advanced enough now to start operating as a Jew. He is out of his intellectual infancy. As soon as he is, the traditional masculine duties fall on him.

BAS-MITZVA

As sometimes happens with hurricanes, the whirling tempest of the American bar-mitzva has spun off a minor whirlwind called a bas-mitzva. The rationale is that girls no less than boys enter into religious obligations when they reach early adolescence, and that therefore there is no real reason why a fuss should not mark the event for girls as well as for boys.

It is easy enough to understand why there was no "bas-mitzva" for thousands of years and why it has sprung up now. Traditionally girls are exempt from advanced Hebrew studies because they are exempt from most of Jewish ritual. Our faith put the formal structure on the men to uphold, leaving the women free for their family tasks; probably the only way the system could work. The bar-mitzva when it came was a minor synagogue formality, not a family Fourth of July. A girl would have been out of her head to agitate for the burdens of scholarship that engrossed her brothers from the age of five onward for the sake of that formality; and parents would have been fools to impose them on her. But when the intensive training of boys dwindled; when the bar-mitzva became a huge festival, earned at the price of some mechanical drilling which a girl could do as well as a boy; when there were no other visible burdens or consequences; when the boy, after the fun was over, dropped all Hebrew study and most observance, the girls and the parents saw no reason why they should not have a "bas-mitzva."

This girl is reading from the Torah at her bas-mitzva.

The difficulty of course has been to provide the proper synagogue solemnity for girls where none has existed since Judaism began. Since there is no custom, improvisation has come into play. The bas-mitzva is often a sort of graduation from Sunday-school training, or at least the completion of one stage. In traditional synagogues the bas-mitzva does not exist. Among the other denominations it has not taken on the pomp and circumstance of the bar-mitzva. In the nature of things it hardly can.

READING 16
Worship

A. Prayer*
MILTON STEINBERG

THE BRIDGE OF PRAYER
Prayer is the bridge between man and God.

With the intellect one figures out that God *is* and also something of what He must be.

In intuition one experiences Him.

In revelation one receives testimony concerning Him, more or less definitive according to the credence given it.

In the good life one charts a course by His light.

In ritual one celebrates Him.

But only in prayer does one establish a soul to soul interchange with Him.

Prayer then consists in two elements: that a soul shall be oriented toward God; and that, whether with words or not, it shall address Him.

Since man turns to God in many moods and designs, prayers are equally numerous and diverse as to temper and purpose. Certain types, however, recur with high frequency, no doubt because they articulate common and elemental emotions.

Of these the most notable are:

- The prayer of *contemplation,* in which man meditates on God and His will;

*From Milton Steinberg, *Basic Judaism* (New York: Harcourt, Brace & World, 1947), pp. 117–25.

- The prayer of *adoration,* in which the greatness and mystery of God are considered;
- The prayer of *thanksgiving,* in which, having experienced God's goodness, man puts into words his gratitude and indebtedness;
- The prayer of *affirmation,* which crystallizes the faith of the believer and his aspirations;
- The prayer of *resignation,* in which, his own devices and strength exhausted, man casts his burdens on the Lord;
- The prayer of *penitence,* wherein the guilty conscience confesses its guilt and appeals for purification from it;
- The prayer of *protest,* the pouring forth of human indignation against the injustices of the world and the voiced demand that they be set right;
- The prayer of *quest,* in which, lost and confused, man gropes for light and direction, sometimes for the very God to whom he addresses his supplications;
- The prayer of *petition,* in which the heart's desires are asked for, whether they be things physical or spiritual, whether for self or for others.

Of these major categories of prayer, examples can be found almost anywhere in life and letters but with extraordinary wealth and profusion in Scripture—the Book of Psalms in particular—in rabbinic literature, and especially in the established Jewish prayer books. . . .

WORSHIP

Man is not himself only, he is a participant in his community. Hence it is not enough that he shall address God in his solitariness; he must turn to Him in his other aspect as well.

Man's prayer as a social being is worship.

Worship does not have to be public, though that is its most usual circumstance; nor need it follow a pre-established program as to text and rite, though it almost always does. Any prayer or ceremonial is worship if it voices either the community or a single person speaking as a member of the group.

The Tradition expects the Jew to set up his private relationship with God, to confront Him when and as the spirit moves him.

"Would that a man might pray the livelong day," was the hope of an ancient rabbi.

But a Jew is also an Israelite, a fellow in the Jewish people. Wherefore Judaism has established a schedule of times and seasons at which he shall come to God in this capacity. It has laid down the principles he shall affirm on such occasions, the ideals he shall assert, even the *personal* expectations which, being a Jew, he ought to entertain. It has gone so far as to work out the very words and ritual gestures in which all these are to be expressed. For this is the nature of the accepted Jewish prayerbooks for weekdays, Sabbaths, festivals, and holy days: they state the fundamental minimal aspirations required of a traditional Jew on his own behalf and cherished by Jewry as a collectivity.

PRECONDITIONS FOR PRAYER

Highly as the tradition esteems prayer—indeed, *because* it values it so highly—it insists that it be discreetly used.

Prayer to be efficacious [effective] must be sincere. It must bespeak genuine, not pretended aspirations.

Prayer to be efficacious must be alive. The dead, mechanical mumbling of words is not a prayer but a travesty.

Prayer to be efficacious must be predicated on true conceptions of God and reality. Not that only metaphysicians and theologians may pray. The simplest person possessed of the most naive notions has equal rights and privileges with anyone else—often, in his spiritual ingenuousness, greater. But there must be behind all errors and misconceptions some bit of valid insight, religious or moral.

The Western Wall in the Old City of Jerusalem is a place of prayer and pilgrimage sacred to the Jewish people.

Prayer to be efficacious must place God's will higher than man's and, when the two conflict, must subordinate the latter to the former. Always it must begin with the postulate, implied or expressed, "May it be Thy will." Always it must close with the thought, verbalized or silent, "Thy will be done."

Prayer to be efficacious must be ethical; not seeking what is contrary to moral principle; not setting the aspirations of any man above the equally legitimate aspirations of his fellow, or above the hopes of men in the mass.

It must come from one possessed of clean hands or from one earnestly desirous of becoming clean. A man shall not approach God while the spoil of the poor is hidden in his household or seek forgiveness for transgressions with the design of sinning again so soon as his prayers are done.

It must reach out for the highest and noblest, not the second-best, of which a man is capable.

Last of all, prayer to be efficacious must not seek the impossible. Of which abuse of prayer the Talmud quotes two telling examples:

A man whose wife is about to bear a baby shall not pray: "May it be Thy will that the child carried by my wife prove to be a boy (or a girl)." Such a prayer, says the rabbi, is nonsensical. For the unborn babe in actuality is already either a boy or a girl.

Again, the rabbis insist, a man who hears a fire alarm sounding in his city shall not pray: "May it be Thy will that the conflagration be not in my home." And that for two reasons: first, such a prayer asks in effect that the misfortune befall another, which is immoral; and second, the fire is already where it is.

In sum, a man shall not pray that facts be not facts.

THE EFFICACY OF PRAYER

Prayer to be efficacious . . .

But what according to the Tradition is the efficacy of prayer? Does it avail?

That God responds to prayer is a basic belief of Judaism.

On the extent of the response the Jewish faithful disagree, some being optimists or maximalists on the issue; others, if not pessimists, are at least circumspect or minimalist.

All Jews acknowledge the conditions and limits of prayer we have listed. Even the most sanguine concede further that it does not replace human effort. One should not address God, fold his hands, and wait for his wish to come true—at least not if one is true to Judaism. One prays but works, too. A sick man calls on God but on his physician also. Otherwise, the Tradition holds, he is a sinner against his own soul and against God who endowed the surgeon with his skill and drugs with their properties.

Given the right use, prayer may, in the Jewish view, achieve the following:

It can first of all—and on this all religious Jews are agreed—release pent-up feelings, crystallize inarticulate thoughts, muster the will, and all in all prove of great psychological worth.

It can further—and on this too there is general assent—tap levels of personality otherwise not to be reached, setting free the full resources of the spirit.

On why prayer possesses this peculiar potency the circumspect and the optimists differ. The former contend that the process is purely naturalistic, being the very normal response of man's psyche to an idea as compelling as that of God. The latter are far bolder, holding that in prayer man is inundated by the divine; an experience quite beyond natural law and not to be accounted for by it.

All religious Jews agree next that prayer exerts an influence on things outside man. But once again there is disagreement on the *how*. The minimalists maintain that prayer sways the physical world only through human agencies. The maximalists insist that quite apart from man it impinges directly on reality.

Then, is the maximalist position that the sky, as it were, is the limit, that prayer can accomplish any result whatsoever?

On this point the maximalists themselves divide. Some argue that prayer must function within natural law as science describes it and that no accomplishment is to be awaited beyond its confines.

Others, super-maximalists as they may be called, contend that nature is but a tool in God's hand. Nothing then can be impossible, not even a miracle. For, as Scripture asks: "Can anything be too wonderful for God?"

Religious Jews, it should be clear by now, run a wide gamut in their evaluation of prayer.

It remains to be pointed out that, while the rule is not absolute, most traditionalists are maximalists, most modernists minimalists.

THE DAILY REGIMEN

This is the normal Jewish day as blocked out by the Tradition and practiced by all Jews in the past and by orthodox Jews to the present. In the main, this regimen is prescribed, being a matter of ritual law. But some of it represents folk-practice or local custom or individual option; all of it, including the legalistically determined elements, is subject in some degree to diversity of interpretation. So, within a framework of uniformity, a fair measure of variety and freedom is achieved.

On awakening and before he so much as stirs, a Jew thinks of his gratitude to God for life and the return of consciousness. "I give thanks before Thee," he prays, "King living and eternal, that Thou hast mercifully restored my soul to me; great is Thy faithfulness."

Then he rises, and with each act in the process of getting up recites an ordained blessing: on washing his hands and face, prescribed as his first duty; on setting foot on the ground; on attending to his bodily needs; on donning an undergarment adorned with the fringes commanded by the Torah. So he refers his every move to God and fulfills the instruction that a man shall be strong as a lion and fleet as a deer to do the will of his Father who is in heaven.[1]

Then he prepares for formal worship. Again he wraps himself in a fringed garment, save that this time it is the large, outer prayer-shawl worn only during religious exercises or sacred study. Next he takes up his *tefilin,* two little boxes encasing selected passages from Scripture, and, by means of the leather thongs with which they are equipped, ties them to himself, so fulfilling in utmost literalness the Biblical commandment: "Thou shalt bind them (i.e., God's words) for a sign upon thine hand, and they shall be for frontlets between thine eyes." One of these containers he fastens to his left arm, next to his heart; a symbolic commitment of heart

---

[1]That the obligations of Jewish observance devolve more fully on males than females is due in part to the fact that Judaism had its beginnings in the Orient. It represents also a deliberate policy of the rabbis who, solicitous over woman's role as a home-maker, exempted her from "all positive precepts [as opposed to prohibitions] in which time constitutes a determining factor." In other words, she is relieved of all clock-bound commitments likely to interfere with her role as wife and mother.

and hand to God's will. The other he affixes to his forehead above his eyes, making a like consecration of his intellect. Finally he ties the leather thong about his left hand in a mystical knot suggestive of the divine name. With each act he recites apposite benedictions. With the last act, moreover, the entwining of the fingers, he pledges himself to God with Hosea's magnificent lines of spiritual espousal:

> I will betroth thee unto Me forever;
> Yea, I will betroth thee unto Me in righteousness, and in justice, And in loving kindness, and in compassion.
> And I will betroth thee unto Me in faithfulness;
> And thou shalt know the Lord.

So, bound to God, wedded to His will, the Jew is ready for his morning devotions which consist in the recitation of Psalms; in prayers, some of personal preference, others affirming the group faith and ideals of Israel; and in passages from Scripture and rabbinic literature included for purposes of religious study.

The Tradition prefers that this order of worship be performed in a synagogue and with a congregation, though it accepts it when executed in private. Whether in one place or the other, it is not brief; as printed in one of the popular editions of the traditional prayerbook, it runs to almost ninety pages and may take as much as an hour to complete.

Not until it is finished and the *tefilin* have been doffed may a Jew partake of food. Ritual, however, continues, attending the breakfast and for that matter all other meals. Hands are washed and a brief benediction is spoken before bread is broken; a longer grace follows the repast. What is more, observances persist thereafter. Twice more, once in the afternoon and once again at dusk, the Jew engages in formal worship. Between times he invokes God's name frequently, since the Tradition ordains benedictions for almost every juncture of his life. Should he partake of food between meals, should he don a new garment, taste a fruit just then in season, see a flash of lightning, hear thunder, catch a glimpse of the ocean or of a rainbow or of trees burgeoning in the spring, encounter one learned in Torah or in secular lore, hear good news or be the recipient of bad—for almost every conceivable contingency there exists a brief but appropriate word of blessing. Furthermore, it is expected that he shall dedicate some period of each day to the study of the Tradition, either by himself or as a member of a class.

And at night on retiring he prays still again in gratitude for sleep, in reaffirmation of his faith, and in self-commitment to divine care; so that the day ends as it began, with the consciousness of God.

One wonders, perhaps, what time remains for work and play. Less, of course, than is available to a person who engages in fewer religious activities or none at all. But more than one would suppose. Most of the

Tefillin are not worn on the Sabbath and festival days, for on those days one needs no other reminder of God and his laws.

observances we have described are performed concurrently with the acts they mark and take no time whatsoever; many others require only a fleeting moment. As for the rest, the Tradition is not perturbed. What, it asks, are the supreme themes of human existence? Are they not God and the good life? Can time, then, be better spent than in their cultivation?

B. The Order of the Service*

EVELYN GARFIEL

THE STRUCTURE OF THE SERVICE

No matter at what point in the long morning service they arrived, Jews of a generation ago seemed always able to "find the place" in their Prayer Books at once, though no one thought of announcing the pages to them. It was not because all Jews were so very learned, that they could accomplish this feat; there is another explanation.

First, of course, everyone recited the prayers often. Men prayed three times daily, and women at least once a week on the Sabbath. Naturally, they were all familiar with the liturgy. But habit and repetition are not the whole answer. The second reason lies not in the people but in the book itself. For the *Siddur* is not a series of hymns, psalms, and meditations strung together by chance or by the whim of some ancient priest. The *Prayer Book* has structure, form that developed out of its history, as we have seen; and that form was carefully guarded by religious law (*Halakhah*). There is a good reason—valid within its own framework—for the location of each prayer in the liturgy. The architecture of the service as a whole is a steadfast pattern common to all the services—morning, afternoon and evening, daily, Sabbath and Festival. Neither minor variations nor the major additions for certain special occasions nor the prayers added by later generations can blur that pattern for those who understand the essential structure of the service.

Two basic prayers dominate this common pattern. One is the *Shema* and the other is the *Amidah* (Standing or Silent Prayer). ". . . and thou shalt speak of them [words of Torah] . . . when thou liest down [at night] and when thou risest up [in the morning] . . .," says the *Shema* (Deuteronomy 6,7). The Rabbis understood this as a direct command to recite these verses evening and morning. Therefore they made the *Shema* the core of the evening and the morning services every day. Tradition— already old in their day—supported them in this, for the *Shema* had for generations been recited in the Temple every day, long before there was a synagogue.

*From Evelyn Garfiel, *The Service of the Heart* (North Hollywood, Calif.: Wilshire Book Co., 1958), pp. 49–51.

The *Amidah,* the second basic prayer, is called by the Rabbis *Hatefillah,* the Prayer. It consists of nineteen separate benedictions, to be said in silence by each person alone, three times a day—morning, afternoon, and night. All the other Psalms and prayers in the *Siddur* are woven into and around this unchanging framework, as introduction, explanation, or conclusion.

On Sabbaths and Festivals there are two major additions to the morning service: the Torah is read, and there is a series of benedictions known as *Musaf* (Addition) which follows the reading of the Torah. The *Musaf* is a substitute for and a reminder of the additional sacrifice offered in the Temple on Sabbaths and Festivals. On Sabbaths and on Fast Days, the Torah is read at the afternoon service as well.

In spite of all these additions, the configuration of the service is not destroyed. The variety gives the service added latitude and interest. Complexity and unity are the qualities that distinguish every work of art. We find them both in the *Siddur* if we know how to look for them. A sonnet has no greater perfection of form than this, the ancient Jewish service of prayer.

THE ANCIENT OUTLINE OF ALL THE SERVICES

I. *Shaharit* (Morning Service)
1. Preliminary blessings and Psalms
2. The *Shema* (including two blessings before and one after)
3. The *Amidah* (Standing or Silent Prayer)
4. Reading of the Torah (on Monday, Thursday, Sabbath, and Festivals)
5. *Musaf* (on Sabbath and Festivals only)
6. *Alaynu* (God's Kingship)
7. Mourners' *Kaddish*
8. Closing Hymn

II. *Minhah* (Afternoon Service)
1. *Ashray,* a Psalm
2. "A redeemer shall come to Zion" (on Sabbath and Festivals)
3. The *Amidah*
4. Reading of the Torah (on Sabbath and Fast Days)
5. *Alaynu*
6. Mourners' *Kaddish*

III. *Ma'ariv* (Evening Service)
1. Short Reading from Psalms
2. The *Shema* (including two blessings before and two after)
3. The *Amidah*
4. *Alaynu*
5. Mourners' *Kaddish*

C. Selected Prayers from the Prayer Book*

INTRODUCTORY PRAYERS

How goodly are your tents, O Jacob, your dwelling places, O Israel. O Lord, through Thine abundant kindness I come into Thy house, and reverently I worship Thee in Thy holy sanctuary. I love the habitation of Thy house, the place where Thy glory dwelleth. Here I bow down and worship Thee, my Lord and Maker. Accept my prayer, O Lord, and answer me with Thy great mercy and with Thy saving truth. Amen.

How lovely are Thy tabernacles, O Lord of Hosts!
My soul yearns, yea, even pines for the courts of the Lord;
My heart sings for joy unto the living God.
One thing have I asked of the Lord, that will I seek after:
That I may dwell in the house of the Lord all the days of my life,
To behold the graciousness of the Lord, and to enter His sanctuary.
Teach me Thy way, O Lord,
And lead me in an even path.
With Thee is the fountain of life,
In Thy light do we see the light.

Almighty God, we have come into Thy sanctuary to commune with Thee. Be Thou our strength, our hope, our guide. Give purpose to our work, meaning to our struggle and direction to our striving. Cause us to understand that only through human betterment, true fellowship and deeds of kindness can we feel Thy presence. May this, our Sabbath worship, bring peace to our hearts and strengthen our desire to live in peace with all our fellowmen. Amen.

WELCOMING THE SABBATH

Come Let Us Sing
Psalm 95

O come, let us sing unto the Lord;
Let us joyfully acclaim the Rock of our salvation.

Let us approach Him with thanksgiving,
And acclaim Him with songs of praise.

For great is the Lord,
A King greater than all the mighty.

In His hands are the depths of the earth;
His also are the heights of the mountains.

*From *Sabbath and Festival Prayer Book* (New York: The Rabbinical Assembly of America and the United Synagogue of America, 1946), pp. 2, 5, 15–16, 19, 28, 39, 117, 119, 123–24, 230–37.

The sea is His for He made it;
And His hands formed the dry land.

> Come, let us worship and bow down;
> Let us bend the knee before the Lord, our Maker.

He is our God, and we are the people He shepherds;
Yea, we are the flock He tends.

> O hearken today to His voice:

Harden not your hearts
As you did at Meribah and Massah,[1]
As in the days of trial in the wilderness;

> When your forefathers tried My patience,
> Yea, they tested Me, though they had seen My work.

For forty years was I wroth with that generation,
A people who erred in their hearts,
And did not know My ways.

> Wherefore I vowed in My indignation
> That they should not enter the land where My glory dwelleth.

The inscription on this prayer book reads: "The Lord is King, the Lord was King, and the Lord will be King forever and ever."

EVENING SERVICE—SABBATH AND FESTIVALS

Reader
Bless the Lord who is to be praised.

Congregation and Reader
Praised be the Lord who is blessed for all eternity.

Praised be Thou, O Lord our God, Ruler of the universe, who with Thy word bringest on the evening twilight, and with Thy wisdom openest the gates of the heavens. With understanding Thou dost order the cycles of time and variest the seasons, setting the stars in their courses in the sky, according to Thy will. Thou createst day and night, rolling away the light before the darkness and the darkness before the light. By Thy will the day passes into night; the Lord of heavenly hosts is Thy name. O ever-living God, mayest Thou rule over us forever. Blessed be Thou, O Lord, who bringest on the evening twilight.

With everlasting love hast Thou loved the house of Israel, teaching us Thy Torah and commandments, Thy statutes and judgments. Therefore, O Lord our God, when we lie down and when we rise up, we will meditate on Thy teachings and rejoice forever in the words of Thy Torah and in its commandments, for they are our life and the length of our days. Day and

---

[1]The names Meribah ("quarrel") and Massah ("trial") were given to the place where the Israelites quarreled and questioned the presence of God when they had no water to drink. See Exodus 7:1-7.

night will we meditate upon them. O may Thy love never depart from us. Blessed be Thou, O Lord, who lovest Thy people Israel.

Deuteronomy 6:4–9

Hear, O Israel: the Lord our God, the Lord is One.

Blessed be His glorious kingdom for ever and ever.

Thou shalt love the Lord thy God with all thy heart, with all thy soul, and with all thy might. And these words which I command thee this day shall be in thy heart. Thou shalt teach them diligently unto thy children, speaking of them when thou sittest in thy house, when thou walkest by the way, when thou liest down and when thou risest up. And thou shalt bind them for a sign upon thine hand, and they shall be for frontlets between thine eyes. And thou shalt write them upon the door posts of thy house and upon thy gates.

A Selected Evening Prayer

Cause us, O Lord our God, to lie down in peace, and raise us up again, O our King, unto life. Spread over us Thy tabernacle of peace. Direct us aright through Thine own good counsel. Save us for Thy name's sake. Be Thou a shield about us. Remove from us every enemy, pestilence, sword, famine and sorrow. Help us, O Lord, to resist temptation. Shelter us with Thy protecting love for Thou art our guardian and deliverer. Yea, Thou God and King art gracious and compassionate. Guard our going out and our coming in unto life and peace, henceforth and forevermore. Yea, do Thou spread over us the tabernacle of Thy peace. Blessed be Thou, O Lord, who spreadest the tabernacle of peace over us, over Israel and over Jerusalem.

KIDDUSH

Praised art Thou, O Lord our God, King of the universe, who createst the fruit of the vine.

Praised art Thou, O Lord our God, Ruler of the universe, who hast sanctified us through Thy commandments and hast taken delight in us. In love and favor Thou hast given us the holy Sabbath as a heritage, a reminder of Thy work of creation, first of our sacred days recalling our liberation from Egypt. Thou didst choose us from among the peoples and in Thy love and favor didst sanctify us in giving us Thy holy Sabbath as a joyous heritage. Blessed art Thou, O Lord our God, who hallowest the Sabbath.

MOURNERS' KADDISH

Magnified and sanctified be the name of God throughout the world which He hath created according to His will. May He establish His kingdom during the days of your life and during the life of all the house of Israel, speedily, yea, soon; and say ye, Amen.

Congregation and Mourners

May His great name be blessed for ever and ever.

Mourners

Exalted and honored be the name of the Holy One, blessed be He, whose glory transcends, yea, is beyond all praises, hymns and blessings that man can render unto Him; and say ye, Amen.

May there be abundant peace from heaven, and life for us and for all Israel; and say ye, Amen.

May He who established peace in the heavens, grant peace unto us and unto all Israel; and say ye, Amen.

SERVICE FOR TAKING OUT THE TORAH

There is none like unto Thee among the mighty, O Lord, and there are no deeds like unto Thine. Thy kingdom is an everlasting kingdom and Thy dominion endureth throughout all generations. The Lord reigneth, the Lord hath reigned, the Lord will reign for ever and ever. May the Lord give strength unto His people; may the Lord bless His people with peace.

Father of compassion, may it be Thy will to favor Zion with Thy goodness and rebuild the walls of Jerusalem. For in Thee alone do we trust, O King, high and exalted God, Lord of the universe.

The Ark is opened.

And it came to pass that when the Ark moved forward, Moses said: Rise up, O Lord, and let Thine enemies be scattered; and let them that hate Thee flee before Thee.

For out of Zion shall go forth the Torah, and the word of the Lord from Jerusalem.

Blessed be He who, in His holiness, gave the Torah to His people Israel.

PRAYERS BEFORE THE ARK—SABBATH

Thou Sovereign of the world and Ruler of mankind, as we stand before the open ark of Thy Torah we gratefully acknowledge Thee to be our

Father and our Law-giver. Thou hast bequeathed unto us Thy Law, a sacred heritage for all time. Give us discernment to know and wisdom to understand that Thy Torah is our life and the length of our days. Teach us so to live that we shall be guided by Thy commandments. May Thy Word ever be a lamp unto our feet and a light unto our path, showing us the way to true and righteous living. Amen.

The Reader takes the Scroll of the Torah

Reader and Congregation

Hear, O Israel: the Lord our God, the Lord is One.

Reader and Congregation

One is our God; great is our Lord; holy is His name.

Reader

Extol the Lord with me, and together let us exalt His name.

Reader and Congregation

Thine, O Lord, is the greatness and the power, the glory, the victory and the majesty; for all that is in the heaven and on the earth is Thine. Thine is the kingdom, O Lord, and Thou art exalted supreme above all. Exalt the Lord our God, and worship at His footstool; holy is He. Exalt the Lord our God, and worship at His holy mountain; for the Lord our God is holy.

Reader

May the Father of compassion have mercy upon a people whom He lovingly tended. May He remember the covenant with the patriarchs; may He deliver us from evil times, curb the evil inclination in the people whom He hath tenderly protected, and graciously grant us enduring deliverance. May He abundantly fulfill our desires and grant us salvation and mercy.

May God help, shield and save all who trust in Him; and let us say, Amen. Ascribe greatness unto our God, and render honor to the Torah.

Blessed be He who in His holiness gave the Torah to His people Israel.

Congregation

And you who cleave unto the Lord your God, are alive everyone of you this day.

Those honored by being called to the Torah, recite the following blessings:

Bless the Lord who is to be praised.
Praised be the Lord who is blessed for all eternity.
Blessed art Thou, O Lord our God, King of the Universe, who didst

The rabbi (right) and the cantor place the Torah scroll on the reading desk.

choose us from among all the peoples by giving us Thy Torah. Blessed art Thou, O Lord, Giver of the Torah.

After a section of the Torah has been read, the following blessing is said:

Blessed art Thou, O Lord our God, King of the universe, who in giving us a Torah of truth, hast planted everlasting life within us. Blessed art Thou, O Lord, Giver of the Torah.

Prayer of Thanksgiving

One who has recovered from a serious illness, or has escaped danger, offers the following prayer:

Blessed art Thou, O Lord our God, Ruler of the universe, who in bestowing good upon man beyond his deserving, hast dealt graciously with me.

The Congregation responds:

May He, who hath dealt graciously with you, continue to bestow His favor upon you.

THE AMIDAH

The Amidah is said standing, in silent devotion.

O Lord, open Thou my lips and my mouth shall declare Thy praise.

Praised art Thou, O Lord our God and God of our fathers, God of Abraham, God of Isaac, and God of Jacob, mighty, revered and exalted God. Thou bestowest loving-kindness and possessest all things. Mindful of the patriarchs' love for Thee, Thou wilt in Thy love bring a redeemer to their children's children for the sake of Thy name. . . .

O King, Thou helper, Redeemer and Shield, be Thou praised, O Lord, Shield of Abraham.

Thou, O Lord, art mighty forever. Thou callest the dead to immortal life for Thou art mighty in deliverance. . . .

Thou sustainest the living with loving-kindness, and in great mercy callest the departed to everlasting life. Thou upholdest the falling, healest the sick, settest free those in bondage, and keepest faith with those that sleep in the dust. Who is like unto Thee, Almighty King, who decreest death and life and bringest forth salvation? . . .

Faithful art Thou to grant eternal life to the departed. Blessed art Thou, O Lord, who callest the dead to life everlasting.

Holy art Thou, and holy is Thy name and unto Thee holy beings render praise daily. Blessed art Thou, O Lord, the holy God. . . .

Thou endowest man with knowledge and teachest mortal man understanding. O grant us knowledge, understanding and discernment. Blessed art Thou, O Lord, who bestoweth knowledge upon man.

Bring us back, O our Father, to Thy Torah; draw us near, O our King, to Thy service, and restore us unto Thy presence in wholehearted repentance. Blessed art Thou, O Lord, who desirest repentance.

Forgive us, O our Father, for we have sinned; pardon us, O our King, for we have transgressed. Verily Thou art merciful and forgiving. Blessed art Thou, O gracious Lord, who art abundant in forgiveness.

Behold our affliction and plead our cause. Hasten to redeem us for the sake of Thy name, for Thou art a mighty Redeemer. Blessed art Thou, O Lord, Redeemer of Israel.

Heal us, O Lord, and we shall be healed; save us and we shall be saved, for to Thee we offer praise. Grant complete healing for all our ailments for Thou, O God, art our King, our faithful and merciful Healer. Praised art Thou, O Lord, who healest the sick among Thy people Israel.

Bless this year unto us, O Lord our God, and bless its yield that it may be for our welfare. . . .

Satisfy us out of Thy bounty, O Lord. Do Thou bless this year that it be for us a year of abundance. Praise be Thou, O Lord, who dost bless the years.

Sound the great Shofar proclaiming our freedom. Raise the banner to assemble our exiles, and gather us together from the four corners of the earth. Blessed art Thou, O God, who wilt gather the dispersed of Thy people Israel.

Restore our judges as of yore, and our counsellors as aforetime, and thus remove from us grief and suffering. Reign Thou over us, O Lord, Thou alone in loving-kindness and mercy and vindicate us in judgment. Blessed art Thou, O Lord, Thou King, who lovest righteousness and judgment. . . .

As for slanderers, may their hopes come to naught, and may all wickedness perish. May all Thine enemies be destroyed. Do Thou uproot the dominion of arrogance; crush it and subdue it in our day. Blessed art Thou, O Lord, who breakest the power of the enemy and bringest low the arrogant.

May Thy tender mercies, O Lord our God, be stirred towards the righteous and the pious, towards the leaders of Thy people Israel, towards all the scholars that have survived, towards the righteous proselytes and towards us. Grant Thy favor unto all who faithfully trust in Thee, and may our portion ever be with them. May we never suffer humiliation for in Thee do we put our trust. Blessed art Thou, O Lord, who art the staff and trust of the righteous. . . .

Return in mercy to Jerusalem, Thy city, and dwell therein as Thou hast promised. Rebuild it in our own day as an enduring habitation, and speedily set up therein the throne of David. Blessed art Thou, O Lord, who rebuildest Jerusalem.

Cause the dynasty of David soon to flourish and may it be exalted through Thy saving power, for we daily await Thy deliverance. Blessed art Thou, O Lord, who causest salvation to come forth.

Hear our voice, O Lord our God, have compassion upon us and receive our prayers in loving favor for Thou, O God, hearkenest unto prayers and supplications. Turn us not from Thy presence without Thy blessing, O our King, for Thou hearest the prayers of Thy people Israel with compassion. Blessed art Thou, O Lord, who hearkenest unto prayer.

O Lord our God, be gracious unto Thy people Israel and accept their prayer. Restore the worship to Thy sanctuary and receive in loving favor the supplication of Israel. May the worship of Thy people be ever acceptable unto Thee. . . .

O may our eyes witness Thy return to Zion. Blessed art Thou, O Lord, who restorest Thy divine presence unto Zion.

We thankfully acknowledge Thee, O Lord our God, our fathers' God to all eternity. Our Rock art Thou, our Shield that saves through every generation. We give Thee thanks and we declare Thy praise for all Thy tender care. Our lives we trust into Thy loving hand. Our souls are ever in Thy charge; Thy wonders and Thy miracles are daily with us, evening, morn and noon. O Thou who art all-good, whose mercies never fail us, Compassionate One, whose loving-kindnesses never cease, we ever hope in Thee. . . .

For all this, Thy name, O our King, shall be blessed and exalted for ever and ever. . . .

May all the living do homage unto Thee forever and praise Thy name in truth, O God, who art our salvation and our help. Blessed be thou, O Lord, Beneficent One, unto whom our thanks are due.

Grant lasting peace unto Israel Thy people, for Thou art the Sovereign

Lord of peace; and may it be good in Thy sight to bless Thy people Israel at all times with Thy peace.

Blessed art Thou, O Lord, who blessest Thy people Israel with peace. . . .

O Lord,
Guard my tongue from evil and my lips from speaking guile,
And to those who slander me, let me give no heed.
May my soul be humble and forgiving to all.
Open Thou my heart, O Lord, unto Thy sacred Law,
That Thy statutes I may know and all Thy truths pursue.
Bring to naught designs of those who seek to do me ill;
Speedily defeat their aims and thwart their purposes
For Thine own sake, for Thine own power,
For Thy holiness and Law.
That Thy loved ones be delivered,
Answer us, O Lord, and save with Thy redeeming power.

May the words of my mouth and the meditation of my heart be acceptable unto Thee, O Lord, my Rock and my Redeemer. Thou who establishest peace in the heavens, grant unto us and unto all Israel. Amen.

May it be Thy will, O Lord our God and God of our fathers, to grant our portion in Thy Torah, and may the Temple be rebuilt in our day. There we will serve Thee with awe as in the days of old.

D. Selected Prayers from *Likrat Shabbat**
SIDNEY GREENBERG

Wisdom from the Ethics of the Fathers

Beloved is man
For he was created in the divine image.

A person who brings pleasure to other human beings
Thereby brings delight to the Creator.

If I am not for myself, who will be for me?
But if I am only for myself, what am I?
And if not now, when?

Say little and do much,
And greet everyone with a cheerful face.

*From Rabbi Sidney Greenberg, comp. and trans., *Likrat Shabbat* (Bridgeport, Conn.: The Prayer Book Press, 1975), pp. 65, 70, 71, 92, 93, 98, 99.

Be a disciple of Aaron,
Loving peace and pursuing peace,
Loving your fellow-men,
And drawing them near to the Torah.

> *Do not say, "I shall study when I have leisure";*
> *You may never find the leisure.*

Do not separate yourself from the community;
Judge not another until you are in his place.

> *He who shames his fellow-man in public*
> *Is not worthy of a share in the world to come.*

Who is wise?
He who learns from everyone.

> *Who is strong?*
> *He who controls his passions.*

Who is rich?
He who rejoices in his portion.

> *Who is honorable?*
> *He who honors his fellow-men.*

The world is sustained by three things:
By truth, by justice, and by peace.

> *It is not your duty to finish the work,*
> *But neither are you at liberty to neglect it.*

In Time of Illness

Faithful Father and Healer,
Out of my distress I call upon You.
Hear me and heal me, O God.

You have already sent the gifts of Your goodness:
The skill of my physician, the compassion of others
Who help me, the concern of those I love.
And I pray that I be worthy of these kindnesses.

Keep me trustful in Your love, O God.
Give me strength for today, and hope for tomorrow;
Keep bitterness far from me; let not despair overcome me.
Give me patience when the hours are heavy,
Give me courage when the hurt is great.

Into Your loving hands I commit my spirit,
Both when asleep and when awake.
You are with me; I shall not fear.
Heal me, O God, and I shall be healed.   Amen.

On Behalf of the Sick

"Hope in the Lord;
Be strong and let your heart take courage."

O merciful Father, we pray for the recovery of _____ ,
who is now ill. Grant him (her) renewed strength and confidence. Give
wisdom and skill to those who are helping to bring healing. Help all who
share the anxiety of this illness to be brave, cheerful, and hopeful.

    Inspire us with courage and faith, and grant Your blessings to all who
call upon You.

    Praised are You, O Lord, Healer of the sick.   Amen.

In the Day of Trouble

O Lord, our fathers trusted in You;
They trusted and You delivered them.

They cried unto You and were saved;
They trusted in You and were not ashamed.

O God, keep not silent;
Hold not Your peace and be not still.

For lo, Your enemies are in an uproar,
They take counsel against Your people.

They have said, "Come, let us destroy them as a people,
That the house of Israel be remembered no more."

They have consulted together with one accord;
Against You do they make a covenant.

O Lord, make them like the whirling dust,
As chaff before the wind.

Fill their faces with shame;
O may they seek You, O Lord,

That they may know You alone are the Lord,
The Most High over all the earth.

O Lord of hosts, restore us;
Cause Your spirit to be with us and we shall be saved.

Reveal Yourself in the majesty of Your triumphant power
Over all the inhabitants of Your world.

May every living creature understand
That You have created it,
And may all with life's breath in them declare:

"The Lord, God of Israel, is King
And His dominion rules over all."

Let Me Return

O Lord, You know the thoughts of men
And read the minds of mortals.
You know that with all my heart I desire to serve You.

Cleanse my mind and purify my thoughts
From the vanities of the world.

Save me from all forms of trouble and distress
Which would put a barrier between me and You,
Shutting me out of Your service.

Remove from my shoulder every man-made burden,
And make me single-hearted in devotion
   to Your commandments,
For by them my spirit lives.

Let me return to You with all my heart,
   in perfect repentance.
"Create for me a clean heart, O God.
And put a new steadfast spirit in me."

Peace Means More Than Quiet

Help us, O God, to lie down in peace;
But teach us that peace means more than quiet.

   Remind us that if we are to be at peace at night,
   We must take heed how we live by day.

Grant us the peace that comes from honest dealing,
So that no fear of discovery will haunt our sleep.

   Rid us of resentments and hatreds
   Which rob us of the peace we crave.

Liberate us from enslaving habits
Which disturb us and give us no rest.

   May we inflict no pain, bring no shame,
   And seek no profit by another's loss.

May we so live that we can face
The whole world with serenity.

   May we feel no remorse at night
   For what we have done during the day.

May we lie down in peace tonight,
And awaken tomorrow to a richer and fuller life.   Amen.

Shabbat, a Sample

When God was about to give the Torah to Israel He summoned the people and said to them: "My children, I have something precious that I would like to give you for all time, if you will accept My Torah and observe My Commandments."

The people then asked: "Master of the universe, what is that precious gift You have for us?"

The Holy One, blessed be He, replied, "It is the world to come!"

The people of Israel answered: "Show us a sample of the world to come."

The Holy One, blessed be He, said: "The Shabbat is a sample of the world to come, for that world will be one long Shabbat."

The Pauses Between the Notes

A great pianist was once asked by an ardent admirer: "How do you handle the notes as well as you do?"

The artist answered: "The notes I handle no better than many pianists, but the pauses between the notes—ah! that is where the art resides."

In great living, as in great music, the art may be in the pauses. Surely one of the enduring contributions which Judaism made to the art of living was the Shabbat, "the pause between the notes." And it is to the Shabbat that we must look if we are to restore to our lives the sense of serenity and sanctity which Shabbat offers in such joyous abundance.

The Shabbat Has Kept Us Alive

A Jew who feels a real tie with the life of his people throughout the generations will find it utterly impossible to think of the existence of the Jew without the Shabbat. One can say without exaggeration that more than the Jew has kept the Shabbat, the Shabbat has kept the Jew.

E. The Tallit*

The tallit is the prayer shawl worn by married men in Orthodox synagogues, and by all males past the age of Bar Mitzvah in Conservative and Reform synagogues. It is a composite garment consisting of two main parts, the garment itself and the tzitzit—fringes on the corners which transform the garment from a piece of cloth to a tallit.

LAWS AND CUSTOMS

The tallit is worn by congregants for the Shaharit (Morning) and Musaf (Additional) Services; by the leader of the tefillot at the Minhah

*From Richard Siegel, Michael Strassfeld, and Sharon Strassfeld, comps. and eds., *The Jewish Catalog* (Philadelphia: The Jewish Publication Society of America, 1973), pp. 51-55.

(Afternoon) Services; some also have the leader wear it for the Maariv (Evening) Services of Shabbat, festivals, and holy days.

Originally the tallit was made out of either linen or wool, but now silk is also acceptable. With regard to the material, there is the concept of shatnez—which is the biblical prohibition against mixing together certain distinct species. Specifically, it is forbidden to wear a garment made of both linen and wool. If you wish to observe this you should be careful about the material you select as well as the material with which the tzitzit are made. Silk goes with everything.

The size of the manufactured silk tallitot commonly found in synagogues today is approximately five feet by two feet. This is by no means a standard for what the size should be. Traditionally, the large tallit was approximately six feet by three or four feet. There are certain advantages to this size:

1. You feel that you are wearing a garment and not a scarf.
2. You can more easily feel enwrapped by it.
3. The symbolisms mentioned later become much more applicable.
The size as well as the design . . . are ultimately determined by the wearer. . . .

Women are not obligated to wear a tallit, nor are they prohibited from wearing one. The importance and need for a prayer robe in which to wrap and immerse yourself during tefillah is certainly equal for both men and women. It is often difficult, however, for women who have been raised in a tradition where only men wear tallitot to readily accept the same type of tallit for themselves. Since any four-cornered garment with tzitzit can be used as a tallit, there are a variety of forms and options available to women. . . . The imagination, creativity, sensibilities, and taste of the wearer are the criteria for making a tallit.

LAWS AND CUSTOMS REGARDING THE TZITZIT

It is a positive commandment to put tzitzit on any four-cornered garment that you wear, as it says in Numbers 15:37–41:

> The Lord said to Moses as follows: Speak to the Israelite people and instruct them to make for themselves fringes on the corners of their garments throughout the ages; let them attach a cord of blue to the fringe at each corner. That shall be your fringe; look at it and recall all the commandments of the Lord and observe them, so that you do not follow your heart and eyes in your lustful urge. Thus you shall be reminded to observe all My commandments and to be holy to your God. I the Lord am your God, who brought you out of the land of Egypt to be your God: I, the Lord your God.

As is apparent, this mitzvah is given in order to remember God, His great love, all of His commandments—and to do them.

While the large tallit is used specifically for prayer, it is a mitzvah in itself to wear a garment with tzitzit *all day*. Traditional Jews, therefore, wear a tallit katan—small tallit—all day and a large tallit just for morning prayers.

The tallit is not worn at night because the mitzvah stipulates that one should *see* the tzitzit. (The implication is that this should be seen by light of day, not by artificial light.)

The tzitzit have to be at the corners; but there is a question as to where the corner is on a four-cornered piece of material. A general rule is that the hole be three or four fingerbreadths from the corner edges.

There is an opinion that the tzitzit should hang on the side of the corner and not on the bottom toward the ground.

There is a custom not to cut the tzitzit to shorten them, but to bite them with your teeth.

HOW TO TIE TZITZIT: RITUAL MACRAME

Before you try tying tzitzit to your tallit, it is advisable to practice with twine or heavy string looped around a chair leg.

Although you can spin or devise your own tzitzit strands, it is easier to buy a tzitzit pack, which is available at most Hebrew bookstores.

There will be sixteen strands in the pack—four long ones and twelve short ones. Separate these into four groups with one long and three short in each. The longer strand is called the shammash and is the one used for the winding.

Even up the four strands at one end and push the group through one of the corner holes in the tallit.

Even up seven of the eight strands (the four being doubled) and leave the extra length of the shammash hanging to one side.

With four strands in one hand and the other four in the other hand, make a double knot near the edge of the material. Take the shammash and wind it around the other seven strands in a spiral—seven turns. Be sure you end the winding where you began—otherwise you may end up with 7½ or 6½ winds. Make another double knot at this point (four over four).

Spiral the shammash eight times around. Double knot. Spiral the shammash eleven times around. Double knot. Spiral the shammash thirteen times around. Final double knot.

Fringe (tzitzit) on a prayer shawl.

This is the common, and halakhically precise type of tying. There are, however, two variations on this:

1. A Sephardic tying adds another dimension to the pattern: each time the shammash is brought around, take it *under* the previous wind before winding it further. This will produce a curving ridge around the tzitzit. This, too, should be practiced before trying it on the tallit.

2. Although not in strict accordance with the halakhah, some tie the tzitzit with the shammash spiraling 10-5-6-5 times respectively.

The symbolism for the numbers is central to the overall symbolism of the tallit. Seven and eight equals fifteen, which in gematria (numerology) is equal to the two letters yod and heh—the first two letters of the Name of God. Eleven is the equivalent of vav and heh—the last two letters of the Name of God. The total—twenty-six—is thus equivalent and representative of YHVH—the four-letter Name of God. Thirteen is equivalent to the Hebrew word Ehad—alef, het, dalet—which means One. So to look at the tzitzit is to remember and know that "God is One."

According to the second way of winding, each section is a different letter of God's four-letter Name.

The central commandment surrounding tzitzit is: "And you should see them and remember all of God's commandments and do them."

How do the tzitzit do this?

In gematria, tzitzit = six hundred. In addition there are eight strands plus five knots. The total is six hundred and thirteen—which, according to tradition, is the exact number of commandments—mitzvot—in the Torah. Just to look at them, therefore, is to remember all the mitzvot.

WRAPPING ONESELF IN THE TALLIT

In the process of putting on and wearing the tallit, its many levels of symbolism become apparent. Only some of this symbolism can be alluded to here. Keep these symbols in mind as you put on and wear the tallit. Other associations will probably occur to you. Nurture them.

There are three steps to putting on the tallit.

1. Before putting on the tallit, inspect the tzitzit to insure that they are still intact and correct. To heighten your awareness of the act, the following verses are said (Psalms 104:1–2):

> Bless the Lord, O my soul: O Lord, my God, You are very great; *You are clothed* in glory and majesty, *wrapped in a robe* of light; You spread the heavens like a tent cloth.

A kabbalistic meditation follows this which leads to greater kavvanah— intention and centering:

> For the purpose of unifying the Holy One, blessed be He and His presence—with a mixture of fear and love, for the purpose of unifying the YH of God's Name (masculine) with the VH of God's Name (feminine) in one complete Unity, in the name of all of Israel, I wrap myself in this tallit with tzitzit. So should my soul and my 248 limbs and my 365 veins be wrapped in the light of the tzitzit which is 613. And just as I am covered by a tallit in this world so should I be worthy of a dignified cloak and beautiful tallit in the world to come—in the Garden of Eden. And through the fulfillment of this command may my soul, spirit, holy spark, and prayer be saved from obstructions. May the tallit spread its wings over them and save them "As an

eagle that stirs its nestlings, fluttering over its chicks." And the doing of this mitzvah should be considered by the Holy One, blessed be He, to be as important as fulfilling in all particulars, details, and intentions, the six hundred thirteen mitzvot that depend upon it. Amen, Selah.

2. Immediately before putting on the tallit, hold it out spread open before you and say the berakhah:

Blessed are You, Lord our God, King of the universe, who has sanctified us with His commandments, and commanded us to enwrap ourselves in [a tallit with] tzitzit.

(Some have the custom of kissing the ends of the crown at this point.)

3. After this, bring the tallit around behind you (like a cape) and, before letting it rest on your shoulders, cover your head with it and allow yourself to feel totally enwrapped, sheltered, and protected. The following is a traditional meditation said at this point:

How precious is Your kindness, God. Man can take refuge in the shadow of Your wings. He is sated with the fat of Your house and from the stream of Your delight he drinks. Because with You is the fountain of life and in Your light do we see light. Send Your kindness to those who (try to) know You and Your righteousness to the good-hearted.

At this point, bring the tallit to your shoulders and wear it well and consciously.

There is one other part in the service in which the tallit is actively used—at the reciting of the Shema.

During the prayer immediately preceding the Shema—the Ahava—the tzitzit are gathered together and held around one finger.

The symbolism for this is at least twofold:

1. It represents the coming together of the "four corners of the earth." You should try to gather the tzitzit as you say: "Hurry, and quickly bring upon us blessing and peace from the four corners of the earth."

2. As the numerical value of the windings of each tzitzit is "God is One," the bringing together is a form of expressing the complete unification of God, and all that this implies. There is a hint of this in the words that come right before the Shema: "You have brought us close to Your great Name, with love and with truth, so that we can praise You and unite You and be in love through Your Name." Immediately following this is the Shema—which is the affirmation of the *actuality* of God's Oneness.

In the third paragraph of the Shema—va-Yomer—for each time that the tzitzit are mentioned (three times) there is a custom to look at them and kiss them. Some even elaborate on this by kissing the tzitzit four times each time—for the four letters of God's Name; or, when wearing tefillin to first touch the shel yad [hand] with the tzitzit, kiss them, then the shel rosh [head], and kiss them again—for each time. When the final words, Adonai Eloheikhem Emet, are repeated by the leader of the service, the tzitzit are kissed for the *fourth* time. (When davening alone, the three words El Melekh Ne-eman preface the Shema. When you have reached the final word, Eloheikhem, then you kiss the tzitzit.)

Following this, the tzitzit should not be immediately dropped, but should be held for a while. They should be released sometime before Ezrat Avotainu, as this deals with the drowning of the Egyptians and indicates a separation—the reality of the divided world as opposed to the unification effected by bringing together the tzitzit.

Some people have the custom of drawing the tallit over the head during various parts of the service to inspire extra kavvanah.

F. Study of Torah*

JACOB NEUSNER

The central myth of classical Judaism is the belief that the ancient Scriptures constituted divine revelation, but only a part of it. At Sinai, God had handed down a dual revelation: the written part known to one and all, but also the oral part preserved by the great scriptural heroes, passed on by prophets to various ancestors in the obscure past, finally and most openly handed down to the rabbis who created the Palestinian and Babylonian Talmuds. The "whole Torah" thus consisted of both written and oral parts. The rabbis taught that that "whole Torah" was studied by David, augmented by Ezekiel, legislated by Ezra, and embodied in the schools and by the sages of every period in Israelite history from Moses to the present. It is a singular, linear conception of a revelation, preserved only by the few, pertaining to the many, and in time capable of bringing salvation to all. . . .

Learning thus finds a central place in a classical Judaic tradition because of the belief that God had revealed his will to mankind through the medium of a written revelation, given to Moses at Mount Sinai, accompanied by oral traditions taught in the rabbinical schools and preserved in the Talmuds and related literature. The text without the oral traditions might have led elsewhere than into the academy, for the biblicism of other groups yielded something quite different from Jewish religious intellectualism. But belief in the text was coupled with the belief that oral traditions were also revealed. In the books composed in the rabbinical academies, as much as in the Hebrew Bible itself, was contained God's will for man.

*Adapted from Jacob Neusner, *The Way of Torah: An Introduction to Judaism,* 2nd ed. (Encino, Calif.: Dickenson Publishing Co., 1974), pp. 43–46.

Schoolboys in Israel.

The act of study, memorization, and commentary upon the sacred books is holy. The study of sacred texts therefore assumes a *central* position in Judaism. Other traditions had their religious virtuosi [experts] whose virtuosity [expertise] consisted in knowledge of a literary tradition; but few held, as does Judaism, that everyone must become such an virtuoso. . . .

The devotion of the Jews to study of the Torah, as here defined, is held by them to be their chief glory. This sentiment is repeated in song and prayer, and shapes the values of the common society. The important Jew is the learned man. The child many times is blessed, starting at birth, "May he grow in Torah, commandments, good deeds."

The central *ritual* of the Judaic tradition, therefore, is study. Study as a natural action entails learning of traditions and executing them—in this context, in school or in court. Study becomes a *ritual action* when it is endowed with values *extrinsic* to its ordinary character, when set into a mythic context. When a disciple memorizes his master's traditions and actions, he participates in that myth. His study is thereby endowed with the sanctity that ordinarily pertains to prayer or other cultic matters. . . . The *act* of study itself becomes holy, so that its original purpose, which was mastery of particular information, ceases to matter much. What matters is piety, piety expressed through the rites of studying. Repeating the words of the oral revelation, even without comprehending them, produces reward, just as imitating the master matters, even without being able to explain the reasons for his actions.

The separation of the value, or sanctity, of the act of study from the natural, cognitive result of learning therefore transforms studying from a natural to a ritual action. That separation is accomplished in part by myth, and in part by the powerful impact of the academic environment itself.

A striking illustration of the distinction between mere learning and learning as part of ritual life derives from the comment of Mar Zutra, a fifth-century A.D. Babylonian rabbi, on Isaiah 14:5, "The Lord has broken the staff of the wicked, the scepter of rulers." He said, "These are disciples of the sages who teach public laws to boorish judges."[1] The fact that the uncultivated judge would know the law did not matter, for he still was what he had been, a boor, not a disciple of the sages. Mere knowledge of the laws does not transform an ordinary person, however powerful, into a sage. . . .

While the talmudic rabbis stressed the act of study without reference to its achievement, at the same time they possessed very old traditions on how best to pursue their task. These traditions included much practical advice on how to acquire and preserve learning. Another Babylonian sage, R. Mesharsheya, advised his sons:

> When you wish to come before your teacher to learn, first review your Mishnah and then go to your teacher. When you are sitting before your teacher look at the mouth of your teacher, as it is written, But thine eyes shall see thy teacher [Isaiah 30:20]; and when you study any teaching, do so by the side of water, for as water is drawn out, so your learning may be prolonged. Be on the dustheaps of Mata Mehasia [a great center of learning] rather than in the palaces of Pumbedita [where Torah was lacking].[2]

Part of that advice is perfectly reasonable. Reviewing before classes, concentrating on the teacher, staying near the great schools—these things would make sense anywhere. On the other hand, the advice to study by a body of water "so that your learning may be prolonged" has little to do with the practical problems of memorizing and reasoning. It rather reflects the rabbis' view of a correspondence between their own study and those aspects of nature which the rabbis looked upon as symbolic of their activities—and they many times compared Torah to living waters.

[1] b. Shabbat, 139a.
[2] b. Keritot, 6a.

READING 17
Jewish Traditions

A. American Judaism
JONATHAN PARADISE

It may be somewhat misleading to draw a profile of the various subdivisions which exist within American Judaism and, thereby, create the assumption that they exist in isolation from one another. To describe the Orthodox, Reform, Conservative, and Reconstructionist as separate "sects" overlooks the great deal of overlap, interaction, and close cooperation that exists in many areas of Jewish life. A significant portion of Jews do not express their Jewish identity through synagogue affiliations. They may participate in Jewish cultural activities conducted in the Jewish Community Center which is supported by the entire Jewish community (no community has competing centers which reflect "denominational" lines). Possibly their "Jewish life" is exclusively bound up in Zionism. Still others may not have any organizational affiliation at all and yet they are quick to identify themselves as Jews.

The various official religious organizations do present a rather distinctive set of beliefs and attitudes. But the above cautionary remarks should be remembered as you read the following descriptions of these organizations.

ORTHODOX JUDAISM

Although all of Judaism has undergone enormous change during the last 150 years, it is safe to say that Orthodoxy has retained the greatest resemblance to classic Jewish patterns. Orthodoxy advocates strict adherence to the *mitzvot* (commandments) set forth by the Halakha (rabbinic law). The Halakha embraces virtually every aspect of life including not only religious ritual and prayer, but matters of daily life. A few of these areas would be diet, conduct of business affairs, and marital life.[1] Orthodoxy maintains that these laws are sacred and divine in origin and have authority equal to that of revealed scriptures.

In keeping with the importance of Halakha in Orthodoxy, the training given in Orthodox schools and especially in rabbinical seminaries stresses legal scholarship. Great prestige is accorded persons who are learned in the Talmud (primarily a legal work).

The main task of the traditional Orthodox rabbi is to teach, study, and give guidance in matters of Jewish law. He is less likely to be involved in public relations, interfaith activity, or psychological counseling. His role in the synagogue service is rather limited since he usually does not lead the prayers and the sermon is not a required feature of Orthodox worship.

The service is entirely in Hebrew and few, if any, of the prayers are omitted. A typical Sabbath morning service lasts about two and one-half hours and is conducted only by males. The use of an organ or other musical instrument during the service would be unthinkable. Women are not called to recite the blessings over the Torah when it is read and are not seated with the men. A partition separates the sanctuary into two areas, the smaller of which is for the women since they are not obligated to participate in public prayer. The Sabbath is a holiday of major importance and, as such, is devoted entirely to prayer, study, and festive meals. The meals, to which guests are frequently invited, are accompanied with singing and special foods. Food must not be prepared on the Sabbath; shopping, smoking, travel by car, or operating other machines are also prohibited. In these and many other ways the Orthodox Jew makes a distinction between Sabbath and weekday.

The Orthodox male covers his head at all times, not only when worshipping. A married woman would not appear publicly with her head uncovered. To be sure, there are many exceptions to the foregoing descriptions of Orthodox practice. For example, some Orthodox men would cover their heads while praying, eating, or studying sacred books but not in other situations.

The role of the rabbi and the mode of synagogue worship in American Orthodoxy have been greatly influenced by non-Orthodox practices during the last generation. As a result, some practices deviate from the above description. For example, in some Orthodox synagogues mixed seating is now tolerated. The rabbi preaches a sermon regularly and performs administrative and pastoral functions which resemble those of

The male who strictly follows Jewish law is not supposed to walk more than four cubits (six feet) with his head uncovered.

[1]Readings 8 and 9 (pages 35–44) give some indication of the importance of law in Judaism and the values the laws seek to embody and make concrete through daily acts.

his Conservative and Reform colleagues. Similarly, the Orthodox synagogue which was traditionally intended only for prayer and study (note the Yiddish word for synagogue is *shul,* meaning "school") has frequently taken on the additional function of social center with clubs, social dancing, and, occasionally, a gymnasium.

Traditional Judaism places heavy emphasis on the centrality of the land of Israel. Many prayers and rituals express the holiness of the land, the yearning to return, the sorrow over the destruction of the temple and the exile of the Jews. For the Orthodox it is both a privilege and a *mitzvah* to live in Israel. It is thus not surprising that most Orthodox Jews are devoted to Israel and that a significant portion of those American Jews who visit and eventually settle there are Orthodox. It should be noted, however, that Orthodoxy does not necessarily include Zionism.

For some time Orthodoxy was faced with the serious erosion of its members' commitment to strict standards of Jewish law. There were those who confidently predicted the disappearance of this sector of American Judaism. This now appears unlikely. During the past fifteen years many new Orthodox congregations have been formed—often consisting of young suburban families. A rather extensive network of parochial schools which promote commitment to Orthodoxy has been developed and is growing steadily. Their graduates are certain to strengthen Orthodoxy.

Although these young Orthodox Jews differ from traditional European Jews in their dress, language, and mannerisms, they are alike in one important respect. Orthodoxy expects its members to place their religion before all other considerations. Whenever an important decision is to be made, the teachings of Orthodoxy should dictate what is to be done. It is expected that the Orthodox Jew would buy a home within walking distance from a synagogue. He would take a job in a community where an Orthodox synagogue existed, where stores sold kosher foodstuffs, and where a Jewish school could offer his children an intensive religious education. An Orthodox male might be limited in the kinds of birth control he and his wife could practice, and abortion is tolerated only in limited circumstances. In all of these areas Orthodoxy expects that religion alone will be the determining factor.

REFORM JUDAISM

Reform Judaism introduced abrupt and far-reaching changes in Jewish beliefs and practices. The exclusive use of Hebrew prayers and the many laws pertaining to diet, Sabbath observance, and numerous other Orthodox practices were declared outmoded or were greatly modified. This new movement had its origins in nineteenth-century

Germany, France, England, and America. It resulted from the desire of Jews to retain their Jewish identity while participating fully in the social and cultural life of their countries. The early leaders of Reform Judaism sought to shift the focus from the rabbinic Halakha to the ethical teachings of the prophets. In their view, it was the latter with their teachings of justice, love, truth, and universal peace which contained the essence of Judaism. In deciding which of the traditional beliefs and practices were to be kept, Reform Judaism stressed human reason over the authority of tradition. The goal was to harmonize secular life and culture with their Judaism. In Europe, and especially in America, Judaism frequently gave way to the style and spirit of the dominant gentile culture. In temple liturgy and mode of worship there was a radical break with earlier practices which were labeled "oriental." The prayers expressing belief in a personal messiah and bodily resurrection of the dead were abandoned. The wearing of a skullcap (yarmulke), prayer shawl (tallit), and phylacteries (tefillin) was discontinued, as was separate seating for men and women.

It was common for Reform congregations to call their synagogue a temple. This reflects the Reform view that Jews no longer need pray for the restoration of the temple in Jerusalem, since each local synagogue is a contemporary temple.

However, the last forty years have seen the reincorporation of increasing amounts of traditional practices. Reform rabbis have called for a renewal of Judaism's emphasis on religious observances both in public worship and home celebrations. Yet a major difference separates Reform from both Conservatism and Orthodoxy. For while affirming the principle of the tradition, there is no detailed written guide which corresponds to Halakha for Reform. Each Jew is free to exercise his individual autonomy, choosing and creating on the basis of commitment and knowledge. Thus, Reform emphasizes flexibility of belief and diversity of views.

Reform Jews always advocated active involvement in causes which sought to advance social justice, civil rights, the antiwar movement, liberal birth control and abortion laws, and the separation of church and state. They conceived of the "election" of Israel as a mission of improving human society and taught that the emphasis on "prophetic Judaism" must be accompanied by a concrete translation into day-to-day action for social justice and peace.

Initially, Reform Judaism rejected the notion of Jewish peoplehood and the Zionist yearnings for a Jewish state in Israel. However, these unfavorable attitudes toward Jewish nationalism were soon abandoned, and Reform Jews now agree with Orthodox and Conservatives that the Jews are a "people" who are bound to one another by more than a common religious faith. Without abandoning their commitment to social messianism, they are increasingly expressing the need to help and seek cooperation with Jews of all persuasions.

Reform Jews also share strong support and identification with the state of Israel. Several of the leading Reform personalities have permanently settled in Israel.

CONSERVATIVE JUDAISM

Conservative Judaism began among Jews who affirmed the need to adapt their religious practices and their general values to Western and American styles. But these Jews reacted against what they regarded as the extreme measures of Reform Judaism. They sought a middle road between retaining traditional forms and teachings of Judaism (hence the name Conservative) while introducing changes that would allow them to enter the mainstream of modern Western society. Conservative rabbis continued the Reform practices of preaching in English and employing some English prayers in the service. The family pew (that is, mixed seating), the Friday evening service conducted after dinner, and the use of an organ with a mixed choir were also features of Conservative worship. However, the standards of Sabbath observance, the predominance of Hebrew in services, and the observance of kosher dietary practices were closer to the standards set by Orthodoxy.

Conservative Judaism has always maintained the principle that the Halakha is an essential element in Judaism. However, Halakha must never become static; it must constantly evolve in response to new conditions and needs. The organization of Conservative Rabbis, the "Rabbinical Assembly," established a law committee which would study issues in Jewish law and then establish guidelines based on new interpretations of the traditional legal sources. Some examples of Halakha rulings which distinguish Conservative from Orthodox are as follows: Conservative Jews are permitted to use electricity on the Sabbath, to travel by car to the synagogue on the Sabbath, to use foods containing gelatin when it has been so chemically altered that it no longer resembles its original form, and to allow women equal status with men in a religious service. The committee also permitted individual congregations to abandon the observance of the second day of all festivals, conforming to the practice in Israel (although, thus far, virtually all congregations continue to observe both days).

Many leaders of the Conservative movement have staunchly supported Zionism as a vital aspect of Judaism. For the masses of Conservative Jews, Zionism is expressed by financial and political support of Israel. It is common for synagogues to organize tours to Israel. Special celebrations are held on Israel Independence Day with a special holiday liturgy. Some Conservative Jews and an increasing number of rabbis have settled in Israel.

A typical Conservative synagogue seeks to provide programs which go far beyond the traditional European *shul,* a house of prayer and study for adult males. It houses club activities and educational programs for every age. Frequently the synagogue will have a restaurant-type kitchen and a "social hall" for serving large dinners. Wedding celebrations, theatrical performances, and large lectures are also held at the synagogue. Some synagogue "centers" even have gymnasiums and swimming pools.

Because the founders of Conservatism wished to avoid excluding varieties of Jewish religious expression, the ideological and ritual guidelines have deliberately been kept very broad.

Theological and philosophical speculation has been relatively unimportant and no new dogmas have evolved which are uniquely Conservative. There is considerable variety in Conservative services. The men wear skullcaps and prayer shawls when required by the service. The prayers are primarily in Hebrew, although English readings are most frequent at Friday evening Sabbath services. Only men may study for the rabbinate or cantorate. It is rare for men and women to sit in separate pews; the "family" pew is common. Women are allowed to participate in conducting a service. While the content of the official prayer book has only slightly departed from the Orthodox version, individual congregations are free to modify the service and insert their own innovations.

Conservative Judaism has enjoyed very rapid growth in the United States. The concept of seeking a middle road appealed to the many Jews who were unwilling to accept the demands of Orthodoxy but equally reluctant to accept Reform's radical break with tradition. For these Jews, Conservative Judaism provides a measure of traditional rituals and symbols combined with flexibility, change, and reinterpretation.

A Conservative congregation. The Conservative movement was started in 1845 in Frankfurt, Germany.

RECONSTRUCTIONISM

For the moment, there is scant justification for treating Reconstructionism as a separate sector on a par with Orthodoxy, Reform, and Conservatism. There are few Reconstructionist synagogues, and it is only recently that a seminary for training Reconstructionist rabbis was established in Philadelphia. Yet, the impact of its philosophy and the innovations proposed by its leader have been profound on all of American Judaism.

The name of the leader who, almost single-handedly, created most of Reconstructionist thought is Mordecai Kaplan. Kaplan proposed the concept of a synagogue/community center. He introduced the ceremony of Bat Mitzvah for girls to parallel the Bar Mitzvah and many other innovations of worship.

The ideology of Kaplan regards Judaism as an "evolving religious civilization." As such, Judaism is more than just a religion. Folkways, customs, language, music, art, rituals, poetry are all part of it and should serve as avenues of Jewish expression. Kaplan stresses the necessity to continue to change and adopt in a "deliberate and planned fashion" the best of the Jewish civilization and the dominant secular culture of the diaspora.

Perhaps the most unusual aspect of Kaplan's teachings is his neutralistic conception of God. He defines God as the "power or process that works for human salvation or self-fulfillment. Thus, God is a process, or an experience, rather than a person or an anthropomorphic representation of the Deity. In this view there is no room for super-naturalism or miracles . . . since these notions cannot be expected to appeal to modern rational man."

Reconstructionists reject the concept of the Jews as a "chosen people." They also deny that the Torah was divinely revealed. The Bible is viewed as a collection of documents which reflect the views of various writers of different ages. In this view, Reconstructionists are simply adopting the position of most modern Bible scholars; yet these and other of Kaplan's views have provoked considerable controversy among religious leaders. In all, Kaplan created a blend of Orthodoxy, Conservatism, and Reform. Like Reform, he insisted on the right of each Jew to determine what was relevant and meaningful for him. He critically examined each prayer, ritual, and dogma to determine its utility and appropriateness for modern, intellectual Jews. He shares with Orthodox and Conservatives heavy emphasis on the importance of Hebrew, the value of rituals, and love for Jewish peoplehood.

B. A Community of Hasidic Jews*
STEPHEN ISAACS

New York, N.Y.—The Williamsburg section of Brooklyn, across the East River from Manhattan, was once one of the elegant resort areas of the East Coast. The Vanderbilts, the Whitneys, the Morgans and others used to ferry over to enjoy the concerts, the beer gardens, the fine hotels.

In the invervening years Williamsburg has undergone great migrations. By now most of the neighborhood has evolved into . . . a rundown collection of hovel-like apartments . . . Unemployment and underem-ployment are widespread. The schools, beset by massive problems of vandalism and discipline, are barely, if at all, teaching.

In the midst of this depressing slumscape lies what is essentially a small, 18th century East European village. This part of Williamsburg has no crime, no drugs, no venereal disease, no graffiti. "To us," says one leader of this community, "juvenile delinquency is a guy who gets caught watching a baseball game on a television set."

*Adapted from an article in the *Minneapolis Star,* March 2, 1974.

This community, near the old Brooklyn Navy Yard, is populated by an unusual remnant of Nazi Germany's insanity: 20,000 to 25,000 Hasidic Jews, fundamental religionists who are as remarkable in their discipline as the early Mormons or the Shakers or the Amish.

The Hasidim do not own television sets. They attend no movies. They dress and think like their forebearers of more than 200 years ago. They pray like them, eat like them, wash like them. They believe they are the true continuum of the true Judaism. They refuse to compromise with the temptations of modernism.

Hasidism was founded in the early 1700s in the Carpathian Mountains by Israel Ben Eliezer, a teacher and clay digger who became a spiritual leader known as the Baal-hem-tov, or "master of the good name." From him spread the word that concentration on intellectual hairsplitting, which had become a mark of being religious for Jews, was false. True piety was in the intensity of feeling put into study and prayer and commitment to God.

Hasidism ("Hasid" in effect means "pious") was a democratic form of Judaism, and it caught fire with millions of Jews in Eastern Europe. Ordinary Jews could suddenly be just as pious, just as worthy, as learned scholars.

In Williamsburg today, Hasidism includes:

- The largest private Jewish school system in the world, including about a dozen buildings, where every boy and girl (separately) learns Yiddish as well as English. The boys study Torah and the Talmud and its commentaries and Hasidic lore.
- A hospital and clinic, with women doctors so women can avoid having strange men touch them.
- An emergency ambulance and oxygen service.
- A synagogue that, on high holidays, accommodates 7,500 worshippers, plus five other . . . synagogues in Williamsburg and Borough Park.
- A private bus service that connects the Hasidic communities.
- Special nursing service in which Hasidic men and women go to community hospitals to help feed fellow Hasidim who cannot care for themselves.
- One of the largest loan societies in New York, with interest-free loans to Hasidim who have business or personal financial need.
- A super kosher butcher shop.
- A bakery for Matzoh, or unleavened bread.
- An employment agency with contacts at 5,000 businesses.
- Summer camps in upstate New York.
- A publishing enterprise which prints a weekly newspaper, Der Yid, and books for the schools, among other things.

- A burial society for those who cannot afford such costs.
- What is said to be the largest mikveh in the history of the world.

A mikveh is a ritual cleansing bath. The immersion must be in natural, pure water. Hasidic men visit one every day, and there is one, tied to artesian wells, underneath their main synagogue.

Across the expressway is the new mikveh for the women, which cost more than $1 million. Hasidim follow orthodox commands that they refrain from sexual relations during menstrual periods and for seven days afterward. The women must immerse themselves before relations can resume.

At the synagogue on a recent sabbath evening, the Williamsburg Hasidim celebrated the birth of fourteen boys in the preceding week, as well as the impending marriage of eight young men the following week. Hasidim usually wed young, and the marriages are "match-made," either by the rabbis or by matchmakers.

Hasidic women ritually shave their heads after the marriages, so they will not be attractive to other men, and on the street they wear scarves or wigs. Women may not sit in the synagogue with the men, so as not to divert the men from the intensity of their prayers. When the women go, they sit in a separate balcony with a latticed screen that shields them from the men's view.

"Our divorce rate is about 1 percent," says Rabbi Friedman, "and most of those are for physical reasons."

All this is about as far as one can get from the women's liberation movement. "What should they want with women's lib?" asks Salomon Feder, who helps administer the school buildings. "They don't have to work. They are in charge of everything in the home, in taking care of the children, in giving love to the children. What is more important? They are the bosses at home, they make the supper, everything."

An American memorial to Jews who died at the hands of the Nazis.

READING 18
Persecution

One cannot devote much time to the study of Judaism without becoming very much aware that Jews have suffered untold pressure and persecution throughout the centuries. The enslavement in ancient Egypt, the Babylonian Captivity, the Spanish Inquisition and expulsion from Spain in 1492 mark only a few of the better-known instances of suffering endured by the Jewish people. The pogroms or terrorist riots against the Jews in Eastern Europe form a part of this story, but nothing carries the horror of the atrocities perpetrated against the Jews in what has become known as the Holocaust of World War II.

To gain some background for the Holocaust we shall look to the historical background of this nightmare in an excerpt from The Burden of Guilt *by Hannah Vogt, a German historian. Secondly, we shall examine some aspects of the "Holocaust" literature and, finally, a few excerpts from a collection of art and writing by children in Terezin Concentration Camp.*

A. The Burden of Guilt*

HANNAH VOGT

Nothing that must be reported about the Third *Reich* is so hard to grasp as the fact that nearly six million Jews were "exterminated according to plan" during this period. This figure is so monstrous that reason refuses to accept it, for the heart cannot fathom its horror. But as we must face

*From Hannah Vogt, *The Burden of Guilt: A Short History of Germany, 1914–1945,* trans. Herbert Strauss (New York: Oxford University Press, 1964), pp. 212–34.

this truth we are pursued by the nagging question as to how these monstrous deeds could have been possible. How could innocent people be treated in this fashion? How can one understand a hatred which had such terrifying consequences? A brief historical resume will provide the answer.

Ever since the overthrow of the Southern Kingdom of Judah and the deportation of a large number of Jews to the capital of Babylonia, Jewish communities existed not only in Canaan but also, at first, in Babylonia, then at the Persian court, in Asia Minor, in Egypt, and in Greece. Jerusalem formed the spiritual center of all these communities. But with the destruction of the temple by the Romans in 70 A.D. the Jews lost their spiritual center. Wherever in the dispersion (Greek: *diaspora*) Jewish communities existed from then on, life revolved around the synagogue and around its most precious possession, the Torah or the Law of Moses. The Jews kept the Sabbath holy and observed the dietary laws and their festivals and ordinances wherever they went.

Loyal to their faith, the Jews did not intermingle or integrate with the people whom they lived among, even if mutual relations were otherwise fairly friendly and peaceful. This was the case for centuries in Europe. True, the Jews were considered strangers and placed under special legislation, but they also frequently enjoyed the special protection of the emperors of the Middle Ages. This, at the time, was not uncommon. As yet, the principle that all men have equal rights was unknown, and different families, estates, or occupations each enjoyed a carefully gra-dated [ranked] legal position. The oldest German law code, for example, the *Sachsenspiegel,* excluded clerics, women, and Jews from the rules of feudal warfare.

It is true that some of these special laws were discriminatory, as, for example, the rules governing the taking of an oath for Jews (they had to stand barefoot, clothed in a sack, upon a blood-smeared pigskin!). More important was the economic discrimination: in many places Jews were forbidden to own or cultivate land, and were excluded from Christian guilds. As a result, they turned to occupations which were not controlled by guild regulations. These included medicine, for example, to which Jews made significant contributions. Initially they also included trading, especially money dealing. Soon the Jews became an indispensable factor in the development of modern economic institutions: they were able to lend money at interest which was forbidden from 1215 on in Christian medieval church laws against usury. They rendered valuable services to economic life but had the frequent experience that debtors would try to cancel their obligations by instigating massacres of Jews. Later on, the laws against usury were relaxed, and the German Christian banking families, such as the Fuggers or the Welsers, also entered the loan business.

The first violent persecution on German soil occurred at the time of the Crusades. A wave of religious excitement whose ultimate causes remain unknown was sweeping Europe. Bands of crusaders and adventurers marched through the lands to wrest Christ's grave from the hands of infidels. Nothing was easier than to arouse these masses to violent acts against the Jews. "Who had nailed Christ to the Cross, and to this day deny his divine character?" Entire Jewish communities perished, as in Worms and Mainz. The Jews could have escaped persecution through baptism, but they usually scorned this escape. They preferred to die by their own hands, together with their wives and children. Such steadfast faith speaks for itself.

Once hatred begins, it resembles a fire which keeps smoldering unless completely extinguished. From then on, the small Jewish minority was always imperiled when famine occurred somewhere, or when epidemics or wars made people afraid. For the superstitious mind of the time, the Jew was cursed, in alliance with the devil. Jews again and again became the scapegoats: they were accused of poisoning the wells, or of defiling the host. In addition, the ghastly lie was spread that the Jews used the blood of a Christian child to celebrate Passover. Still, the Jews were by no means the only victims of medieval religious fanaticism and superstition. Heretics were persecuted and witches burned for the same reasons.

This changed only with the Enlightenment. It directed the light of reason into the dark recesses of popular superstitions, and so ended belief in witchcraft. It demanded religious toleration and an end to the use of force in matters of faith. For this reason, the relationship of the Christian to the Jew also had to be given a new meaning. Lessing's drama *Nathan the Wise* expressed the new spirit in the most beautiful and humane form.

With the Enlightenment there arose a new sense of justice. All mankind was to enjoy equal rights, the privileged were to blend with the under-privileged. The more these ideas were accepted among broad groups, the more it was felt undignified that Jews were forced to dwell in segregated quarters (or ghettoes), that they were excluded from certain occupa-tions, that they had to pay "duty" (the so-called *Leibzoll,* a head tax) when crossing a frontier as if they were things. The ghettoes were dissolved, and the Jews "emancipated," which meant they were given equal rights with the other citizens. This development occurred in Germany between 1797 and 1812.

This, however, did not yet solve all the problems. Now people began to take offense because centuries of segregation had left their mark on Jewish customs, language, and gestures. For example, Jews had become accustomed to lacing their German with Hebrew words, Hebrew being the language of the synagogue. Precisely because Jews now had "equal rights" they were felt to be "different"; and since people everywhere tend to look askance at minorities, people were not at all ready to abandon the old religious hatreds.

This hostile attitude was reinforced by the fact that the Jews were emancipated at the same time as the old, relatively secure guild economy gave way to a new competitive economy. Now people no longer produced in answer to a fixed demand but for an uncertain market. The word was now: "To each according to his ability! Only accomplishments count!" In the new, tougher climate many were yearning for the past. But among those favored by the new economic freedom were also many Jews. They successfully took up many occupations from which they had previously been excluded. Centuries of experience had prepared them for the new world of the market and of business. Thus, craftsmen and petty traders frequently came to believe that their livelihoods were endangered by Jewish competition, while, in reality, they suffered under the new competitive system. Once more, Jews were to serve as scapegoats.

Meanwhile, genuine emancipation continued, as one or two generations erased the imprint which the ghetto had left on the Jew. Many Jews were baptized. Services in Reform synagogues followed the pattern of the Protestant service. Most Jews did not adhere any more strictly to their traditions than Catholics or Protestants did to their Christian faith, for there had been a general loosening of all religious ties. For the most part, they also ceased to consider themselves as a people, or a nation. In Germany, they felt German, in France French, in England English. Everywhere in Germany they took a leading part in intellectual life, helped to preserve traditions, or to sponsor modern developments. They were conservative, liberal, or socialist, but they were Germans, and wanted to be nothing else. Thus, at last, conditions existed under which the medieval hatred of the Jews could have disappeared, just as the medieval fear of witchcraft had disappeared.

Then, however, the unexpected happened. It appeared as if people in Europe could not free themselves from old, deeply rooted hatreds. Since the old religious rationalizations were no more modern or progressive, they searched for new ones, and found them in the "race doctrine." This doctrine had originated with the natural sciences that had brought about the great technological progress of the nineteenth century. But instead of working with reliable scientific methods, it brought forth arbitrary evaluations, and, from the very start, turned into a pseudo-science. Charles Darwin derived the origin of animal species from the "struggle for existence," in which the stronger or better adapted species survives while the weak and poorly adapted species perishes.

On this basis, people were now being subdivided into various sub-species, called "races," a concept previously used only in animal husbandry. In the absence of precise taxonomic standards [classifications] each scientist had the field for himself. Some distributed people among three, other among five, twenty, or more races and sub-races.

If these scientists had limited themselves to categorizing physical characteristics, their doctrines would have been innocuous. They claimed, however, that physical characteristics were correlated with certain intellectual and psychological characteristics. Thus the French Count Gobineau declared those people grouped together as "Aryans" by philologists [specialists in language as it relates to cultural history] on the basis of language similarities, to be a separate race. He claimed that this race alone was creative, intelligent, and dynamic. Negroes, however, he considered as cowardly, insensitive, easily excitable, and of mediocre intelligence.

Such "scientific" results, of course, flattered the pride of the European, who just at that time was preparing to extend his rule over the entire globe. Scientifically, their evidence was zero. Not one scrap of conclusive evidence has ever been put forward to prove that millions of members of one particular race are endowed with like intellectual and psychological characteristics. Any unprejudiced observer can see that all groups include intelligent and stupid people, lazy and diligent ones, courageous and cowardly men, the brilliant and the dull. Such differences appear even in small families whose members probably resemble each other physically.

Since the delineation of races depended entirely on each scientist's whim, it was more than easy to declare the Jews a "race" too. This step was taken by Houston Stewart Chamberlain, an Englishman by birth, in a book *The Foundations of the XXth Century*. He described Teutonic or Nordic man as a noble and privileged creature while assigning primarily negative characteristics to the Jews. To meet the possible argument that Jesus, after all, was Jewish too, he simply changed his line and claimed that Jesus could not possibly have been a "Jew by race" (*Rassenjude*).

A perusal of antisemitic literature (the word was first used in 1880) shocks the reader into recognizing that here the old religious hatred reappears in a modern guise. Characteristically, it deals not with "the Jews" in the plural but speaks of "the Jew" as if he were a demon or a devil. To this demon it ascribes supernatural powers: a Jew decomposes the "host nation" like a bacillus [disease-producing bacterium]; he dilutes the nation with his alien spirit (even in cases where the Jews represent only 0.5 percent of the population); he aims to rule the world. Antisemitic caricatures used to portray the Jew with all the features of the medieval devil.

Antisemitism served the double purpose of arousing primeval instincts—the fear of demons and a mania for persecution—and of allowing people to think that they were in step with "advanced natural science *Weltanschauung.*" With the same "scientific methods" it could have been proven just as easily that the misfortunes of the world stemmed from people with red hair.

This transformation of the medieval hatred of the Jew into racial antisemitism was to have disastrous consequences. In the Middle Ages, Jews could escape the alleged "curse of God" through baptism. The claim that they were "an inferior race" made them objects of persecution without allowing them either to stand up to their tormentors or to escape from them. As long as they were faced with traditional hatred, Jews could fall back on their proud and ancient faith. Their general defamation as a race left no defense. It hit all Jews as a group, or the fantasy image of *the* Jew. Whatever the individual Jew accomplished, whether he made great inventions, contributed to cultural life, fought bravely in wars, or donated his possessions to charity, made no difference to the antisemite. He either considered it an individual exception, or Jewish virtues and accomplishments were considered a mere camouflage for the hidden inner depravity of the Jew. In the face of antisemitism, each Jew suffered torment without a chance of escaping, like an innocent man cast out from society, torment as Jacob Wassermann has described it in moving words:

> In vain you hide away. They say: that coward, he crawls away, his bad conscience drives him to it. In vain you mingle with them and offer them your hand. They say: how does he dare, the Jew, to intrude? In vain you keep faith with them, as a comrade in arms, or as a fellow citizen. . . . In vain you live with them, or die with them. They say: he is a Jew. . . .[1]

Thus antisemitism violated the basic moral law that each man must be judged only by his deeds and thoughts. After 1945, we Germans rejected the accusation that we were collectively guilty for the crimes of the Nazis—and these crimes were, in truth, committed also "in the name of our people," while accusations which antisemites hurled against the Jews rested on nothing else but evil lies. In this way we can fathom the depth of the injustice which the antisemites, with impunity, were allowed to spread for decades.

But why was such an unjust doctrine of hatred accepted by all social strata, by educated as well as ignorant people? A number of reasons can be propounded, none of which, of course, should be used to excuse the immorality of antisemitism. The nineteenth century ushered in fundamental economic and social changes, during the course of which the individual frequently lost his way in a maze of social relations he dimly understood. For any aggravation and any pain, antisemitism offered a simple, crude remedy: the Jews were to blame for it all. As the citizens took a greater part in determining their own lives, each individual was asked to accept more responsibility for the government, and to determine

---

[1]Jakob Wassermann, *Mein Weg als Deutscher und Jude* (Berlin: Fischer Verlag, 1921), p. 122.

his life by his own efforts. This burden became too great, and it was decidedly simpler to fight "Judah" than to improve conditions. In addition, class differences began to disappear as society progressed. Work and income increasingly became the only determinants of social status and replaced occupation or descent. In this situation, even mediocrities could easily fancy themselves as members of an elite: "The very moment one treats the Jew as an inferior and harmful creature, then he immediately feels he is a member of an elite."[2]

To nationalists, antisemitism was a useful weapon, since nationalism could be as easily stimulated attacking an "internal enemy" as by fighting against an "external" one. From its inception, antisemitism was thus closely allied with nationalism, while liberalism and socialism generally gave it a wide berth. Before the First World War, antisemitism was, for this reason, generally confined to the radical right, e.g., the Pan-Germans, and to those middle-class groups who suffered under social pressures, and had to protect themselves, on the one hand, against the competition of big business and, on the other, from the danger of "sinking into" the proletariat. As a result, they settled on the Jew as their sole enemy, responsible for capitalism and socialism alike. A few right-radical associations and student corporations also excluded Jews from membership. Violence was rare. The Jews did not really feel threatened by this antisemitism; they considered it as an ugly mental aberration, which, as yet, affected only a few of their fellow-citizens.

For various reasons, the situation of the Jews in Germany deteriorated after the First World War: national pride had been deeply hurt and humiliated by the war-guilt clause and other articles of the Treaty of Versailles. As nationalism spread, antisemitic propaganda followed in its wake. With the adoption of parliamentary democracy, the citizen, burdened with greater responsibilities, felt insecure and searched for easy solutions and remedies for all his difficulties. Finally, increasing attention was centered on the Jews when a large number of so-called "eastern Jews" emigrated from what were once Austrian and Russian areas in Poland.

The economic dislocation of inflation and the subsequent depression combined with nationalistic passions, monarchist dreams, and anti-democratic sentiments to form the unholy alliance which was to destroy the Weimar Republic. What role did antisemitism play in this? Did Hitler grow strong because he preached the most outspoken and vulgar type of antisemitism? Was "Death to the Jews!" the slogan which sent the majority of the German people marching under his banner?

The answer to these questions is probably "No." Surely the struggle against Versailles, against the "parliamentary talking shop," and the

[2]J.-P. Sartre, *Anti-Semite and Jew* (New York: Schocken Books, 1948).

adoption of a vague socialism played a greater role in winning masses of voters. Still, the sobering doubt remains of why the slogan "Death to the Jews!" which screamed out from many Nazi posters, and was spread by many newspapers, did not frighten more people by its undisguised brutality.

Nazi propaganda was never soft, but it reached its peak of crudeness, falsehood, and vulgarity in its attacks on the Jews. The majority of the German people did not read such party papers as the "Angriff," or the "Volkischer Beobachter," before Hitler "seized power," but with the advent of "co-ordination" (Gleichschaltung) the "nauseating, hideous brew"[3] of antisemitic propaganda became daily fare in all newspapers. Even the minds of children were poisoned by books picturing the "hellish features" of the Jew. So-called "scientific" works flooded the market in which sick and evil minds poured out their hatred without restraint. Since antisemitism had now become the official Weltanschauung of the state, one must wonder why violence against the Jews was still sporadic. The fact was that the German people were being indoctrinated but had not yet been conditioned to violence against individuals. Many Germans continued to buy in Jewish stores and went to Jewish physicians, and ultimately Hitler had to resort to laws and government measures to carry through his anti-Jewish policies.

On March 28, 1933, the Nazi party bosses organized a boycott of Jewish stores. Uniformed S.A.[4] men daubed Jewish stars on the shop windows of Jewish stores, and picketed them with outsized signs demanding: "Don't buy from Jews!" Jewish merchants were intimidated and suffered damages, but their customers were not so easily driven away.

Paragraph 3 of a Decree for the Restoration of the Professional Civil Service [sic] provided the basis for dismissing "non-Aryan" officials (April 1933). Typically in this early period Hitler was still restrained by Hindenburg, who protested against the clause in this decree which permitted the removal from office of Jewish war veterans.

Hitler did not dare take the next large step until the Reich Party Congress in Nuremberg in 1935, when the Nuremberg Laws reduced Jews to the category of second-class citizens. Marriages and extra-marital relations between Jews and "citizens of German blood" were forbidden. Racial crime (Rassenschande) became a favorite theme of Streicher's hate sheet "Der Sturmer." Although the Nuremberg Laws did not touch already existing marriages between Aryans and non-Aryans, increased pressure was subsequently brought to bear on the Aryan partner to sue for divorce. These race laws drove many people to suicide, including the poet Jochen Klepper and the actor Joachim Gottschalk, to

[3]Franz Bohm, Antisemitismus, an address delivered on March 13, 1958. Private printing.
[4]Abbreviation for Sturmabteilung, a Nazi militia organized about 1924.

mention the most famous cases. Both men had Jewish wives and killed not only themselves but their wives and children as well.

Another discriminatory measure introduced in August 1938 made it obligatory for Jews to use only Jewish first names, and to add the names Israel or Sara if they had any forbidden first names. This measure was to help in identifying Jews more easily, but, ironically, it implicitly admitted that Jews did not really differ physically or intellectually from the rest of the populace.

A string of similar antisemitic decrees followed upon the assassination of Ernst vom Rath, a councillor at the German legation in Paris, by Herschel Grynszpan, a Polish Jew, on November 9, 1938. It started with the burning down of synagogues in Germany by S.A. troops, acting under orders. Altogether 267 synagogues went up in flames that night; in addition, 815 stores were destroyed, 20,000 Jews arrested, and 36 killed. In his press, Goebbels had the nerve to pass off these acts of arson which he had organized and directed in person as "a spontaneous reaction of the German people." It would, however, be truer to say that many people reacted with spontaneous indignation as the scales fell from their eyes about the true character of the Nazi regime. But they were not indignant enough to resist openly.

The cue was now provided for the party leaders to put their sick fantasies into practice. By a horrible perversion of justice, the victims, the aggrieved, the despoiled—the Jews—were ordered to "atone for their crimes" with a fine of one billion marks. Another decree stated:

> Paragraph 1: All the damage caused by the indignation of the people about the propaganda attacks of international Jewry against Nazi Germany in Jewish business premises and dwelling units on November 8, 9, and 10, 1938, is to be repaired at once by the Jewish owner, or the Jew who did business on the premises.
>
> Paragraph 2: The expense of the repair is to be borne by the owners of the Jewish business premises and dwelling units concerned. Insurance claims by Jews of German nationality are confiscated in favor of the *Reich*.

Other orders followed in close succession. First came the Exclusion of Jews from German Economic Life, and then Jews were forbidden to engage in business or crafts and could no longer be employed in an executive capacity. The Minister of Education ordered the removal of Jewish pupils from German schools. Many cities established a so-called "Jew ban," which meant Jews were forbidden to enter certain residential sections, or to visit movie houses, museums, and theaters.

At this time, many Jewish families decided to emigrate if they possibly could. They escaped the worse fate which, after the outbreak of the war, awaited those who would not or could not leave.

This systematic and calculated chicanery was stepped up even more after the outbreak of the war. Beginning in 1940, Jews in many places could do their shopping only at fixed hours. Later, Jews were restricted to only a few designated stores. In September 1941, the Jewish Star Decree followed, according to which Jews 6 years and over had to wear in public "a hexagonal star, the size of a palm, bordered in black, made of yellow material, bearing the inscription 'Jew' in black letters, affixed to the left side of their garments at the height of the breast." The use of the star of David, a religious symbol, as a stigma was especially vindictive.

In countries occupied by German troops, where people had not lost their normal sensitivity through eight years of Nazi propaganda, the introduction of the decree led to many demonstrations of solidarity: on the streets people greeted Jews wearing the star with demonstrative cordiality, and non-Jews pinned yellow flowers or Jewish stars made of paper on their clothes. King Christian of Denmark announced in a message that all Danes were equally close to his heart, that he himself would be the first to wear the Jewish star, and that he expected all loyal subjects to follow suit, whereupon the Nazis withdrew their decree in Denmark. A decree on forced labor followed in October 1941. As far as possible, Jews had already been "forced to serve" as factory workers under a law proclaiming a universal obligation to work. Now the government-determined wage scales were declared inapplicable for them, and they were not permitted any bonuses, maternity benefits, or family allowances. Even the rules governing safety at work were dropped for Jewish workers!

It is embarrassing to enumerate the many petty humiliations to which the law was bent. In 1942 the *Reich* Law Gazette was filled with such decrees: all Jewish dwellings were to be marked by the star of David; Jews were not permitted to keep pets; Jews were forbidden to have their hair cut by Aryan barbers; Jews were not allowed to own electric appliances, record players, typewriters, bicycles; Jews were not allowed to visit heated public shelters, etc.

But these systematic, calculated annoyances had long since been overshadowed by an incomparably more terrifying threat. In November 1941, a decree Concerning the Deportation of Jews was announced. It read:

> Jews who do not hold jobs essential for the economy will be deported to a city in the east in the course of the next few months. The property of the Jews so deported will be confiscated for the German *Reich*. Each Jew may keep 100 Reichsmarks and 110 pounds (50 kg) of luggage.

Beginning as early as the spring of 1940, the S.S.[5] had re-established ghettoes in such Polish cities as Lublin, Lodz, Cracow, and Warsaw. The Jews were herded into designated parts of the towns, and the entire area was surrounded with fences and cordoned off with signs which warned: "No trespassing, Jewish quarter." At that time, Poland had 2.9 million

[5]Abbreviation for Schutzstaffel, the military and police unit of the Nazi party.

WOHNGEBIET DER
JUDEN
BETRETEN
VERBOTEN

The ghetto in Krakow, Poland.

Jews. These unfortunate people had been unable to emigrate, for they were mostly small farmers, tradesmen, and craftsmen and could not possibly obtain money for the voyage. They fell prey as helpless victims to the S.S.

On the pattern of these Polish ghettoes, an entire ghetto-city was established in 1941 in Terezin (Theresienstadt in Bohemia). It was to serve as a forced residence for German Jews, primarily for leading Jewish functionaries. In Germany, the rumor was spread that this camp was "especially humane," that the Jews were permitted to develop their own culture and put on plays and concerts. The only purpose of this legend was, in the last analysis, to soothe people's conscience. Those who heard that their Jewish acquaintances were transported to Theresienstadt late at night or early in the morning could perhaps rest content that after all conditions there were not too bad. In reality, this camp, like all other camps, was a well-organized hell where a man's mind withered under the narrow compulsions of collective life before his body died of hunger. For many, however, Theresienstadt was only a station on the way to the extermination camps established for the "final solution of the Jewish question."

On July 31, 1941, Goring issued instructions to Heydrich, the S.D.[6] chief, to submit a comprehensive draft for the carrying out of the "final solution of the Jewish question." It is difficult to determine Goring's precise intentions. The letter speaks only of emigration and evacuation. But where could the Jews have been evacuated to at that time? Hitler had attacked Russia on June 22, 1941. Not only were the Polish Jews in his net but also their co-religionists in Holland, France, Czechoslovakia, the

[6]Abbreviation for Sicherheitsdienst, the Nazi security service.

Balkan countries, and western Russia. What was to happen to them? Among the S.S., plans were circulated for the deportation of all Jews to the island of Madagascar, off the African coast.

Since such plans were impractical, the doctrinaires around Himmler decided to "exterminate" the Jews. The minutes of a meeting held at the Grosse Wannsee to plan the "final solution" (known as the Wannsee Protocol) read as follows:

> As a further possibility of solving the question, the evacuation of the Jews to the east can now be substituted for emigration, after obtaining permission from the Fuehrer to that effect. However, these actions are merely to be considered as alternative possibilities, even though they will permit us to make all those practical experiences which are of great importance for the future final solution of the Jewish question.
>
> The Jews should in the course of the Final Solution be taken in a suitable manner to the east for use as labor. In big labor gangs, separated by sex, the Jews capable of work will be brought to these areas for road building, in which task undoubtedly a large number will fall through natural diminution. The remnant that is finally able to survive all this—since this is undoubtedly the part with the strongest resistance—must be treated accordingly, since these people, representing a natural selection, are to be regarded as the germ cell of a new Jewish development, in case they should succeed and go free (as history has proved). In the course of the execution of the Final Solution, Europe will be combed from west to east.

Nowhere is the bureaucratic make-believe language of the S.S., the language of inhumanity, revealed more horribly than in this document. Following this blueprint, the S.S. began to call its subsequent mass murder "special treatment." Faced with tremendous numbers of absolutely helpless human beings, the executioners of the Third *Reich* were seized with a frenzy of extermination.

At first, "special treatment" consisted in mass shootings. The Jews were dragged out of their ghettoes and ordered to dig ditches in remote places. Next, every man, woman, child, and aged person had to strip naked, and carefully place his clothing and his shoes on piles. Then, five to ten people at a time had to step up together to the edge of the ditch, and were mowed down with a tommy gun. After the mass graves had filled with 500 to 1000 bodies, they were covered with lime and earth. It is reported that Himmler was so nauseated when he witnessed this "method," that he recommended from then on, as a "more humane means," the use of poison gas (to be released in vans or specially constructed chambers camouflaged as shower rooms). Suitable facilities for this form of mass extermination were constructed in the large extermination camps of Auschwitz, Maidanek, and Treblinka. Huge crematoria were built, and the bodies were burned around the clock.

To top this absolutely infernal system the Jews themselves were ordered to operate the entire machinery of murder. They had to remove

Deportation from a Polish town.

the piled-up bodies from the gas chambers and to operate the crematoria. The only hope remaining to these workers in their ghastly work was, perhaps, to escape death.

Today, some people refuse to face up to these appalling facts. But can we be so cowardly as to evade even in our imaginations the suffering that real people, people such as you and I, had to bear in harsh reality?

When those Jews who were still free learned about the ultimate destinations of their deported co-religionists, they sought, by any available means, to go underground and live "illegally." Help was offered in Holland, where a large segment of the population proved its mettle [moral strength], and there were similar cases in Germany, though not nearly enough.

The dangers were very great, indeed. Those underground had no more ration cards, the only means of obtaining food during the war years. They had to share the scanty rations of their protectors, and lived in constant danger of discovery. The "illegal" people also suffered many dreadful hours during air raids on German cities, where they had the alternative of staying unprotected in their apartments, or risking discovery by going to a public air-raid shelter.

For the many who found this escape barred, the end was always the same: first, work to exhaustion in factories "essential for the war," each day filled with fear that relatives incapable of work had received orders for deportation to the east. . . . This would come for everyone some day. . . . In the last moment, many chose to die by their own hands. . . . At collection points, the deportees were robbed of their last belongings. Then, for days, the trip in overcrowded cattle-cars. If Theresienstadt was the destination, it could mean a small respite. If it was one of the notorious extermination camps, incoming transports were led to "selection." Men were separated from women, children torn away from parents. The sick, the aged, the weak, and the children were sent to the left at "selection": their destiny was death. Those still considered capable of work were sent into the barracks and had to work as slaves for their miserable food until they died of hunger or epidemics, or were themselves selected for extermination. The threat of death hung ever present over all; the smell of the crematoria lay like a cloud over the camps.

Nor was this all. The S.S. guards held daily roll-calls in these camps, too, and forced the emaciated prisoners, in their garb of rags, to stand in rain, snow, sun, or wind until all inmates had been counted. Woe to any of these human beings who lost his precarious hold on life and died unnoticed in a barrack on a heap of rags! Then the prisoners were counted and re-counted and 24, even 48, hours might pass before the prisoners were allowed to disband. Those who fell down were kicked or beaten.

This lust for extermination was revealed to its full extent in the copious records where all murders were listed with bureaucratic pedantry. An S.S. Economic and Administrative Main Office was founded exclusively for such purposes as collecting and packaging all the possessions of the murdered, from tons of clothing to eye glasses, artificial teeth, gold teeth, and women's hair, and "utilizing" them. Man was not only exterminated as if he were vermin, he was also made into matter and exploited as a "source of raw material" for the war economy.

This was the result of the Final Solution:

Country	Jewish Pop., Sept. 1939	Jewish Losses	Percentage of Jewish Losses
1. Poland	3,300,000	2,800,000	85.0
2. USSR, occupied territory	2,100,000	1,500,000	71.4
3. Rumania	850,000	425,000	50.0
4. Hungary	404,000	200,000	49.5
5. Czechoslovakia	315,000	260,000	82.5
6. France	300,000	90,000	30.0
7. Germany	210,000	170,000	81.0
8. Lithuania	150,000	135,000	90.0
9. Netherlands	150,000	90,000	60.0
10. Latvia	95,000	85,000	89.5
11. Belgium	90,000	40,000	44.4
12. Greece	75,000	60,000	80.0
13. Yugoslavia	75,000	55,000	73.3
14. Austria	60,000	40,000	66.6
15. Italy	57,000	15,000	26.3
16. Bulgaria	50,000	7,000	14.0
17. Others	20,000	6,000	30.0
	8,301,000	**5,978,000**	**72.0**

Nobody will ever fully appreciate the suffering behind these figures: the humiliations, the shame, the agony. We cannot escape it by saying that we did not know about it and had never wanted it to happen. However true this may be, where were we when we should have opposed the beginnings? One of the most impressive short stories of Leo Tolstoy bears the title: "If you let the flame rise, you will never extinguish it!" We let the flame of hatred rise and did not extinguish it while there was still time. We allowed posters and songs to spread hatred and abuse while we were still at liberty to fight against them. This first sin of omission gave rise to all the later crimes.

To the injustice committed in our name we must not add the injustice of forgetting. While relatives still mourn their dead, can we forget because the shadows of the past are painful to us? There is no restitution for such enormous suffering. But by preserving the memory of the victims, we can perform a sacred duty imposed upon us by the guilt we bear toward our Jewish fellow-citizens.

B. Writings of the Nazi Holocaust*
ERNST PAWEL

Note: the following text is based on the original script delivered by Mr. Ernst Pawel, novelist and critic, on closed-circuit television, and is now available on 16 mm. film or videotape. For information on rental or purchase, write to: Audio-Visual Department, Anti-Defamation League of B'nai B'rith, 315 Lexington Avenue, New York, N.Y. 10016, or contact the regional office nearest you.

> The last, the very last,
> So richly, brightly, dazzlingly yellow.
> Perhaps if the sun's tears would sing
> against a white stone . . .
>
> Such, such a yellow
> Is carried lightly 'way up high.
> It went away I'm sure because it wished to kiss the world goodbye.
>
> For seven weeks I've lived in here,
> Penned up inside this ghetto
> But I have found my people here.
> The dandelions call to me
> And the white chestnut candles in the court.
> Only I never saw another butterfly.
>
> That butterfly was the last one.
> Butterflies don't live in here,
> In the ghetto.

This poem was written by a child, a child who was gassed and burned shortly after writing it. Somehow it seems both callous and inappropriate to talk about this poem, this painful and lingering echo of a soul, in terms of a particular class of literature. Yet this is one difficulty which has to be confronted in any discussion of what has come to be called *holocaust literature:* i.e., the effort required to disregard the traditional . . . categories in this particular instance, and to accept instead *as literature* the entire range of voices trying somehow or other to cope with, or articulate, an experience without historic precedent. This experience, because of its very nature, defies in the end all such efforts; after all, language—being human—has its limitations when it comes to dealing with the unspeakable. Nonetheless, inadequate and fragmentary though the efforts may be, they have meaning and remain of vital importance to us, the survivors.

For in a sense we are all survivors.

*Adapted from a film lecture by Ernst Pawel, in *Teacher's Study Guide: Writings of the Nazi Holocaust* (New York: Anti-Defamation League of B'nai B'rith, no date), pp. 5–13.

What we, that is, our generation, have to live with—and I don't just mean Jews, but all of us—is the fact that the Nazi holocaust was an end to a certain kind of innocence. In the light of what happened, we know now that there is practically no limit to the horror and brutality which men are capable of perpetrating under certain conditions. And what the so-called holocaust literature has done is to force us to face this fact. Of course there is no guarantee that it won't happen again—and, to repeat, I don't just mean to Jews, but to any minority; but if we know as much as it is possible to know of how it came about, our chances of preventing it from recurring may be a little better.

As literature, then, these writings are unique in both their function and scope. They are, of course, also unique in terms of their subject matter. If I briefly refer—as I will—to the "facts" in which they are rooted, I do so not in order to rake up questions of guilt and punishment once again nor to parade the grim and gruesome statistics you will find fully documented in the records of the Nuremberg Tribunal, but for another reason entirely. Take Anne Frank's *The Diary of a Young Girl,* for example. Though it unquestionably is a moving document in its own right, it is nonetheless crucial for us to keep in mind that it is our knowledge of what happened after the last line was written, rather than the story itself, which gives it a dimension no amount of art or candor could possibly convey.

What are these "facts" then? The most important is Adolph Hitler's "Final Solution," so called because it refers to the planned and calculated murder of six million Jews by gas, bullets, torture, starvation, disease. Most of these murders were committed in a series of death camps especially constructed for the purpose, the largest of which was Auschwitz, in Poland.

Under questioning, Rudolf Hoess, Auschwitz's commander, had this to say about his work:

> I commanded Auschwitz until December 1, 1943, and estimate that at least 2,500,000 victims were executed and exterminated there by gassing and burning, and at least another half million succumbed to starvation and disease. These figures represent about 70 to 80% of all the persons sent to Auschwitz as prisoners. Included among the executed and burned were approximately 20,000 Russian prisoners of war.
>
> In June 1941 I visited Treblinka to find out how they carried out their exterminations. The camp commander told me that he had liquidated 80,000 in the course of six months. He was mainly concerned with liquidating the Jews from the Warsaw ghetto. He used monoxide gas, and I did not think his methods were very efficient. So when I set up shop at Auschwitz, I used Cyclon B, which took from 3 to 15 minutes to kill the people in the death chamber. We knew when the people were dead because their screaming stopped. . . . After the bodies were removed, our special commandos took off the rings and extracted the gold from the teeth of the corpses.

Another improvement we made was that, where at Treblinka the victims almost always knew what lay ahead, at Auschwitz we tried to fool them into thinking that they were going through a disinfection process.[1]

For reasons not too difficult to understand, the butchery of millions of people with such an unprecedented brutality literally paralyzes the imagination, and this no doubt is the reason why so very little "fiction" in the conventional sense has come out of this experience. Among firsthand accounts, there is the work of Elie Wiesel and Miguel De Castillo who, though basing their stories on what they themselves lived through, attempt nonetheless to transform their personal experience into something that is both more objective and of greater symbolic meaning. (Their work, incidentally, is available in English.) There exist as well a number of novels by authors who fortunately did not have to undergo these horrors themselves—John Hersey, Richard Ellman, George Steiner and Leon Uris.

. . . The most significant part of holocaust literature consists of straightforward accounts in the form of diaries and records that have survived even where their authors did not, and of personal recollections penned after the liberation by those who did survive. However, it is the more ambitious literary attempts at transcending personal experience and seeking a larger meaning that finally have the greatest import and the most relevance to our present discussion. For it is literature in the sense in which we have just defined it that has the real power to translate facts and figures into something accessible to the emotions as well as the intellect, obliging us to experience at least some small part of the agony frozen into these statistics. We may refuse to look, of course, as so many did even while the camps were in full operation. But, like them, we do so only at our own risk.

How did it all start? Here is one writer's account:

In his heavy, slow step, his fat hands swinging against his thighs, the teacher walked peacefully back to his desk. When he was on the platform again, he stiffened his neck and, taking up the pointer, he thrust it forward in a gesture of command. "And now," he cried in a raging tone . . . "Dogs, Negroes and Jews, step forward."

For a moment Ernie Levy attributed those words to Herr Geek's incomprehensible sense of humor, but when the students did not laugh as the teacher stared furiously at Ernie's dark curls, the boy understood that the phrase was directed solely at the Jews. Immediately, he slipped to the side to take up his position as a Jew in the center of the aisle. . . .

"Jews," Herr Geek cried, "When I give an order to the class in general, it means that I am addressing myself to the German students and not to their guests."

[1]Whitney F. Harris, *Tyranny on Trial* (Dallas, Texas: Southern Methodist University Press, 1954), p. 336.

> Rigid in his military posture, only his lower jaw moving, Herr Geek launched a confused, menacing diatribe at the "Jewish guests." These last . . . were to know that Herr Geek would always find a way to make himself understood when he wished to address himself to them—for example, by beginning the phrase with the name of an animal.[2]

This, then, is a typical example of how it began: with prejudice and its inevitable bedfellow, segregation. Yet for the Nazis to achieve one of their primary goals, which was *total* segregation of the Jews, a long and determined effort was necessary. There were, it must be remembered, a number of Germans who actively helped their "non-Aryan" friends and neighbors throughout the duration of the Hitler regime. Similarly, some of the clergy openly condemned the atrocities and persecutions—the outstanding example being that of Father Bernhard Lichtenberg of St. Hedwig's Cathedral in Berlin, who, after repeated arrests and warnings, asked to be allowed to share the fate of his Jewish brethren. (His wish was duly granted.) But there are few saintly figures like Father Lichtenberg in this world, and even the number of ordinary people who are willing to stand up and be counted as their brothers' keepers is frighteningly small. Moreover, and perhaps even more important, the true picture of what really was happening did not become clear for a very long time, not even to the victims themselves.

A striking and, at the same time, pathetic example of this "ignorance" can be found in Anne Frank's *Diary*. Of all the books to have come out of the Nazi holocaust none had moved more people, and moved them more profoundly, than this book, written by a young Jewish girl who was killed on the threshold of life. Just one girl out of all the millions killed; yet, because of this very fact, someone in whom we can all recognize some part of ourselves and for whom we can personally mourn—as we cannot mourn for the other faceless millions.

Here is Anne Frank's pathetically naive entry of May 22, 1944—at a time when millions of her fellow Jews had already been killed:

> It is being rumored in underground circles that the German Jews who emigrated to Holland and who are now in Poland will not be allowed to return here; they once had the right of asylum in Holland, but when Hitler has gone they will have to go back to Germany again.

Anne Frank wanted to, or had to, believe that the German Jews she speaks of were all still alive, rather than victims of the gas chamber. Not even in her wildest nightmare could she have imagined her former compatriots capable of gassing not only adults but children like herself, and then processing the thousands and thousands of corpses into soap.

[2]Andre Schwartz-Bart, *The Last of the Just* (New York: Atheneum Publishers, 1960).

Nor was she alone in this belief. The majority of the Jews, and even the Nazis, blinded themselves in one way or another to the terrible reality.

Which may be just as well. But this ignorance or innocence, this very human refusal to believe "the unbelievable," however necessary it may be from the viewpoint of preserving sanity, was an important factor, perhaps *the* most important factor in the terrible success of Hitler's "Final Solution." And it is for this reason that we, the living, can no longer afford the luxury of such illusions.

Here is another quote, this time from the diary, *Scroll of Agony,* of the Hebrew scholar Chaim A. Kaplan, killed at Treblinka. The entry is dated July 26, 1942, and by this time Kaplan no longer had to guess. *He knew.*

> A whole community with an ancient tradition, one that with all its faults was the very backbone of world Jewry, is going to destruction. They came and divided the Warsaw ghetto into two halves; one half was for sword, pestilence and destruction, the other half for famine and slavery. The vigorous youth, the healthy and productive ones, were taken to work in the factories. The old people, the women, the children were all sent into exile. There was only one decree—death.

An inevitable question looms up at this point. Once this stage of certainty, of knowledge had been reached, why did the Jews go to their death without a last-ditch resistance? Or, as the historian Emmanuel Ringelblum asks in his diary: "Why are they all so quiet? Why does the father die, and the mother, and each of the children without a single protest?"

Kaplan, for one, has an answer. Here it is: "A mother refused to surrender her baby. The Nazis immediately grabbed the baby and hurled it out of the window. . . . During a deportation two powerfully built porters fought their captors. The next morning the Nazis avenged the mutiny of the two porters by killing 110 Jews."

Some other answers or explanations that have been offered are:

1. Lack of weapons (only a few dozen guns were available even in the largest revolt, that of the Warsaw ghetto).
2. The young were restrained by a sense of collective responsibility— i.e., the fact that the Nazis retaliated at the ratio of a hundred or even a thousand to one.
3. Many of the others—the old, the women, the children, the sick—i.e., the bulk of the ghetto population—had been reduced to impotence by hunger and disease. "Under a hundred pounds you just don't rebel," one of the survivors has said, according to Andre Malraux.

While it is certainly true that the life led by the vast majority of Jews in pre-War Europe failed to prepare them for anything approaching armed resistance, it is perhaps even more to the point that the spiritual values for which they lived (ranging from cosmopolitan liberalism to religious orthodoxy) prevented the sort of militant action which, though ultimately suicidal, might at least have led to the killing of a significant number of their enemy. The only ones in a position to break out of this traditional mold were the young, most of whom were members of some political or youth organization, and whose actions set up tensions within the Jewish community that have yet to die down and that touch upon the very essence of faith. In any case, the fact remains that those who considered it preferable to die rather than to kill, to die as a man rather than to accept the value system of the enemy and live as a murderer, were certainly no less heroic than those who chose to die by fighting in the rebellions of Warsaw, Treblinka and hundreds of other small and unrecorded actions.

Alexander Donat, in his *Holocaust Kingdom,* eloquently argues this point:

> Try to imagine Jesus on the way to Golgotha suddenly stopping to pick up a stone and hurling it at one of the Roman legionnaires. After such an act, could he ever have become the Christ? Think of Gandhi, and Tolstoy, too. For two thousand years we have served mankind with the Word, with the Book. Are we now to try to convince mankind that we are warriors? We shall never outdo them at that game.

This attitude was shared by Anne Frank and her parents who, once their hideout was discovered, offered no resistance to their captors. *Not,* however, by the well-known psychologist and author, Dr. Bruno Bettelheim, who (echoing to some extent the attitudes of present-day Israeli youth) has charged that the behavior of the Franks, though typical of thousands of families caught in a similar trap, was criminally wrong, short-sighted and stupid; that Mr. Frank, instead of teaching his daughter history and Latin, could have put his time to much better use by exploring possible escape routes, and acquiring some weapons so that, if all else failed, he would have been able to kill at least a Nazi or two before being killed himself.

On the face of it, this is certainly a reasonable and plausible point of view. Yet I suspect that, in order for Mr. Frank to have shared it, he would have had to have been clairvoyant enough to know what we know today; to have had our perspective on recent historical events. It is true, of course, that fear tends to blind men to reality, makes them cling to illusions and act irrationally. This is Dr. Bettelheim's main point. But it is also possible to take the attitude that Mr. Frank, improvident and impractical though he may have been, was struggling desperately against almost impossible odds to maintain what *he* regarded as supremely important, i.e., human values and human dignity; and that he strove, by whatever limited means were at his disposal, to counteract the dehumanization which the enemy was everywhere seeking to impose.

Dachau, a former ammunition factory, held more than 206,000 prisoners between 1933 and 1945; 32,000 deaths can be certified.

In any case, by one road or another, they almost all reached the "Heart of Darkness"; fell victims to the "Final Solution." The physical agony suffered requires no further comment. But what comes through in all the books written on the subject is the truly terrifying torment of the spirit—the feeling of complete isolation from the rest of the world—the feeling (amply justified) that in their hour of agony they were abandoned by nearly all of mankind. We are concerned here not with the moral implications of this failure of mankind (though there were notable exceptions, such as the case of the Danes who saw to it that almost no Jews fell into Nazi hands); we are concerned, rather, with the impact this failure had on the spirit of camp inmates. The eyes and ears of humanity seemed shut, and not a move, not even a token gesture was forthcoming to bring, if not help, at least a message of hope.

And beyond this human silence lay the even more terrifying silence of God. It is all too easy today to reaffirm the lesson of Job, to reassert the truism that God's ways are not man's ways. But to have gone through that hell on earth and to have retained one's faith required a kind of heroism rare among men. To cite just one example:

The SS seemed more preoccupied, more disturbed than usual. To hang a young boy in front of thousands of spectators was no light matter. The head of the camp read the verdict. All eyes were on the child. He was lividly pale, biting his lips. The gallows threw its shadow over him.

This time the Lagerkapo refused to act as executioner. Three SS replaced him.

The three victims mounted together onto the chairs.

The three necks were placed at the same moment within the nooses.

"Long live liberty," cried the two adults.

But the child was silent.

"Where is God? Where is He?" someone behind me asked.

At a sign from the head of the camp, the three chairs tipped over.

Total silence throughout the camp. On the horizon the sun was setting.

"Bare your heads," yelled the head of the camp.

His voice was raucous. We were weeping.

"Cover your heads."

Then the march past began. The two adults were no longer alive. Their tongues hung swollen, blue-tinged. But the third rope was still moving; being so light, the child was still alive. . . .

For more than half an hour he stayed there, struggling between life and death, dying in slow agony under our eyes. And we had to look him full in the face. He was still alive when I passed in front of him. His tongue was still red, his eyes were not glazed.

Behind me I heard the same man asking:

"Where is God now?"

And I heard a voice within me answer him:

"Where is He? Here He is—He is hanging on this gallows. . . ."

That night the soup tasted of corpses.

This passage, from the deeply moving autobiographical novel, *Night,* by Elie Wiesel, is one of the relatively few examples of "fiction" written by a survivor. The following passage, on the other hand, is completely factual and is taken from the diary of Leon Wells, a man assigned to the death brigade but who escaped and lived to testify at Nuremberg. The book is called *The Janowska Road:*

> At seven o'clock in the morning we have formation in our yard. We are counted, and the young man who had been appointed our leader reports our number to the storm trooper guards. After the report we scatter about the yard. The breakfast arrives from the concentration camp by truck. Ten men go out to unload breakfast. In addition to our breakfast, the truck is loaded with corpses, those who were killed yesterday in the concentration camp. And so, from now on, every morning with our breakfast we shall also receive corpses.

The silence of man, and the silence of God—the two questions framing the gateway to an end beyond understanding. An operation conducted on a truly fantastic scale, . . . not by beasts in the guise of human beings, but by clockwork executives in charge of a giant . . . murder machine aimed at the extermination of ever more and more millions. An operation which ultimately took precedence over all other tasks, including the continuation of the war—to the point where, at the very end, with Allied and Soviet armies already penetrating into the heartland of Germany, precious vehicles were still being diverted in vast quantities for no purpose other than mass murder. And not only of Jews, at this point, but of *all* so-called inferior races. A murder which continued unabated until 9½ million non-Jews had been killed as well.

The classic example is Babi Yar, a ravine in Kiev, where the Nazis first exterminated all of Kiev's Jews and then killed hundreds of Ukrainians routinely, day in and day out, for the next two years. A butchery graphically described by Anatoly Kuznetsov in his book, *Babi Yar:*

> Meanwhile, routine executions went right on in Babi Yar as before. But the dead were no longer buried; they were tossed into the furnaces at once. Prisoners on their last legs, those who couldn't work anymore, were also dumped in—alive.
>
> Gas vans often came from town with living passengers. They drove right up to the furnaces before the gas was turned on. From inside came muffled cries, followed by wild banging on the doors. Then all was quiet. The Germans opened the doors, and prisoners unloaded the bodies. They were warm, moist with sweat, and perhaps still half-alive. They were laid on the pyre.

But, if dehumanization was the prelude to death, the victims' attempts to remain human represented the transcendence of death. "We are all going to die very soon," Jorge Semprun quotes one of the Jewish doctors at the Auschwitz prison hospital as saying. "But as long as we are alive, let us live like human beings."

. . . Or listen to Joseph Bor as he describes a performance of Verdi's *Requiem* at the Terezin concentration camp:

> And did the listeners appreciate the music? Of that he had no doubt; he felt the deep-held breath in the auditorium, and the intensity of emotion. Did they even understand the speech of the music, did they grasp what it was trying to say to them? "I cannot speak to you in words, I am addressing you in music, but listen to me, you prisoners in a Jewish concentration camp: The end of the war is coming. We who are the seed of Abraham will tread no more the way of the Cross. For you, too, suffering is at an end. We'll walk no more in darkness and insecurity; the day of life is dawning. Listen to what the choir is singing to you. *Libera me.* Do you understand? Freedom, freedom!"

In concluding, I don't want to imply that the image of the Jew as it emerges from holocaust literature ranges simply from martyr to hero. Rather, it is—first and last—the image of a victim. The manner in which men deal with the forces that victimize them varies not only from one man to the next, but also within the same man, depending on circumstances. Many responded to the systematic dehumanization of the Nazis by becoming themselves less than human—brutalized, ready to work for and with the assassins. Others, again, were intent only on their own physical survival. And yet, in each and every one of these books, there also emerges (even under the most extreme conditions) cases of individuals whose strength and heroism defy conventional terms and standards. In fact, the mere existence of these writings is itself an eloquent testimony to the strength of the human spirit.

We are all of us—Jews and non-Jews alike—survivors of this experience. And one of the prices of survival is the awesome knowledge that it happened, that it could happen again in our time, and that only we ourselves stand in the way of such an event. This, I think, is the true message and meaning of holocaust literature.

I want to take leave of you as I began—with another poem by a dead child:

I'd like to go away alone
Where there are other, nicer people,
Somewhere into the far unknown
There, where no one kills another.

Maybe more of us,
A thousand strong
Will reach this goal
Before too long.

C. Children's Writings*

. . . We got used to standing in line at 7 o'clock in the morning, at 12 noon and again at seven o'clock in the evening. We stood in a long queue with a plate in our hand, into which they ladled a little warmed-up water with a salty or a coffee flavor. Or else they gave us a few potatoes. We got used to sleeping without a bed, to saluting every uniform, not to walk on the sidewalks and then again to walk on the sidewalks. We got used to undeserved slaps, blows and executions. We got accustomed to seeing people die in their own excrement, to seeing piled-up coffins full of corpses, to seeing the sick amidst dirt and filth and to seeing the helpless doctors. We got used to that from time to time, one thousand unhappy souls would come here and that, from time to time, another thousand unhappy souls would go away. . . .

From the prose of 15-year-old Petr Fischl (born September 9, 1929), who perished in Oswiecim in 1944.

Fear

Today the ghetto knows a different fear,
Close in its grip, Death wields an icy scythe.
An evil sickness spreads a terror in its wake,
The victims of its shadow weep and writhe.

Today a father's heartbeat tells his fright
And mothers bend their heads into their hands.
Now children choke and die with typhus here,
A bitter tax is taken from their bands.

My heart still beats inside my breast
While friends depart for other worlds.
Perhaps it's better—who can say?—
Than watching this, to die today?

No, no, my God, we want to live!
Not watch our numbers melt away.
We want to have a better world,
We want to work—we must not die!

Eva Pickova, 12 years old, Nymburk

On a Sunny Evening

On a purple, sun-shot evening
Under wide-flowering chestnut trees

Fantasy *by Raja Englanderova, 14 years old. Of the 15,000 children who came to Terezin, only 100 survived. Raja was one of the survivors.*

*From *I Never Saw Another Butterfly: Children's Drawings and Poems from Terezin Concentration Camp 1942-1944* (New York: McGraw-Hill Book Co., 1964), pp. 14, 45, 53.

Upon the threshold full of dust
Yesterday, today, the days are all like these.

Trees flower forth in beauty,
Lovely too their very wood all gnarled and old
That I am half afraid to peer
Into their crowns of green and gold.

The sun has made a veil of gold
So lovely that my body aches.
Above, the heavens shriek with blue
Convinced I've smiled by some mistake.

The world's abloom and seems to smile.
I want to fly but where, how high?
If in barbed wire, things can bloom
Why couldn't I? I will not die!

1944 Anonymous
Written by the children in Barracks L 318 and L 417,
ages 10–16 years.

The Flower Seller *by Helena Mandlova, 13 years old. A collage of paper cut from office forms.*

A contemporary (1962) photograph of Auschwitz.

READING 19

Disaster*

ABRAHAM JOSHUA HESCHEL

1945 . . . A new conception: The world is a slaughterhouse. Hope is obscene. It is sinful to remain sane.

Six million lives gone. Wherever we dwell, we live in a graveyard. Only one way out, the way to the inferno.

1945 . . . Is this what is left of us: chimneys in the extermination camps?

What shall come after the holocaust: nights of despair, no dawn, never, but endless shrieks? Anguish forever, no relief, life is gall, history a scourge? Has the world lost its soul? Have civilization and humanity nothing in common?

Has Auschwitz ended our future as well?

Three out of four Jews in Europe—dead. Two out of five of us anywhere in the world—dead. Will the spirit of those who survived be reduced to ashes? The Allied Armies which freed the concentration camps came upon tens of thousands of emaciated bodies, skeletons, dry bones. "Son of man, can these bones live?" Judaism was reduced to dry bones, faith in God was on trial. Will this people, crushed, battered, crippled, tortured, find strength to survive?

What should have been our answer to Auschwitz? Should this people, called to be a witness to the God of mercy and compassion, persist in its witness and cling to Job's words: "Even if He slay me yet will I trust in Him" (Job 13:15), or should this people follow the advice of Job's wife,

*Adapted from Abraham Joshua Heschel, *Israel: An Echo of Eternity* (New York: Farrar, Strauss and Giroux, 1969), pp. 111–15.

"Curse God and die!" (Job 2:9), immerse itself into the anonymity of a hundred nations all over the world, and disappear once and for all?

Our people's faith in God at this moment in history did not falter. At this moment in history Isaac was indeed sacrificed, his blood shed. We all died in Auschwitz, yet our faith survived. We knew that to deny God would be to continue the holocaust.

We have once lived in a civilized world, rich in trust and expectation. Then we all died, were condemned to dwell in hell. Now we are living in hell. Our present life is our afterlife. . . .

We did not blaspheme, we built. Our people did not burst forth in flight from God. On the contrary, at that moment in history we saw the beginning of a new awakening, the emergence of a new concern for a Living God theology. Escape from Judaism giving place increasingly to a new attachment, to a rediscovery of our legacy.

How would the world have looked at the Jewish people if the survivors of the concentration camps had gone the path of complete assimilation? Flight from God? From Judaism?

What would be the face of Western history today if the end of twentieth-century Jewish life would have been Bergen-Belsen, Dachau, Auschwitz? The State of Israel is not an atonement. It would be blasphemy to regard it as a compensation. However, the existence of Israel reborn makes life less unendurable. . . .

We are tired of expulsions, of massacres; we have had enough of extermination camps. We are tired of apologizing for our existence. If I should go to Poland or Germany, every stone, every tree would remind me of contempt, hatred, murder, of children killed, of mothers burned alive, of human beings asphyxiated.

When I go to Israel every stone and every tree is a reminder of hard labor and glory, of prophets and psalmists, of loyalty and holiness. The Jews go to Israel not only for physical security for themselves and their children; they go to Israel for renewal, for the experience of resurrection.

Is the State of Israel God's humble answer to Auschwitz? A sign of God's repentance for men's crime of Auschwitz?

No act is as holy as the act of saving human life. The Holy Land, having offered a haven to more than two million Jews—many of whom would not have been alive had they remained in Poland, Russia, Germany, and other countries—has attained a new holiness.

So many lives of people whose bodies were injured and whose souls were crushed found a new life and a new spirit in the land. The State of Israel, as it were, sought to respond to the prophet's advice: "Strengthen the weak hands, and make firm the feeble knees" (Isaiah 35:3).

In 1937, the period of Nazi persecution and expulsion of the Jews from Germany, I concluded a book about Don Isaac Abravanel, who lived during the time of the expulsion of the Jews from Spain in 1492, with the following words:

The Jews, who had played a leading role in the politics, economics and social affairs of their country left (had to leave) their Spanish homeland. The conquest of the New World was achieved without them. Had they remained on the Iberian peninsula they would surely have participated in the deeds of the Conquistadores. When the latter came to Haiti they found 1,100,000 inhabitants; twenty years later only 1,000 remained.[1]

In 1492 the Jews, who were desperate, had no inkling what an act of grace was involved in their misery. Driven out of Spain, they had no part in the atrocities soon to be carried out in the New World.

And yet, there is no answer to Auschwitz. . . . To try to answer is to commit a supreme blasphemy. Israel enables us to bear the agony of Auschwitz without radical despair, to sense a ray of God's radiance in the jungles of history.

[1]Abraham J. Heschel, *Don Jizchak Abravane* (Berlin: Erich Reiss, 1937), p. 30.

A group of Hasidim arriving in Israel from the Soviet Union.

A color guard parades the flag during an Israeli Independence Day celebration.

READING 20
Israel

A. Israel: A Dream and a Nation*
MILTON STEINBERG

ISRAEL—TRADITIONALIST CONCEPTIONS

Judaism, the faith of Israel, includes also a faith *in* Israel, in the significance of the role of the Jewish people in history.

For the traditionalist that faith embraces four articles: the Election, the Covenant, the Mission, and the Vindication in time-to-come.

The Election is the doctrine that God chose Israel out of all the nations of the world to be the recipient of His revelation, the central figure in the drama of human salvation.

Why this people in particular?

In part because of the merits of the first fathers, whose righteousness was so great as to win this high calling for their descendants.

In part also because, according to one rabbinic theory, only this people was willing to accept the disciplines and hardships incidental to being elected. In this point, an ancient legend relates that God, when He was about to reveal the Torah, offered it in turn to every nation on earth, only to have it rejected because of its exacting moral demands. Israel alone received it and then . . . less out of heroism than impulsiveness.

The Covenant is the agreement between God and Israel.

*Adapted from Milton Steinberg, *Basic Judaism* (New York: Harcourt, Brace & World, 1947), pp. 91–98.

As the word implies, the agreement is two-sided. If God selected Israel, Israel consented to be selected, and in that fact may be said not only to have been chosen by God, but to have chosen Him in turn.

Under the terms of their mutual understanding, Israel as one contracting party undertakes to do God's will without reckoning cost or consequence. God, for His part, makes Israel His particular treasure, a people near to Him.

No more exalted honor can be conceived than the Election. But it presents no special privileges. Quite the reverse. It entails obligations and hardships.

More, not less, is expected of Israel by virtue of its unique station. Tribes ignorant of God and His will or uncommitted to them may be forgiven their sins and lack of respect. Not so a kingdom of priests and a holy nation which has given its solemn, pledged word: "All that the Lord hath spoken will we do and obey." Wherefore the prophet warns the Jewish people in God's name:

You only have I known of all the families of the earth;
Therefore I will visit upon you all your iniquities.

What is more, peril, not security, accompanies the Election. The advocate of justice and mercy must expect the assault of wicked men, the hostility of evil institutions. Against him the powers of darkness cannot but conspire to blot out his name, to silence his truth.

Such are the terms of the Covenant. They make a hard bargain, committing a people for all time to the role portrayed in the latter chapters of Isaiah, that of God's servant, willing to suffer if only he may serve.

But to what end the service?

Which query leads to the doctrine of the Mission.

Israel lives not merely to know God and do His will but, by preachment and example, to communicate His truth and way to the nations, so that blind eyes may be opened, the prisoners come forth from dungeons, and in the end all men be induced to form one band to do the right with a perfect heart.

The goal and final objective of the Mission are then none other than the deliverance of mankind. But in that happy event, when it has come to pass, what will be the servant's portion?

Israel will be present at the final outcome to experience his Vindication. His time of service ended, his commission discharged, he will partake, as he deserves, of the universal redemption he has labored so mightily to bring to pass.

His children, so long dispersed and persecuted, will be reassembled in their ancient land, there to enjoy peace and security proportionate to the bitterness and length of their exile.

The Jewish religion, so long mocked at and scoffed, will be universally recognized as the true faith.

The ruined Temple in Jerusalem will be rebuilt to stand as a house of prayer for all nations.

It is a glowing justification which the traditionalist foresees for Israel. But here too—and nothing could be more typical of the Jewish spirit—not the Jewish people alone comes into its own but all men with it; its deliverance being, when all is said and done, a part, essential but still a part, of the redemption of the whole human family.

ISRAEL—MODERNIST REINTERPRETATION

Modernists have done a quite thorough job of reworking the traditional conception of the Jewish people, rejecting some of it outright and accepting the rest only with radical alterations.

In their eyes, the doctrines of the Election, Covenant, Mission, and Vindication are all to be explained . . . as the projections of historical forces. To interpret them so does not necessarily dispute their validity; it does, however, set them in a drastically different light.

All ancient peoples, modernists point out, assumed themselves to be chosen of their gods, such a belief on the part of Jews being, to begin with, only one instance of a universal notion. Yet the Jewish conception speedily became unique. No other nation of antiquity ever came to the point of regarding itself as chosen not for its own advantage but for service.

But why did the Jews alone reach this elevation? Because, modernists respond, of two factors: the first and more potent, the genius of the prophets; the second, the misfortunes that befell the Jewish community of Palestine. Zealous that all things should advance God's design, the prophets came inevitably to look on their own people as dedicated to that purpose. At the same time, the military defeats, poverty, and political instability of the Jewish state inclined Jews to seek their group *raison d'etre* [reason for being] in directions other than conquest and prosperity.

When first conceived and for long afterward, the notion of Israel as a chosen people had substantial warrant in facts. In all the ancient world only the Jews possessed a tenable God-faith, a humane morality, and a hope for the human future.

The rise of Christianity and Mohammedanism gave further support to the Jewish claim to Election, for both of these religions viewed Israel as the original chosen people which had, however, subsequently forfeited its distinction. The Jew naturally accepted from the Gentiles the testimony favorable to himself and disregarded the rest.

Then, in the Middle Ages, the doctrine of the Election took on heightened importance for Jews, supplying them with self-respect, purposefulness, and confidence at a time when the whole world conspired to dispirit them and break their strength.

This is the outline story of the evolution of the Election, Covenant, Mission, and Vindication as modernists reconstruct it.

But what of the present validity of these doctrines?

Here modernists disagree among themselves.

Some hold that, while such ideas may once have had a reason for being and may even have been true in a fashion, they ought no longer to be retained: first, because they draw . . . contrasts between Israel and the nations; and second, because these contrasts are no longer factually defensible, the Jews these days being no more conspicuous for dedication to God's purposes than some other groups.

The typical modernist is less radical on the issue. He denies outright any interest in drawing contrasts, an occupation he finds distasteful. But he is not so ready to forget the history of the idea of the Election or so indifferent to its potential future uses.

He points out that in literal fact the Jews were the first to choose God in the sense of consecrating themselves to Him. They constitute therefore the original chosen people. Then, too, they have consistently made the doing of His will their collective purpose. Wherefore they may be said to have been a chosen people continuously. And as for the present, they may, if they so will it, go on with their historic role. They need only dedicate themselves, as did their fathers, to God's law and design. Let them choose Him once more, and they are again chosen. The Election lives, the Covenant is in force, the Mission goes forward, and the Vindication waits the predestined moment. Israel is as always the servant of God.

So holds the right-wing modernist.

But, one asks, what of the other peoples of the world?

Let them, too, choose God, he answers, and they also are chosen.

LAND AND LANGUAGE

Judaism looks upon Palestine and the Hebrew tongue as sacred.

They are sacred, both of them, for their associations. It was in the Holy Land and in Hebrew that revelation came to the prophets and was imparted by them to Israel and mankind. Palestine was the site of many of the supremely memorable incidents in Jewish history, and Hebrew was the medium for most of the precious utterances of the Jewish soul. One cannot revere the Tradition without coming by transference to revere the idiom in which it spoke and the earth from which it sprang.

Both are sacred for the uses to which they are put. It is in Hebrew that a Jew prays, worships, and conducts his spiritual exercises, entirely if he be a strict traditionalist, in part large or small if a modernist. In either case at every high moment in his spiritual career some Hebrew phrase is likely to be sounded.

Similarly the consciousness of Palestine pervades every phase of his religious life. The Scripture he reads, the prayers he recites, the rabbinic literature he studies are full of references to it. And as for Jewish rites and observances, having been fashioned in the Holy Land, they reflect their native scene. Like other faiths Judaism acknowledges the cycle of the seasons. But the calendar it follows is Palestinian in form and inspiration. Passover marks the ripening of the first grain, Pentecost the gathering of the first fruits, Tabernacles the final harvesting—all as they occur in the Holy Land. Always Palestine sets the pitch of Judaism's awareness of the agricultural and pastoral.

Land and language are sacred, last of all, for their place in the vision of the future.

Except for extreme modernists, all religious Jews regard Palestine and the Hebrew tongue as involved in some fashion in the destiny of Israel and mankind.

Many a traditionalist believes that the reconstitution of Israel on its ancestral soil is a precondition to the Messianic era. When the dispersed Jews of the world have been brought home by the Messiah, Torah will go forth from Zion, the word of the Lord from Jerusalem, swords will be beaten to plowshares and spears to pruning hooks.

Less rigid traditionalists and the bulk of modernists see the future in a less mystical light. To them Palestine and the Hebrew language contribute in natural course to the triumphant outcome of the human adventure.

For long centuries the growth of Judaism has been hampered by dispersion and persecution. But when a Jewish Commonwealth has come into being, when outcast Jews have found peace, when the Hebrew language and literature have taken root in their native soil, the Tradition will have a fresh chance at free, spontaneous unfolding. Its circumstances will be favorable as they have not been in two thousand years. And not in Palestine only, but throughout the world. For Palestine then will be a free heart pumping the blood of health and vigor to all the Jewries of the dispersion.

Who knows what revelations the people of revelations shall have to speak at that time? This much is certain: the Jewish people everywhere will be the stronger for the Homeland and its revived Hebrew culture, and therefore the better able to labor for the advent of that ideal society which it was the first to project and after which it has striven so long and mightily.

B. Eretz Yisrael*

NATHAN AUSUBEL

In a geographic sense, unquestionably the most passionate, and also the most enduring, love affair in all history has been that which has persisted between the dispersed remnants of the Jewish people and their historical homeland. From the ancient Biblical chronicle itself it would seem that this fervent attachment for Zion has enjoyed a continuity that has been uninterrupted for about four thousand years. It began as far back as the Jewish folk-memory can go in point of time: during the legendary period of the Hebrew Patriarchs—the presumed "Founding Fathers" of Israel. Eretz Yisrael was the name of the "Promised Land" which, according to the Scriptural account, God had guaranteed in the most solemn covenants he entered into with Abraham, Isaac, and Jacob, and subsequently with Moses and with the Jewish people itself during the manifestation of God at Mount Sinai. The Land of Israel thus has for the Jews a holy and awesome significance.

By the beginning of the eighth century B.C.E., the tradition of the inseparability of the Jewish people with God, the Torah, and Eretz Yisrael had already been fully established. "For out of Zion shall go forth the Torah, and the word of the Lord from Jerusalem," exulted the Prophet Isaiah. Several centuries later, the Prophet of the Babylonian Captivity, Ezekiel, recalled the ancestral homeland as *Eretz Chayyim*—"the Land of the Living." He implied thereby that Jews living in exile could be counted only as being among the dead. (*Bet Chayyim* is one of the Hebrew names for "cemetery.")

It is hardly possible to grasp the character of the emotional turmoil in the hearts of the Jewish people after the Temple had been sacked, Jerusalem destroyed, and the Kingdom of Judah ended so ingloriously by the Roman legions of Titus and Vespasian in 70–73 C.E. Thereupon, the Jewish people went into perpetual mourning, banning all luxury, all gaiety, and even the solace afforded by instrumental music. This grief, the Rabbinic Sages said, would be lifted only when the Messiah would come to re-establish the remnants of Israel on Mount Zion.

The realistic and highly intelligent Romans understood only too well the true character of the Jew's love for Eretz Yisrael. In their own selfish political interests, they did everything to curb and frustrate it. The early Church Father Eusebius notes in his *Ecclesiastical History* that, after the disastrous uprising in 132 against the Romans, the Jews were "strictly forbidden to set foot in the region around Jerusalem, by the formal decree and enactment of [the Roman Emperor] Hadrian, who commanded that they should not, even from a distance, look on their native soil."

*Adapted from Nathan Ausubel, *The Book of Jewish Knowledge* (New York: Crown Publishers, 1964), pp. 143–44.

Nevertheless, Jews found ways to avoid the harsh decrees. Maimonides, the twelfth-century rabbi-philosopher of Spain, states that "even after the Destruction [of the Temple], they gathered in Jerusalem on the Festivals, coming from all the surrounding regions."

The longing for the Jewish Homeland continued to be agonizing for the pious. Away from Eretz Yisrael, they felt orphaned and emotionally insecure. Not a few in every generation felt an overwhelming urge to journey to the Holy Land. They went there inspired with the Prophet Ezekiel's affirmative conception: to "live" in the *Land of the Living.* This traditional view is also found expressed in the medieval Cabalistic writing, the Zohar: "It is a great privilege for a man to live in the Holy Land. There the dew of heaven falls upon him in benediction; he sinks his roots deep into its life, which is holy."

Many are the instances cited in Rabbinic and medieval religious literature which dwell on the passionate love for Zion among Jews. In the Talmud, it is recorded how the noted Rabbinic scholar Ullah had left his home in the Land of Israel and gone to settle among the Jews of Babylonia. As he lay dying and recalled how distant he was then from Eretz Yisrael, he started to weep. His colleagues and his students tried to console him. They pleaded with him: "Do not weep so! We promise faithfully to carry your body to Eretz Yisrael and there bring it to eternal rest." "Of what use will that be to me?" lamented Ullah. "See, I'm losing my jewel [i.e., his soul] in this unclean land!" How he longed, said he, to surrender his soul while nestling in "the lap of my mother [Eretz Yisrael]" and not to have to surrender it while "in the lap of a strange woman [Babylonia]!"

But though many of the pious wished to settle in the Land of Israel in order to find a greater spiritual meaning for their lives, many more felt a compelling need to go there that they might die on holy soil. This compulsion was no doubt brought about by the terrible massacres of the Jews by the Crusaders and by the violence that the Church and state of medieval and later times engaged in while attempting to baptize the Jews.

There was much pathos in the journeys to Zion. The "exiles" were like footsore wanderers going home again. Many perished from hunger on the way. Others met with death at the hands of robbers, or of fanatical Christians or Mohammedans.

With the sixteenth century, in the wake of the many calamities that had struck at the Jews in Europe, and at a time when they had sunk back into ignorance and superstition in Eastern Europe, the practical Cabala ensnared the minds of tens of thousands of Jews. The return to Eretz Yisrael, which had been a thin but perpetual stream until this time, now turned into a virtual torrent. Large communities of devout Jews formed in Jerusalem, Hebron, Safed, and Tiberias.

The zealots of the Return greatly increased in numbers in the second half of the eighteenth century with the mass-arrival of sectarian Chasidim from Poland, Galicia, and the Ukraine. In a mystical sense, the Chasidim were both the inheritors and the continuators of the Cabalist doctrines and outlook and way of life. Probably the most compelling reason for their return was their wish to be buried in the sacred soil of Eretz Yisrael so that, when the Messiah would come and the first trumpet blast announcing the Resurrection would sound, they would lose no time in rising from their graves.

The Jewish cemetery in the Valley of Jehoshaphat, at Jerusalem, presents an appalling spectacle. It consists of a forest of graves tumbling over one another. The older tombstones have long since crumbled and disappeared to make way for the new ones.

A folkway still practiced outside of Eretz Yisrael is the sprinkling of a little earth from the Holy Land into the open graves of tradition-minded Jews at their burial. It is a vicarious way of satisfying the yearning of the pious Jew of the Dispersion for being united, in a physical sense at least, with the Holy Land. That this custom must have originated during the Middle Ages is indicated in the somewhat tentative report by a medieval rabbi: "I have heard that earth from the Holy Land, when it is sprinkled upon the eyes, navel and between the legs of those who die outside of that country, is considered equal to being buried in Eretz Yisrael itself."

There can be little doubt but that cumulative emotional and psychological factors in the religious-national attachment of the Jews to the historic land of their forefathers for so many years determined the inevitable geographic direction Zionism took. The establishment of the State of Israel in Eretz Yisrael in 1948 bears witness to this timeless and enduring love.

C. The Jewish State and Judaism*
ISIDORE EPSTEIN

The rebirth of the Jewish State after a submergence of about two thousand years is one of the great miracles of the ages. . . . Miraculous, too, must be accounted the ingathering, in the course of the first decade of the State's existence, of one million destitute exiles from about sixty different countries, and their integration into the economic, social, and cultural structure of the country. No less astonishing and unprecedented is the rapid development of the new State, the expansion of its agricultural settlements and industries, and the exploitation of its resources. Equally astonishing is the creation, out of what was once a wilderness, of a modern welfare state with a rich social and cultural life,

*Adapted from Isidore Epstein, *Judaism: A Historical Presentation* (New York: Penguin Books, 1959), pp. 319–20, 322.

with schools, universities, research institutes, social services, labour organizations, hospitals, libraries, museums.

On the cultural side, the creative activity of the State is evident in the growth of its fine arts, music, poetry, drama, but particularly in the great revival of the Hebrew language and literature. In the religious sphere, too, though Israel is a democracy where religion is a matter of choice, and though indeed widespread non-observance is noticeable, there has been notable progress. Evidence of this is the fact that much of what constitutes the Jewish way of life has found and is finding its way more and more into the fabric of the Jewish State. Saturday is the national day of rest. On this day all government offices are closed. No ship loads or unloads at Israeli ports. No aircraft lands or takes off; no train runs. Shops and cinemas are closed; public bus services are suspended. What applies to the Sabbath applies also to the religious festivals. The dietary laws, Biblical and Rabbinic, are strictly observed in the Army, as well as in other public institutions and services under government control, such as the police, schools, hospitals, and prisons. The law of personal status (marriage and divorce) conforms to traditional Jewish law and is under the exclusive jurisdiction of the Rabbinical Courts, except for the non-Jewish population who have recourse to their respective religious tribunals.

State religious schools cater for the wishes of observant parents. . . . Not since the destruction of the Temple has there been such a large concentration of Torah and Jewish learning in Israel as there is today. . . . Many leading Rabbinic sages from all parts of the world have taken up residence in the State of Israel, all contributing to the enrichment of spiritual life and to the fostering of religious knowledge throughout the length and breadth of the country. There is also a very significant literary production in the religious field. Books and publications on every aspect of Jewish thought and teaching are appearing in quick succession, transmitting the wisdom of the ages to the sons and daughters of the new Israel.

At the same time it should be noted that there is no interference whatsoever in the private life, beliefs, and practices of the individual. The link between 'Religion and State' in Israel is no greater than it is in most Western countries, including Great Britain. Israel has as yet no constitution, but in its proclamation of Statehood, full religious freedom is guaranteed to all citizens of whatever creed. In Israel there is no State Religion. Yet despite this religious freedom, the majority even of the non-observant elements, which number about fifty per cent of the population, are not unaware of the fact that . . . such public association with Jewish tradition is necessary for the maintenance of world Jewish unity. . . .

. . . The restoration of the Jewish people as a unified political group after a dispersion of 2,000 years, marked by unparalleled persecutions and sufferings, is identified in the mind of the Jew of today with the purposes of God for Israel, and through Israel for the whole of humanity. Down all the ages the Jew has felt deeply his integral relationship with mankind as a whole. In the self-same spirit the new-born Jewish State feels that the vindication of the Jewish faith and hope of thousands of years is destined to prove of extreme significance for all nations in a world torn by crises, tensions, and the fear of wholesale destruction.

. . . There is no question that the influence of the Jewish state on world Jewry has been profound. It has not only imparted to many Jewries a new dignity, and a sense of moral and physical security, such as they had hitherto not possessed, but has also inspired a renaissance of Hebrew culture, given rise to a deeper appreciation of Jewish values, stimulated Jewish studies, and intensified Jewish spiritual loyalties. Among the Reform it has led to a restoration of many Jewish national traditions and religious practices which they had discarded, and among the Orthodox it has inspired a greater confidence in promoting their principles. Everywhere it has tended to secure Jewish solidarity and to foster among Jews a sense of unity based on their common historical and cultural traditions and their common spiritual aspirations for the future. It is thus not fantastic to expect that sooner or later even those children of the House of Israel who are still estranged from their people will come to draw fresh inspiration from Zion and Jerusalem whence the Torah and the word of the Lord will go forth, as foretold by the prophets of old.

Israeli Independence Day celebration in Jerusalem.

Glossary

*Italic words in the definitions are defined elsewhere in
the Glossary.*

Amidah (lit. "standing," i.e., prayer recited while standing). Central
segment of all prayer services. Contains as many as nineteen
separate sections: (1) praise to God of the Patriarchs, (2) praise of
God's power, (3) praise of God's holiness, and prayers for: (4)
knowledge, (5) repentance, (6) forgiveness, (7) redemption, (8)
healing of the sick, (9) good crops, (10) ingathering of dispersed
Israel, (11) righteous judgment, (12) punishment of wicked and
heretics, (13) reward of pious, (14) rebuilding of Jerusalem, (15)
restoration of King David's dynasty, (16) acceptance of prayers, (17)
thanks, (18) restoration of the Temple service, (19) peace.

Ashkenazi (pl. *Ashkenazim;* lit. "German"). A member of one of the two
major divisions of Jews—those of central or eastern European
origin. The Ashkenazim differ from the Sefardim in their customs,
rituals, and dialect. See *Sefardi.*

Bar mitzvah (pl. *b'nai mitzvah;* lit. "son of the Commandment"). Ceremony marking new status of 13-year-old boy who is now obliged to
perform all religious duties of an adult. The boy often conducts the
Sabbath service, chanting from the *Torah* portion and from the
Prophets. The service is often followed by a festive party and receipt
of gifts from family and friends.

Bat mitzvah (also spelled *bas mitzvah;* pl. *b'not mitzvah;* lit. "daughter of
the Commandment"). Ceremony for girls parallel to *bar mitzvah.* A
recent development in Judaism.

Ben (pl. *banim;* lit. "son"). Frequently used in Hebrew names. Often
abbreviated as "b."

Berit (also spelled *brit* or *berith;* lit. "covenant"). Abbreviation of berit
milah, the covenant of circumcision. The physical sign of the
covenant; surgical removal of the foreskin of the penis on the eighth
day after birth. See *Mohel.*

Cabbala. See *Kabbalah.*

Cantor (Heb. *hazzan*). A professional singer who leads the chanting of the prayers. In some synagogues, the cantor often performs with a choir.

Chanukkah. See *Hanukkah.*

Chasid. See *Hasid.*

Chuppah. See *Huppah.*

Conservative Judaism. A religious movement committed to Jewish nationhood, the land of Israel, Hebrew prayer, and adapting Jewish law to modern life. Began as an attempt to find a middle ground between *Reform* and *Orthodoxy.*

Daven (lit. "to pray, worship"). To recite the prayers used in daily services and festivals. A Yiddish term.

Diaspora. The dispersion of Jews outside of Israel.

Eretz Yisrael (lit. "the land of Israel"). The land promised by God to the patriarchs, part of the divine covenant. Love for Eretz Yisrael and its holiness became a theological concept.

Etrog (also spelled *ethrog*). A fruit used with the palm branch in the *Sukkot* celebration.

Gemarah (also spelled *Gemara*). The second part of the *Talmud,* consisting of commentary on, and interpretation of, the *Mishnah.*

Haggadah (also spelled *Aggadah;* pl. *Haggadot;* lit. "telling, narration"). In a broad sense, the nonlegal contents of the *Talmud* and *Midrash.* In its more narrow meaning, a special book containing the ritual account of the exodus from Egypt and the spiritual meanings of *Passover;* used at the Passover *Seder* banquet.

Halakhah. The legal rulings of traditional Judaism, including the early codes, such as *Mishnah,* as well as contemporary rulings.

Hanukkah (also spelled *Chanukkah;* lit. "dedication"). Holiday (beginning 25th of Kislev [in December]) commemorating the victory of the Maccabees over the Syrian Greeks and rededication of the Temple in 165 B.C.E. Marked by kindling of candles for eight days.

Hasid (also spelled *Chasid;* pl. *Hasidim;* lit. "pious one"). A member of a mystical religious group noted for its great piety and fervor. Orthodox in practice, the Hasid stresses serving God in joyful, enthusiastic, even ecstatic prayer.

Hasidism (also spelled *Chasidism*). The sect of the Hasidim.

Havdalah (lit. "separation"). Ceremony to separate the holy from the secular. Recited at conclusion of Sabbath and festivals. Symbols include wine, spices, and the light of a braided candle.

Holy Ark. A holy cabinet, usually built into the eastern wall of the sanctuary. Contains the *Torah* scrolls, crowns, and breastplates. Congregation rises when it is opened.

Huppah (also spelled *Chuppah*). The wedding canopy under which the marriage ceremony is performed.

Kabbalah (also spelled *cabala, cabbala, kabala*). A system of mystical interpretation of the Scriptures developed by early rabbis.

Kaddish. An Aramaic prayer, offering praise to God, recited at close of principal segments of the service. Also recited by mourners.

Kashrut (lit. "fitness"). The dietary laws. See *Kosher.*

Kavvanah (lit. "to devote, intent"). Devotion in prayer.

Ketubbah. A marriage contract detailing the obligations of the bride and groom to each other. In the past it was an important legal document that specified the obligations of the husband to his wife. Today it stresses the moral responsibilities of the couple.

Kiddush (lit. "sanctification"). A ceremony proclaiming the holiness of the incoming Sabbath or festival. It consists of a prayer given usually before the evening meal over a cup of wine or two loaves of Sabbath bread.

Kippah (pl. *kippot*). The head covering worn by Orthodox and Conservative males. Practices vary; some wear kippot at all times, others only when praying or studying sacred texts. Also known as yarmulke.

Kohen (pl. *Kohanim;* lit. "priest"). A descendant of the priestly tribe. Accorded the honor of being called first to read from the *Torah.*

Kosher (also spelled *kasher;* lit. "proper, fit"). Conforming to Jewish laws regulating suitability for use. Usually applied to food.

Levite (from *Levi;* pl. *Levi'im*). A descendant of the tribe of Levi. Given the honor of being called to the *Torah* after the *Kohen.*

Lulav (pl. *lulavim;* lit. "branch"). Palm branch used in the service on festival of *Sukkot.*

Menorah (pl. *menorot*). A candelabrum. Most ancient symbol of Judaism. A seven-branched menorah was used in the ancient Temple.

Mezuzah (pl. *mezuzot;* lit. "doorpost"). A rolled parchment containing first two paragraphs of the *Shema,* inserted into a case which is attached to the right doorpost(s) of the home.

Midrash (pl. *midrashim*). Interpretation of Scripture. May teach a moral or legal concept. Also refers to collections of sermonic interpretations.

Mikveh (pl. *mikvaot*). A ritual bath intended to cleanse one of impurity. Often is part of the conversion ceremony.

Minyan (pl. *minyanim;* lit. "number, count"). A minimum of ten adults (age 13 or over) required for congregational worship. Orthodox and some Conservative congregations count only males for this purpose.

Mishnah (also spelled *Mishna*). Hebrew code of law compiled around 200 C.E. by Rabbi Judah the Prince. The first part of the *Talmud.*

Mitzvah (pl. *mitzvot;* lit. "commandment"). Laws prescribed by the *Torah* and by rabbinic law. Later also used in the sense of "a good deed."

Mohel (pl. *mohalim*). A person authorized to perform ritual circumcision (i.e., not merely a hospital surgeon).

Ner Tamid (lit. "perpetual lamp"). A lamp which is always kept burning. Usually hung above the *Holy Ark.*

Nigun (pl. *nigunim;* lit. "to play an instrument"). A traditional folk melody.

Orthodoxy. A modern term for strictly traditional Jewry. Orthodox Jews believe in the revelation of Sinai and the binding authority of both the written *Torah* and the rabbinic law. They resist radical deviations from traditional practices and beliefs.

Passover (Heb. *Pesach*). Festival (beginning 14th of Nisan [in April]) commemorating the exodus from Egypt.

Pentateuch. The Torah, the first five books of the Hebrew Bible: Genesis, Exodus, Leviticus, Numbers, Deuteronomy.

Pentecost. See *Shavuot.*

Pesach. See *Passover.*

Phylacteries (Heb. *tefillin*). Leather cases with straps worn by adult (age 13 or over) males in morning service (not on Sabbath). Cases contain parchment with four paragraphs from *Torah:* Exod. 13:1–10, Exod. 13:11–16, Deut. 6:4–9, and Deut. 11:13–21. The cases are placed on forehead and left arm. Generally not used by Reform Jews.

Pidyon haben (lit. "redemption of the first born"). A short religious ceremony conducted when a male child is 30 days old, whereby the father donates a small sum of money, symbolic of the biblical injunction of Exod. 13:1–16, to redeem the first-born son. A *Kohen* or *Levite* is exempt from the obligation.

Purim. Joyous festival (celebrated on 14th of Adar [in February or March]) commemorating deliverance of Persian Jews from extermination. (Cf. Book of Esther.) Holiday marked by costume parties, performance of farces, considerable drinking and revelry.

Rabbi (lit. "my master teacher"). Originally a title of honor when addressing sages. Today, title of anyone graduated from a rabbinical seminary.

Reb. A title of respect.

Rebbe. A rabbi or spiritual leader, especially of the Hasidic sect.

Reconstructionism. A movement based largely on teachings of its founder, Mordecai Kaplan. Denies belief in a supernatural God. Stresses centrality of Jewish community in shaping Jewish beliefs and practices. Staunchly Zionist. Liturgical practices share much with *Reform* and *Conservative Judaism.*

Reform Judaism. A religious movement advocating thorough-going adaptation of Judaism to conform to modern life. Regards *halakhah* as nonbinding. Stresses importance of ethics and morality.

Rosh Hashanah. Jewish New Year (celebrated on 1st of Tishri [in late September or early October]). Introduces period of soul-searching and repentance. Marked by special prayers and sounding of the *shofar.*

Sanhedrin. The highest legislative body and court of appeal during the time of the Second Temple in Palestine.

Seder (pl. *Sedarim*). Home celebration on the first night of *Passover,* conducted by family members. The celebration is repeated on the second night by Orthodox, Conservative, and some Reform Jews. Contains prayers, songs, reflections on meaning of freedom and slavery. Special foods are served at a festive meal.

Sefardi (also spelled *Sephardi;* pl. *Sefardim;* lit. "Spanish"). A member of one of the two major divisions of Jews—those of Mediterranean or Middle Eastern origin. The Sefardim differ from the Ashkenazim in their customs, rituals, and dialect. See *Ashkenazi.*

Sefer torah (also spelled *sepher torah;* pl. *sifrei torah;* lit. "book of Law"). A handwritten parchment scroll of *Torah.*

Shavuot (lit. "weeks"). Major festival (observed on 6th and 7th of Sivan [in June], seven weeks after *Passover).* Combines spring festival of "first fruits" with commemoration of giving of *Torah* at Mt. Sinai. Also called Pentecost.

Shema (also spelled *Shemah;* lit. "Hear!"). The first word of Deut. 6:4: "Hear, O Israel: The Lord is our God, the Lord Alone!" Proclaims the unity of God. (Cf. Deut. 6:4-9, Deut. 11:13-21, Num. 15:37-41). A major feature of morning and evening prayer service.

Shiva (lit. "seven"). Seven days of mourning following the burial of a close relative.

Shofar. A ram's horn; sounded like a trumpet before and during *Rosh Hashanah* and the conclusion of *Yom Kippur.*

Sukkah (pl. *sukkot;* lit. "tabernacle" or "booth"). A small temporary structure which is erected prior to the festival of *Sukkot.* Families take their meals in the Sukkah in commemoration of the forty years of wandering in the wilderness after the exodus from Egypt.

Sukkot. Fall harvest festival of thanksgiving (beginning on 15th of Tishri [in October]). See *Sukkah.*

Tallit (pl. *talliyot or tallitot;* lit. "prayer shawl"). A four-cornered cloth with fringes worn by all male adults at morning services and by those officiating at afternoon and evening services. This practice is not followed by Reform Jews.

Talmud. The collection of Jewish law, theology, and legend produced in rabbinic academies in Babylon and Palestine from 200 to 500 C.E. Became a primary written authority for Judaism until modern times. Consists of the *Mishnah* and *Gemarah.*

Tefillin. See *Phylacteries.*

Torah (lit. "teaching"). In narrow sense, the *Pentateuch;* in extended meaning, all learning which is regarded as linked to the sacred traditions of Judaism.

Tzitzit (also spelled *tsitsit, zizit*). Fringes of the *tallit.*

Wailing Wall (Western Wall). The last remnants of Herod's temple in Jerusalem. The main object of traditional Jewish pilgrimages. Since 1967, the Wailing Wall has become a major shrine.

Yahrzeit (lit. "year's time"). Anniversary of the death of a parent or close relative.

Yahweh (also spelled *YHWH*). A transliteration of the four Hebrew letters used as a symbol or substitute for God's name. Jews avoid pronouncing the name out of respect.

Yarmulke. See *Kippah.*

Yeshivah (pl. *yeshivot*). A Talmudic academy.

Yiddish (lit. "Jewish"). Originally a Jewish dialect of German with a mixture of Hebrew and Slavic words. Written in Hebrew alphabet, Yiddish was the language of Eastern European Jews. Survives today primarily in North America, Latin America, and Israel.

Yom Kippur. Day of Atonement, a fast day for penitence (10th of Tishri [in late September or early October]).

Zionism. The modern political movement to reestablish a Jewish state in Palestine. Founded in 1897 by Theodor Herzl.

Zizit. See *Tzitzit.*

Zohar. Mystical book with kabbalistic commentary on the Bible and stories of the mystical life of Simeon bar Yohai.